Turkish Migration, Identity an

TRANSNATIONAL PRESS LONDON

Turkish Migration Series

Politics and Law in Turkish Migration

Family and Human Capital in Turkish Migration

Göç ve Uyum

Turkish Migration, Identity and Integration

Little Turkey in Great Britain *(forthcoming)*

Journals by TPL

Migration Letters

Remittances Review

Göç Dergisi

Journal of Gypsy Studies

Kurdish Studies

International Economics Letters

Border Crossing

Transnational Marketing Journal

Turkish Migration, Identity and Integration

Editors:

Ibrahim **Sirkeci**

Betül Dilara **Şeker**

Ali **Çağlar**

TRANSNATIONAL PRESS LONDON
2015

Turkish Migration, Identity and Integration

Edited by Ibrahim Sirkeci, Betül Dilara Şeker, Ali Çağlar

First Printing: 2015

Paperback

ISBN 978-1-910781-12-8

Cover Photo: "Language course" by Altay MANÇO

TRANSNATIONAL PRESS LONDON
12 Ridgeway Gardens, London, N6 5XR, United Kingdom
www.tplondon.com

Contents

Acknowledgements

This book has been possible with the effort of a large group of academics from all over the world. We are grateful to so many friends and colleagues who reviewed the papers over several rounds. We thank *Migration Letters* journal for permission to reprint three articles authored by Sarah Hackett, Katharina Hametner, and Steffen Poetzschke which nicely complement this volume. For their help with the editing process, we would like to thank Mehmet Ali Dikerdem from Middlesex University for his thorough copy-editing of the manuscript as well as editorial support by M. Rauf Kesici, Tuncay Bilecen, and Therese Svensson, research fellows at Regent's University London Centre for Transnational Studies. Sparing significant time for this edited book, our families and friends for tolerating us being absent from many chores and for their continuous support deserve a big thank you.

About the Authors

Ayşegül Akdemir Ayşegül Akdemir received her Bachelor's degree from Bogazici University, Istanbul, in Sociology in 2009 and Master's degree in Conflict Studies at the University of Augsburg, Germany in 2011. She is currently working on her PhD in Sociology at the University of Essex, UK. Her thesis is on the transnational social space and identity of Alevis in Britain. Her research interests are transnational migration, identity, gender and qualitative research methods.

Ömer Alkın finished the Master of Arts in Media Cultural Studies at Heinrich Heine University in Düsseldorf with a thesis about research processes in screenwriting theory. At the moment he works as a lecturer for film and Visual Culture at the Institute for Art History in Düsseldorf and has practical experiences as assistant director and script consultant for feature and short films. With his topical PhD he analyses socio-filmic constructions of emigration and emigrants in Turkish emigration cinema from a Visual Culture Studies perspective.

Claudia Arnold (lic.phil.hist.) is a Sociologist and Member of the Research Staff at ISGF. She is co-director of the "Centre for intercultural prevention of addiction and for health promotion" in Zurich (www.fisp.ch). She is a graduate of sociology, social psychology and economics. She has many years of experience in social research and in the field of gender monitoring.

Feray J. Baskin is a doctoral candidate in anthropology at Indiana University, USA. She has two MA degrees in French linguistics (University of Leiden in the Netherlands and Indiana University, Bloomington, USA) and one in anthropology (Indiana University). For her master thesis (titled Du céfran à l'envers backwords French) from the University of Leiden she analyzed the uses of verlan, a slang language and identity marker, popular in France among youth in housing project neighbourhoods. Her dissertation research focuses on the correlation between the influence of media on linguistic practices and the outcomes of integration of Turkish immigrants in France.

Nir Billfeld is an Economist specializing in Econometrics and Labour Economics, and a PhD student in Economics at the University of Haifa, Israel. In recent years he has worked and is still working as a Lecturer of Econometrics class in the faculty of Applied Mathematics at Ort Braude College, and guides students in writing seminar paper in Econometrics. He has experience in Economics consulting and implementation of advanced Econometrics estimation methods. Nir deals in recent years in developing new models to estimate systems of simultaneous nonlinear equations and big data analysis.

Yakup Çoştu is Associate Professor in Sociology of Religion Department, Faculty of Divinity, Hitit University, Çorum, Turkey. He is a graduate of Ondokuz Mayıs University, Samsun (BA, MA, PhD). Dr. Çoştu has conducted research in the UK (2007-2008 SOAS, London University and 2012 London Metropolitan University) and Germany (2012 Osnabrück University). He has published several books, book chapters and articles in national/international peer reviewed journals as well as being a frequent participant to international conferences at home and abroad. Dr Çoştu serves as editor for Hitit University Journal of Social Sciences Institute while also serving at editorial boards of Journal of Academic Researches in Religious Sciences.

Feyza Ceyhan Çoştu is PhD Candidate at the Philosophy and Religious Studies Department, Social Science Institute Hitit University, Çorum, Turkey. She is a graduate of Gazi University, Ankara (BA, MA). She has worked at the several private schools as philosophy teacher.

Ali Çağlar is a Professor of Political Science at Hacettepe University, Ankara, Turkey. He is a graduate of Hacettepe University in the Department of Social Work and Social Services. In 1983, he was a recipient of the İhsan Doğramacı Achievement Award. Prof Çağlar previously worked at Cumhuriyet University, Middle East Technical University, as a Research Assistant in the Sociology Department prior to joining Hacettepe University in 1995 as an Assistant Professor. He got his PhD in Sociology at the University of Surrey in the UK in 1994. Prof Çağlar served in the OSCE Kosovo Mission as international election trainer in Prizren from June 2001 to January 2003. He has also served as Secretary General to the Interuniversity Council of Turkey in 2011-2012. Since 2011, he has been the Vice Rector at Hacettepe University. His main areas of research and expertise are security studies, crime, policing, terrorism, asylum and migration studies. Professor Çağlar has extensively published in these fields in national and international academic journals in addition to authoring three books.

Corina Salis Gross is Social Anthropologist and Head of Research Unit at the Swiss Research Institute for Public Health and Addiction (ISGF, www.isgf.uzh.ch), and Associate Researcher at the Institute for Social Anthropology at the University of Berne (www.anthro.unibe.ch). She worked as a research assistant in the Planning Department of the Health and Welfare Directorates of the canton of Bern. Her doctoral thesis was on cultural representations of death in nursing homes submitted at the Institute of Ethnology of the University of Bern. Between 1992 and 2005, she was a research assistant at the Institute. She has been a visiting scholar at Harvard University in Boston, United States.

Björn Gustafsson is Senior professor at the Department of Social Work, University of Gothenburg, Sweden and Research Fellow at the Institute for the Study of Labor (IZA), Bonn, Germany. His expertise area spans from Social policy and Social Assistance to immigrants, Poverty, and income distribution. His most recent publications include "Are China's Ethnic Minorities Less Likely to Move?" appeared in *Eurasian Geography and Economics* and "Data for Studying Earnings, the Distribution of Household Income and Poverty in China" (with Li Shi and Hiroshi Sato) appeared in *China Economic Review.*

Sarah Hackett is Senior Lecturer in Modern European History, School of Humanities and Cultural Industries, Bath Spa University, United Kingdom. Her research focuses on European Muslim immigration in the post-1945 era, particularly to Britain and Germany. She is the author of *Foreigners, Minorities and Integration: The Muslim Immigrant Experience in Britain and Germany* (Manchester University Press, 2013). Dr. Hackett joined Bath Spa University in 2013 having previously taught at the University of Sunderland. During February 2014, she was a visiting lecturer at the University of Southern Denmark's Centre for Contemporary Middle

East Studies. During March 2015, she was a visiting lecturer at the University of Bergen's Department of Archaeology, History, Cultural Studies and Religion.

Katharina Hametner is a lecturing at Sigmund Freud Private University Vienna, Austria. Katharina Hametner is a psychologist and PhD-scholar at the University of Vienna. She is also founding member of ikus. Her research interests include critical migration and racism studies, qualitative methods, cultural Psychology, and identity and Habitus theory.

Yehudith Kahn is an economist specializing in economic research on the Middle East. She is a lecturer at the Department of Economics and Management Tel Hai Academic College. She holds a PhD in Economics magna cum laude from the Aix Marseille 3- University, France. Her main research field is migration and labor market. In recent years, Dr Kahn is investigating the effects of migration on poverty and inequality in the Middle East, mainly in Turkey, Egypt and Morocco. Her main research field is migration and labor market.

George Leeson is Co-Director of the Oxford Institute of Population Ageing and Senior Research Fellow in Demography at the University of Oxford. He is Senior Research Fellow at Kellogg College, Oxford, as well as being a member of the Oxford Martin School. He is responsible for the Global Ageing Survey carried out in three waves in more than 20 countries in Europe, North and South America and Asia and including approximately 45,000 persons aged 40-79 years. His other research includes the demographic inequalities of global ageing, the changing populations of Europe, migration and migrants in Europe, longevity and centenarians.

Torun Österberg is a Senior Lecturer and Researcher at the Department of Social Work, University of Gothenburg, Sweden. Her work focuses on neighbourhoods and place. Her recent paper titled "the increasing importance of place: neighbourhood differences in metropolitan Sweden, 1990-2006" was published in *China Journal of Social Work* in 2013.

Deniz Özalpman is PhD candidate at the Department of Communication of the University of Vienna, under the supervision of Professor Katharine Sarikakis. She is investigating the emergence of global media audiences and global texts through the case study of Turkish television drama series in European and Arabic local contexts. She is part of the team of Media Governance and Industries Research Group at Department of Communication, University of Vienna.

Steffen Pötzschke is a researcher at GESIS – Leibniz-Institute for the Social Sciences (Mannheim, Germany). As a member of the Cross-Cultural Surveys team he participated in the research project "The Europeanisation of Everyday Life: Cross-Border Practices and Transnational Identities among EU and Third-Country Citizens (EUCROSS)" which was financed by the 7th Framework Programme of the European Commission. He holds a master's degree in International Migration and Intercultural Relations from the Institute for Migration Research and Intercultural Studies (IMIS) at the University of Osnabruck, Germany. His research interests are: transnationalism, the transformation of identities and belonging, and the political participation of emigrants.

Michael P. Schaub is a senior lecturer in psychology at the University of Zurich and the scientific director of the Swiss Research Institute of Public Health and

Addiction ISGF, a WHO Collaborating Centre, associated with the University of Zurich. He is a trained psychotherapist with a strong clinical and scientific background in the area of substance use disorders. He completed his Ph.D. in 2005 on the topic of cannabis use, its associated personality dimensions in the general population, and co-occurring mental-health problems in vulnerable persons. In 2012 he received his postdoctoral lecture qualification (Habilitation) for psychology, with the specialization for "treatment and diagnostic of substance use disorders" at the University of Zurich. Dr. Schaub has published more than 50 peer-reviewed papers in scientific journals. He is scientific expert in addiction research for the World Health Organization WHO and at the United Nations Office on Drugs and Crime UNODC.

Ibrahim Sirkeci is Ria Financial Professor of Transnational Studies and Marketing and the Director of the Regent's Centre for Transnational Studies (RCTS) at Regent's University London (UK). He holds a PhD in Geography from the University of Sheffield (UK) and a BA in Political Science and Public Administration from Bilkent University (Turkey). Prior to joining Regent's University London, Sirkeci had worked at the University of Bristol. His main areas of expertise are Human Mobility, Labour Markets, Remittances, and Segmentation. He is the editor of several journals including *Migration Letters* and *Transnational Marketing Journal*. His books include *Transnational Marketing and Transnational Consumers* (Springer, 2013), *Migration and Remittances during the Global Financial Crisis and Beyond* (World Bank, 2012 with J. Cohen and D. Ratha), and *Cultures of Migration, the global nature of contemporary mobility* (University of Texas Press, 2011 with J. Cohen). He has been chairing the *Turkish Migration Conferences* since 2012.

Betül Dilara Şeker is Assistant Professor of Psychology and Head of Department for Psychology at Celal Bayar University, Manisa, Turkey. She is a graduate of Ege University where she has completed her PhD in Social Psychology. Before joining Manisa Celal Bayar University in 2012, Dr Şeker has worked at Van Yüzüncü Yıl University. She has moved to academia after a spell as a teacher working at Ministry of Education. She has carried out research in London while she was a post-doctoral visiting researcher at Regent's Centre for Transnational Studies at Regent's University in 2013. Her recent research mainly focuses on acculturation, and migrant integration.

Ali Faruk Yaylacı is Assistant Professor in the Faculty of Education, Recep Tayyip Erdogan University in Rize/Turkey. He was born in 1972 in Ankara. He received undergraduate degree from Educational Sciences Faculty at Ankara University in 1994. He had master degree from Educational Management and Planning Program in 1999 and doctoral degree from Educational Management and Supervising Program in 2004 at Ankara University. He worked as a teacher and principal in Turkey and Belgium. His research interests in educational sciences, sociology and philosophy are in the areas of educational management, organization theory, migration and European Turks.

Filiz Göktuna Yaylacı is Assistant Professor in the Department of Sociology at Anadolu University, Eskisehir/Turkey. She was born in 1979 in Salihli/Turkey She received undergraduate degree from Sociology department at Anadolu University in 2002. She had master degree from Sociology Department in 2005 at Anadolu

University and doctoral degree from Department of Communication Design and Management Program in 2012 at Anadolu University. Her research interests in sociology and communication are in the areas of migration, social communication, identity, stereotypes, particularism, integration, European Turks, and multicultural societies.

Nilüfer Korkmaz Yaylagül earned a PhD in Anthropology from Hacettepe University, Turkey in 2008 and began her teaching career as lecturer at Akdeniz University, Department of Gerontology in November 2009. She has been a Visiting Fellow at the Oxford Institute of Population Ageing (2012), the University of Oxford, UK where she has carried out a post-doctoral research about health and older Turkish migrants. For the last six years, Dr Yaylagul has been involved in teaching sociology and anthropology of ageing and cross-cultural gerontology at Akdeniz University. She has particular interest in migration in old age, social policy and long-term care in developing countries and support provisions.

Suzan Yazıcı who is a specialist in Family Medicine has studied Gerontology and Geriartrics at Malta University at 2002-2003. She works at Akdeniz University Department of Gerontology since 2009 as academic staff. She carried out a post-doctoral research about first generation Turkish immigrants with collaboration of Copenhagen University Center for Healthy Aging. Her personal research areas of interest are Successful Aging, Health Promotion and Aging and Driving at Old Age.

Introduction

Ali Çağlar, Ibrahim Sirkeci, Betül Dilara Şeker

Turkish migration to Europe and beyond for over five decades resulted in strong minorities in many countries. Sizeable Turkish communities have formed in Germany, the Netherlands, Austria, Switzerland, and the UK. The dynamic nature of international human mobility, changing attitudes, and policies towards immigration have brought these diaspora populations under spotlights. This book is comprised of leading research and scholarship on the most recent manifestations of issues related to Turkish migration, identity, strategies and patterns of integration, which have been selected to offer a wide array of case studies while providing multidisciplinary perspectives.

As touched upon briefly in the Foreword, politics and law have emerged as the two main facets of contemporary migration management. Traditional immigration countries have tampered with their immigration laws and have sporadically experienced the politics of mobilisation against immigration. Traditional source countries, on the other hand, have rapidly turned into destination countries during the last two decades. However, the fact remains that there are still countries with surplus populations and others who do not want any more migration. This situation is essentially in line with the hypotheses of the culture of migration and conflict model which predicts conflicts, tensions, disagreements among national level actors (Sirkeci & Cohen, 2016; Sirkeci, 2003; Sirkeci, 2009).

Following the collapse of the Ottoman Empire, there were large population movements between Anatolia and neighbouring territories including the compulsory population exchanges between the newly formed Turkish Republic and Greece between 1923 and 1926. Similarly, there were relatively large flows of population during the nation building era of the early Republican period where non-Muslim properties were nationalised. While the majority of non-Muslim minorities left Turkey, Muslim Turks moved in the opposite direction from the countries gaining independence after the collapse of the Ottoman Empire. However what has put Turkey firmly on the international migration map are the mass labour migrations of the 1960s and 1970s. Following the energy crisis of the early 1970s, Turkish emigration found new destinations in Arab countries, Australia, and the former Soviet Republics in addition to the already established culture and routes of migration corridors created historically between Turkey and certain Western European destinations. Thus we have seen continuity in flows to these countries despite policy changes tightening immigration and transformations in the need for foreign labour in these countries. Initial flows have been

1

replaced by family migrations, refugee flows, asylum seeking migrants, and in more recent times the arrival of undocumented migrants in large numbers.

Given this, we can identify five distinct periods in recent Turkish migration history: 1) the migration of mainly unskilled and skilled workers dominating the initial period from 1961 to 1973; 2) migrations due to family reunions dominating the second period until 1980; 3) Following the military intervention of 1980, Turkish or Kurdish refugees seeking asylum in Europe, along with flows of contract workers to Arab countries in the 1970s and 1980s; 4) flows of undocumented persons to Western Europe during the late 1990s and 2000s; 5) the boom in migration to Turkey with Turkey turning into an immigrant receiving country in the 2000s and 2010s. Along with these dominant flows, there is always the case of flows of highly skilled independent movers, albeit in much smaller scale. The last two periods are also marked with the emergence of a Turkish culture of migration which ensures steady outflows but also attracts inflows.

The Turkish Ministry of Foreign Affairs claims that more than 5 million Turkish citizens are now living outside Turkey, around 4 million of which reside in Western Europe, 300.000 in North America, 200.000 in the Middle East and 150,000 in Australia[1]. Although this number is relatively low in comparison to Turkey's population (6%), it is nevertheless significantly large when compared to some smaller European Union member countries. According to Turkish official statistics (YTB, 2011), the overwhelming majority of Turkish migrants and family members live in Germany (2,500,000), France (541,000), the Netherlands (384,000), Belgium (160,000), Switzerland (120,000), Austria (112,000), and the United Kingdom (180,000-250,000) (Sirkeci & Esipova, 2013) if we exclude former Turkish citizens naturalized in these countries. The Turkish Ministry of Labor and Social Security statistics[2] also reveal that an important portion of Turkish

---

[1] See for details, http://www.mfa.gov.tr/the-expatriate-turkish-citizens.en.mfa (Date Accessed: 25.01.2015). United Nations reports about 2,545,214 Turkish born outside Turkey by around year 2000 (http://data.un.org/ Accessed: 25:01.2015).

[2] Between 1972 and 2009, the number of Turkish citizens who obtained German citizenship is 777,904. Between 1946 and 2008, that number for Dutch citizenship is 259,958. Between 1985 and 2008, Turkish citizens who chose Belgian citizenship amounts to 130,374. Austrian citizenship between 1999 and 2009 is 88,597. Between 1991 and 2008, the number of Turkish citizens who obtained French citizenship is 71,323. The number of Turkish citizens in these countries as of 31 December 2010 are respectively; Germany 1.629.480, Netherlands 372.728, Belgium 39.419, Austria 110.678, and France 459.611. (Çalışma ve Sosyal Güvenlik Bakanlığı, http://www.csgb.gov.tr/csgbPortal/diyih. portal?page=yv&id=1) (Date Accessed: 26.01.2015). The number between 1980 and 2011 for British citizenship is 78,296 and the number of Turkish born people in England and Wales increased from 52,396 in 2001 to 91,115 in 2011 according to the UK Census (Sirkeci & Esipova, 2013:6).

migrant workers and their families have acquired the citizenship of their host countries. The majority of these populations are built around communities which arrived in the 1960s and 1970s. However, the dominant feature of these population flows have changed over time. For example, family-related population movements (reunification and marriage) are different in terms of legal mechanisms, but they are part and parcel of the overall mobility. After the energy crisis of the 1970s, the volume of family migration rose mostly due to restrictions in other migration categories. On the other hand, asylum seeker and refugee flows dominated the period from the 1980s until the 2000s when other migration channels were tightened. The total number of asylum applications by Turkish citizens in industrialised countries between 1980 and 2011 was 1,033,000 (Sirkeci and Esipova, 2013:3). Although the volume of asylum seekers from Turkey has sharply decreased over the last decade, as of July 2014, the total number of refugees originating from Turkey was 65,900 while that of asylum seekers reached 10,252 according to the UNHCR.[3] Variations of mover categories in countries can be seen in response to local legislations. For example, in the UK, due to further restrictions on immigration, many Turkish citizens arrive with visas based on the Ankara Agreement of 1963[4] which gives special advantages but limits settlement options. Besides, up to 3 million Turkish movers who had previously returned to Turkey should be taken into account while speaking of Turkish migration and integration.

Contract-workers arrived in Turkish migration history with sizeable moves to Arab coutries and former Soviet Union countries in the 1970s and the total numbers reached nearly 150,000. These flows are relatively small in the rich variety of current migration flows from Turkey. Similarly, a significant number of Turkish students study abroad, and some stay while some return. The total number of Turkish students abroad grew from 37,000 in 2007 to 53,000 in 2012 (OECD, 2014).

Overall, we can confidently claim that there is now an established Turkish culture of migration, which is particularly strong between Turkey and several destination countries including Austria, Germany, the Netherlands, Switzerland, Sweden, the UK, and France. In the 25 years since 1987, on average annually about 85,000 Turks moved in to the OECD countries while, over 45,000 moved out (OECD, 2014). The number of Turks moving to OECD countries declined to around 60,000 in the decade leading upto 2013. These steady moves created strong diaspora populations including over 1,969,979 Turkish citizens and 1,720,892 Turks naturalized in their countries

---

[3] 2015 UNHCR country operations profile – Turkey, http://www.unhcr.org/pages/49e48e0fa7f.html, (Date Accessed: 31.01.2015).
[4] See Sirkeci, I. et al. (2016). *Little Turkey in Great Britain*. London: TPLondon.

of residence within the OECD area by the end of 2012 (OECD, 2014). Due to the changing economic balance between Turkey and destination countries as well as the established culture of migration, some popular destination countries have become source countries as we saw sizeable number of Turks moving to Turkey (Sirkeci and Zeyneloglu, 2014). It is becoming more of a pattern of mutual flows between Europe and Turkey, whereas Turkey emerges as a key destination for those in relatively deprived parts of the world.

Migrants' remittances are not included in this volume, but they constitute a significant part of Turkish migration studies. Over the decades, these initially small sums of money sent by an increasing number of Turkish movers have contributed to Turkey's economy remarkably in the last fifty years, helping to cover the balance of trade deficits.

As a destination, Turkey had to fast track new legislation as sudden arrival of over 2 million Syrian and Iraqi refugees, as of April 2015, has shifted the paradigm. Steady slow growth of European immigration as well as efforts to control irregular migration were the basis for the new legal framework. Syrian and Iraqi arrivals turned all attention to conflicts and integration. Thus ambition to become a full member of the European Union (EU) cannot be the only guiding criteria for Turkish migration policy. Soon Turkey will possibly need to revisit both the newly adopted *Law on Foreigners and International Protection* (April 4, 2013) and the readmission agreement with the EU, governing the treatment of unauthorized migrants originating from or transiting through Turkey. Another important change came as Turkish citizens were for the first time allowed to vote at their place of residence in the 2014 parliamentary and presidential elections. This change is a sign of Turkey's intensifying relations with its diaspora populations and further transnationalisation of Turkish politics.

Nevertheless, multiple loyalties and transnational practices make identity an even more complicated issue often interwoven with the issues of integration. Despite being classified as Turks or Turkish nationals in most registers, there is a rich variety of ethnic and religious segments in this broad group, Turks, Kurds, Alevis to name a few. Identity is often not a simple response to the question "who are you?" as it relates to time, space and the temporal context of affairs. Nevertheless, limited data on ethnic and religious identity continue to restrain researchers' imagination. Thus movers from Turkey appear as men, women, Muslims, Alevis, Kurds, Turks, and others in the literature. Diaspora associations indicating movers' ties with their cities, towns, and villages of origin in Turkey.

Identity is a complex phenomenon as it is often multiple, interchangeable, situational, confrontational and subjective. Certain identities are given while some others are acquired. Inherited identities come with belongings such as family, clan, race, and ethnicity and the acquired are for example occupational and educational identities. Among migrants from Turkey, Turkish and Kurdish are the dominant ethnic identities while Sunni and Alevi are dominant religious identities. These overlap and/or cross cut political identities and quite often contested. Sirkeci (2003) maps Turkish Kurds identity positions in Germany where Turk may appear both as part of "us" and "other". Hence Turks and Kurds may contest each other but sometimes, they come together as the "immigrant other" facing members of the English or German host society. It is important to note that identity building is an open ended process to an extent and built and rebuilt over time. Migration experience sometimes highlights certain identities while also adding new dimensions to existing ones or bringing new ones into individuals' portfolio of identities. Identity is also temporal. Individuals and groups may emphasise an ethnic identity more strongly at certain times than others. For example, annual Kurdistan festivals are such occasions among the Kurds in Europe. Nevertheless, a political stance may bring together Kurds and Turks as it happened during the Gezi Park protests.

"Preservation of our culture and traditions" is a commonly mentioned phrase among conservative segments of Turkish immigrant populations in Europe (see for example, chapter 9 of this book). The elements of these "culture and traditions" become part of the identity yet be unpacked by their daily routines, religious rituals, literature and language, life styles, values, customs, and what they watch and so on. Regulations, rules, and attitudes in the host society do also have an impact on identity formation. Macro level integration policies do also shape identities for good or worse. Kastoryano (2000:132) pointed to that by revealing some differences between the Turkish migrants in France and those in Germany. To what extent, foreign governments are allowed to interact with diaspora communities also have an impact. Turkish Religious Affairs (see chapter in this book) is an example of that.

Identity issues are closely linked with the issue of integration which is not a concern for Turks abroad or Turkey alone. All countries with large or small populations of immigrants (and immigrant origin) are somehow interested in this agenda. After a long cycle of academic debates over terminology including assimilation and integration it seems we are settled with a redefined or revised version of integration to address the process of different populations encountering each other (Alba & Foner, 2015:4-8). Following their discussion, we may adopt a broadly defined concept of integration as "the extent to which immigrants, and especially their children, are able to participate in key mainstream institutions in ways that position them to advance socially and materially" (Alba & Foner, 2015: 8).

Although cultural differences between host and migrant groups appear more often in public debates, one key area of concern is rather economic: labour market performances, disadvantages and discrimination. Across Europe, not only third country nationals but also migrants from other EU countries face serious labour market penalties (Khattab et al. 2011; Johnston et al., 2010). These (un)employment experiences do have a bearing on identities too.

Spatial concentration and isolation also matter. Immigrants tend to concentrate in certain areas characterized by migration history, economic attractiveness, and many other factors depending on country and time. For example, Turks in Germany concentrate in a few cities (Kastoryano, 2002), while over 64%[5] of 169,771 Turks and Kurds live in London according to the 2011 UK Census (ONS, 2015). "Little Istanbul" in Berlin (Kaya, 2000:11), "Istanbul in 200 meters" in Cologne (Sirkeci, 2003:68) are examples of enclaves connected with Turkey but also creating transnational living spaces through enclaves which economically enable migrants. It is also part of a historic phenomenon of ethnic segregation and unemployment (Friedrichs, 1998). Yet, similar to many other immigrant minority groups in Europe, they face difficulties in the labour market (Sirkeci & Açık, 2015). Given the variety of policies and models of integration across Europe, Turkish migrants' integration has to be studied case by case. Nevertheless, it has to be noted that it is an interactive process involving both movers and non-movers in both sending and receiving countries, as well as their institutions. Legal frameworks play a critical role in the process.

EU's *Common Agenda for Integration* asserts that the promotion of fundamental rights, non discrimination and equal opportunities for all are key integration issues. The EU legislation provides a strong framework of anti-discrimination (EU, 2005). The European Council on Refugees and Exiles (ECRE) (ECRE, 2002) draws a structural framework of integration for the EU including the following topics: "Institutional arrangements, access to the labor market, access to vocational training, discrimination in the labor market, recognition of overseas qualifications, education, the education of migrant children, housing, health, family reunion, data on migrants, and financing integration". There is also one important set of guiding principles for all member states embodied by the European Union. The actions suggested are shown in the *Handbook on Integration, the INTI Preparatory Actions* and *the*

---

[5]Once the Turkish Cypriots are excluded, this figure is 43% for the Kurds and 70% for the Turks from Turkey resident in the UK.

proposed European Fund for Integration (EU, 2005). According to the provisions of this book; integration is a dynamic, two-way process of mutual accommodation by all immigrants and residents of member States. Integration implies respect for the basic values of the European Union. Employment is a key part of the integration process and is central to the participation of immigrants. In order to make the contributions of immigrants to host society, and to make such contributions visible; basic knowledge of the host society's language, history, and institutions is indispensable to integration. Efforts in education are critical to preparing immigrants, and particularly their descendants, to be more successful and more active participants in society. Access for immigrants to institutions, as well as to public and private goods and services, on a basis equal to national citizens and in a non-discriminatory way is a critical foundation for better integration. Frequent interaction between immigrants and member State citizens is a fundamental mechanism for integration.The practice of diverse cultures and religions is guaranteed under the Charter of Fundamental Rights and must be safeguarded.The participation of immigrants in the formulation of integration policies and measures, especially at the local level, supports their integration.

Above and beyond these general principles, it is the specific practices in each migrant-receiving country that blueprint the real framework of integration: For instance, Germany's Federal Office for Migration and Refugees refers to integration as a long-term process with the aim of including everyone in society who lives in Germany on a permanent and legal basis. Immigrants should have the opportunity to participate fully in all aspects of social, political and economic life on an equal footing in order to become part of German society. Their responsibility is to learn German and to respect and abide by the Constitution and its laws (UNHCR 2013: 14). Since 2011, in Germany, if an immigrant does not participate in an integration course, his/her residence permit can only be extended for one year, until he/she has successfully completed the integration course (Urso and Schuster, 2013:33). However, some Turks think integration is impossible in the way Germans expected it to be. Especially with respect to religion and tradition, many Turkish migrants think that what Germans anticipate is assimilation not integration. However, some others acknowledge that they are contented with their position and they get on well with the local Germans because they know the German language, they abide by the local rules and they are employed (Şahin 2011: 151-52). Thus integration has features relating to the community and wider population but also it is an individual journey which connects movers and non-movers, locals and newcomers.

Turkish movers abroad have settled in many countries and have been subject to various integration processes. Recently, Turkey has suddenly faced

7

its biggest challenge of immigrant intergration with millions of Syrians fleeing their country amid armed clashes between radicals, moderates and government forces.

The impact of the global economic crisis, the rise of threats such as ISIS in Iraq and Syria, and anti-immigration discourses warrant more studies on Turkish and other movers in Europe and beyond. In this edited volume, we brought together a set of studies tackling different aspects of Turkish migration and immigrant experiences abroad.

Pötzschke's opening chapter summarises mobility patterns of Turks in Europe drawing upon the data gathered through a project on the Europeanisation of everyday life (EUCROSS). Kahn and Billfeld compares the incentives for Turks to return home with Moroccan and Egyptians. They look at the ways in which return decisions are revised over time.

In the following chapter, Yaylagul and colleagues draw our attention to the uses of health services by Turkish refugees in London using a life course approach with life history method. Gustafsson and Osterberg outline the patterns of child poverty among the movers from Turkey in Sweden drawing on Swedish official statistics.

Akdemir explores the identity formation processes among Alevis in London with and emphasis on their struggle to rights and recognition. Then we switch to the continent, as Ali Faruk Yaylacı delineates the perceptions of identity among Turkish teachers in Belgium using a case study method. Pursuit of identity processes continues with chapters by Baskin and Hametner who bring us fresh insights and discussion on identity, integration and racism among Turkish women in France and Austria. Filiz Yaylacı's chapter explores the ways in which communication strategies and practices among Turkish immigrants in Belgium play a role in determining identity and belonging. She has conducted qualitative interviews with 55 immigrants from Posof and Emirdag as well as recording observations in Belgium.

Gross and colleagues focus on a known characteristic of Turkish populations and their experiences in smoking cessation in Switzerland. Following two chapters by Alkın and Özalpman introduce us to movies and audience. Alkın looks at German cinema on Turkish immigrants and immigration and also on emerging Turkish-German cinema which are discussed with reference to two periods. Deniz Özalpman looks at a Turkish drama series with a focus on illustrating the use of Grounded Theory in Turkish migration studies.

Hackett's chapter examines Turkish Muslims in Hamburg drawing upon oral history interviews and focusing on positive aspects of their entrepreneurial attitudes. Yakup Çoştu and Feyza Çoştu in the final chapter, investigate the Diyanet Vakfı (Turkish Religious Foundation) in the UK and immigrants perceptions about and utility of these religious organisations in terms of identity formation and community building.

We do hope this volume will be of use to the students, academics, researchers and practitioners in the field. There is a fast growing literature on Turkish migration and we aimed at laying another brick.

Chapter 1: Mobilities of Turkish migrants in Europe

Steffen Pötzschke

Introduction

While recent studies have investigated intra-European mobility of EU citizens (Favell, 2008; Recchi & Favell, 2009) and the transnationalisation of selected European societies (Mau, 2010) the main goal of this paper is to shed light on border crossing mobility practises of Turkish migrants residing in member states of the European Union. Particularly, it is of interest to investigate whether the third-country migrant status influences the extent to which these individuals make use of the common European mobility space. To allow for an assessment of this question, their data will be contrasted with that of intra-European migrants from Romania. Existing studies, such as Neumayer (2006), clearly show the impact of visa regulations on international mobility. One of his arguments is that for citizens of most countries in the world from a practical point of view, the national passport is less important than the visa it contains (or lacks). Therefore, it could be assumed that the question of whether or not Turkish migrants reside within the Schengen area has a direct impact on their intra-European mobility. To review this issue, survey data collected both in signatory and non-signatory countries of the Schengen agreement is used in the analysis.

The first part of the paper provides an overview of the data used, while the second part presents some insights in physical and non-physical mobility of Turkish migrants. The final part of this text discusses the results of regression analysis, which uses intra-European mobility as a dependent variable and, among others, country dummies, different socioeconomic characteristics and communication with individuals abroad as independent variables.

Data and method

This paper is based on data gathered by the project "The Europeanisation of Everyday Life: Cross-Border Practices and Transnational Identities among EU and Third-Country Citizens (EUCROSS)", funded by the European Commission in the 7th Framework Program. As part of the quantitative EUCROSS survey, computer assisted telephone interviews were conducted with 1,000 nationals in Denmark, Germany, Italy, Romania, Spain and the United Kingdom (UK). Furthermore, with the exception of Spain, additional interviews with 250 Turkish[1] and 250 Romanian migrants were conducted in each country. Data collection started in early 2012 and was completed in early 2013. For sampling purposes, the term "nationals" was understood strictly in its legal sense, i.e., each contacted adult who held the nationality of the survey country (possibly in conjunction with other nationalities) was eligible for the respective national sample. To be included in the migrant samples individuals had to possess Romanian and Turkish nationality respectively, without being naturalised in the country of residence (CoR). Furthermore, they actually had to be migrants in the original meaning of the term. Therefore, members of the so called second (or a later) generation who were born in the CoR were not recruited for these samples.

Table 1.1. Average age, age at migration, duration of sojourn in CoR (in years), gender (in per cent)

	Age		Age at migration		Duration of sojourn		% female	
	Turks	Romanians	Turks	Romanians	Turks	Romanians	Turks	Romanians
Denmark	41.2	33.4	20.8	26.3	20.4	7.1	47.2	41.0
Germany	46.2	48.8	19.1	33.4	27.1	15.5	56.1	56.8
Italy	33.9	42.2	24.9	29.3	9.0	12.9	43.8	59.8
Romania	40.7	---	29.0	---	11.7	---	31.2	---
Spain	---	36.8	---	28.5	---	8.2	---	58.7
United Kingdom	38.5	33.6	26.1	28.5	12.4	5.1	43.0	48.6

Source: EUCROSS (2013). Turks: N=1235; Romanians: N=1225.

Turkish migrants surveyed by EUCROSS are on average younger than the interviewed CoR nationals. However, as Table 1.1 demonstrates, they are slightly older than intra-EU migrants from Romania. The smallest gap between all three groups occurs in Germany, where, at the same time, respondents of both migrant samples show the highest mean age. The interviewed Turkish citizens also migrated at a younger age and have already lived significantly longer in the respective CoR than Romanian migrants. The only exception from this rule is Italy, where Romanians on average stayed four years longer than Turks.

On the one hand, the longer duration of sojourn in Denmark and Germany is likely to be related to the history of Turkish labour migration between the late 1950s and the early 1970s. Both countries ceased their active labour recruitment policies in 1973, however in neither of these cases this did

---

[1] Throughout this paper the terms "Turks", "Turkish" or "Romanian" etc. refer to nationality in a strictly legal sense, i.e., to the fact whether or not a person is formally a citizen of the respective state. On the contrary, it is not used as an ethnic description. Therefore, the term "Turk" refers for example to Turkish citizens of Kurdish ethnicity as well.

end the immigration of Turkish citizens as originally intended. Instead it changed its nature from mainly work orientated mobility to migration patterns of family reunification (Herbert, 2003; Liversage, 2009; Soysal, 2003). This interpretation is supported by the fact, that "family and love" was mentioned as the main reason for migration in both countries whereas "work" and "education" dominated in Italy, Romania and the UK (data not presented).

On the other hand, the earlier mentioned differences in duration of sojourn between the surveyed countries is partially also resulting from the EUCROSS sampling itself. As mentioned, the migrant sampling frame excluded naturalised individuals. However, in contrast to Germany and Denmark, laws allow immigrants to retain their original nationality when they become British citizens. Therefore, it has to be assumed that, in direct comparison, a higher share of Turkish immigrants acquired CoR citizenship in the United Kingdom over time than in those countries where they would have had to renounce Turkish nationality (King et al., 2008b; Pötzschke et al., 2014). Hence, it seems reasonable to assume that a higher share of Turkish long term residents in the UK, compared to Denmark and Germany, wasn't eligible for the respective EUCROSS migrant sample. With the exception of the sample in Romania the gender distribution was reasonably balanced across all Turkish samples.

Physical and non-physical mobility of Turkish migrants

Table 1.2 offers an overview over the international mobility of both migrant groups surveyed in EUCROSS with respect to the last 24 months before the interviews.

The data show that in most countries a considerably lower number of respondents in the Turkish compared to the Romanian samples visited another EU member state within the last two years before the survey. Besides Turks in Romania, those living in Germany were least likely to have done so. This is remarkable considering Germanys geographical position and the fact that it is a Schengen state, which provides (most of) its foreign residents with the possibility to visit neighbouring countries without any further formalities. Turkish migrants residing in the UK, a state which is not part of the Schengen area and does not share a land border with another EU-member state (with the exception between Northern Ireland and Ireland) are on the contrary, much more likely to have visited another EU country. In fact, the respondents of this sample are in this regard only a few percentage points behind those living in Denmark, which in turn is a Schengen country, shares a direct border with another Schengen state and, due to its smaller size, offers less possibilities for extended mobility within its own borders.

Table 1.2. Recent trips (within last 24 months) in per cent

	EU countries		Countries outside the EU		Country of origin	
	Turks	Romanians	Turks	Romanians	Turks	Romanians
Denmark	48.8	67.2	12.8	18.4	88.0	84.4
Germany	28.2	58.8	9.1	18.4	82.5	78.4
Italy	61.6	54.0	22.8	9.6	76.0	88.0
Romania	9.2	---	17.6	---	89.2	---
Spain	---	30.8	---	7.2	---	73.2
United Kingdom	44.4	57.7	14.1	17.4	87.1	86.3

Source: EUCROSS (2013). Turks: N=1250; Romanians: N=1248.

Nonetheless, while the percentage in Germany is lower in comparison to that measured in the other EU-15 countries, still more than one in four Turkish migrants living there visited another EU country at least once in the 24 months preceding the survey. Furthermore, it has to be considered that the specific item only asked for visits, which included at least one overnight stay. However, the qualitative data collected in the second stage of the EUCROSS project indicates that respondents tended not to consider countries they passed when traveling to the country of origin (CoO) by car (Pötzschke et al., 2014).

The fact that less than ten per cent of the Turkish respondents in Romania visited other EU countries is not that surprising considering that their CoR is situated at the periphery of the current European Union and in direct proximity of their CoO. While visits to non EU states were in general less common to Turkish than to Romanian migrants, the contrary holds true for visits to the CoO, both with exception of the samples in Italy. On average, 85 per cent of the Turkish migrants who participated in EUCROSS visited Turkey at least once during the preceding 24 months. With respect to the small group of people who showed a total abstinence of international mobility in the same period it is again Turks in Germany who stand out with 14.3 per cent. This is nearly double the value measured for Turkish migrants in Denmark. All others are in between. Once again, these figures are higher for the Turkish migrants than for Romanians in all countries, with the exception of the UK where the means of both groups are at 9.3 per cent.

With regard to both physical and non-physical mobility, personal networks on an international scale are highly important. Therefore Table 1.3 shows the basic parameters of both surveyed migrant groups' networks, using the aggregated values of the individual samples.

When asking respondents for the existence of personal contacts (friends, family, etc.) abroad, the questionnaire offered "a few", "a lot" and "none" as substantive answer categories.

It is plain on first sight that the personal networks of both surveyed migrant groups have a clear focus on people who hold the respective CoO nationality. Nearly 85 per cent of all interviewed Turks and 78 per cent of the Romanian migrants still have contact to nationals of their CoO who also live there. This, of course, does not come as a surprise since the respondents are first generation migrants. It can therefore be assumed that most of them would have left (some) friends and family behind. More than half of the respondents in both groups know people of their own nationality in third countries.

Table 1.3. Personal networks abroad in per cent

	People from CoO, living in CoO		People from CoO, living neither in CoO nor in respondent's CoR		People from third countries	
	A few	A lot	A few	A lot	A few	A lot
Turkish migrants	14.6	70.1	38.6	18.1	17.4	7.0
Romanian migrants	35.5	42.7	44.2	20.4	22.8	5.9

Source: EUCROSS (2013). Turks: N=1250; Romanians: N=1248.

Nevertheless, Table 1.3 also shows that nearly one in four Turkish migrants knows third country nationals who are not residing in his or her own CoR. However, there are considerable differences between the samples. While 47 per cent of the Turkish respondents in Italy reported such contacts, only a single Turkish migrant in Romania did (data not presented). The respective values of the remaining three samples vary between 18 and approx. 30 per cent. The data furthermore reveals that the majority of these third-country nationals are residing in other EU member states.

Considering international communication as a major form of non-physical or communicative mobility (Urry, 2007), EUCROSS also examined the frequency in which respondents were in contact with the aforementioned acquaintances abroad and which means of communication they used. The data shows that the communication behaviour of a considerable share of Turkish respondents in all five surveyed countries is frequently transcending national borders (table not presented). With the exception of Turkish migrants in Romania at least half of all migrants talk to someone abroad once a week or more often. In fact, telephone or telephone-like conversations (e.g., via Skype) present the most frequently used channel of communication with friends and family abroad in four of the five samples. This finding is in line with the assumption of a growing transnationalisation of migrant communities world-wide. Since it is unlikely that respondents have dramatically good or bad news to report each week, it is moreover safe to assume that for most migrants at the beginning of the 21st century, long-distance calls have lost their main character as emergency signals or short life signs to those left behind in the CoO (Pries, 2008). In fact, messages sent via social networking sites, which are the second most commonly used means of international communication for the Turkish migrants analysed here, are likely to be sent in such cases today (without being limited to this function). More than 56 per cent of all Turkish respondents in Denmark and still 20 per cent in Germany used such services on a weekly basis. E-mails and letters which are usually much longer than the aforementioned messages and substantially less direct than telephone calls, are sent least often (the share of respondents who used this way to communicate with people abroad at least once a week ranged from 13.5 per cent in Germany to 34.8 per cent in Italy).

Regression analysis

In order to analyse the effects of the formal status as EU citizens, social networks, non-physical mobility and other independent variables on intra-EU mobility six regression models were computed. The dependent variable was of a dichotomous character and indicated whether or not respondents had visited another EU country during 24 months prior to the survey.

The three models presented in Table 1.4 include both Romanian and Turkish migrants. A dummy which separates both groups is at the same time a measure of the influence of EU citizenship. Model one, which only includes the aforementioned dummy shows that the effect of citizenship status on physical mobility in Europe is highly significant. Thus, Romanian respondents were significantly more likely to have undertaken such travels.

When socioeconomic variables are included (M2) the model shows highly significant effects of indicators such as a positive subjective evaluation of the respondents' current economic situation, higher education levels and the knowledge of third languages (i.e., besides the CoO and CoR language). On the contrary, gender, introduced as a dummy for females, and age are negatively related with physical mobility within the EU.

Finally, upon the introduction of variables measuring social networks and non-physical mobility (transnational communication) the picture changes again. First and foremost, age loses significance as does the nationality dummy. The latter is especially interesting as it indicates that the absence of the status as EU citizen is less important than other included factors. In this model (M3) the economic situation and higher education levels still show a positive effect on European mobility.

Table 1.4. Logistic regression models for recent physical mobility of Romanian and Turkish migrants within the European Union (unstandardised regression coefficients)

	M1	M2	M3
Romanian migrants *(baseline: Turkish migrants)*	0.620***	0.275**	0.190
Current economic household situation		0.255***	0.203***
Education *(baseline: lower secondary education or less)*			
Intermediary secondary		0.377*	0.457*
Higher secondary		0.510***	0.616***
University		1.288***	1.237***
Knowledge of additional language/s		0.496***	0.311*
Female		-0.309***	-0.333***
Age		-0.0143**	-0.00523
Duration of stay in CoR		0.0114	0.00872
Partner's origin *(baseline: no partner or partner from CoO)*			
CoR			-0.0654
Other EU country			0.368
Third country			-0.0887
Social contacts in CoR - Number of family members, in-laws and friends originally			
from CoO			-0.104
from CoR			0.148*
from 3rd country			0.255***
Social contacts abroad - Number of family members, in-laws and friends originally			
from CoO and living there			-0.227**
from CoO living neither there nor in CoR			0.433***
from third country living in any country but CoR			0.269**
Frequency of communication abroad via			
Telephone or VoIP (Skype etc.)			0.161**
Mail or e-mail			0.00821
Social networking sites			-0.0256
Consumption of TV content in a third language			0.0894**
Constant	-0.473***	-1.661***	-2.495***
Cragg & Uhler R^2	0.031	0.149	0.235
N	2,498	2,406	2,264

*** p<0.001, ** p<0.01, * p<0.05

Furthermore, the results show positive effects of the respondents' social networks in the CoR and abroad. The fact that the acquaintance with CoR nationals and third country nationals who live in the CoR has a significant positive effect on European mobility indicates that social integration into European societies and European mobility facilitate each other. The highly significant positive correlation between mobility and the existence of contacts abroad (excluding CoO nationals in the CoO) underlines that mobility is furthermore reliant on opportunity structures. At the same time, one can assume that the causal relationship between these variables works in both directions as travels abroad might provide the respondents with new contacts.

Looking at the pseudo R^2 values (Cragg & Uhler R^2) it is obvious that the third model is much more suited to explain the varying degrees of intra-European mobility, since the respective value rises from 0.03 in the first model to 0.24 in the third.

In the three models of Table 1.5 only Turkish migrants are considered. Model 1 is restricted to the measurement of the relation between the dependent variable and the Turkish migrant groups in the different countries, using Turkish migrants in Denmark as a baseline. It shows a highly significant negative effect of the German and Romanian country dummies. Turks living in Italy, on the other hand, are significantly more likely to have visited other EU countries than their co-nationals in Denmark. However, the model shows no significant effect of the UK dummy. These results are remarkable as they suggest that – in case of the surveyed Turkish migrants – there is not necessarily a direct relation as to whether a CoR is situated within the Schengen area and intra-EU mobility. This becomes especially clear regarding the surveyed EU-15 countries in which the residence outside of Schengen has no effect on intra-EU mobility while there are significant differences between those four countries which are part of the Schengen space. The negative effect of the Romanian country dummy, on the other hand, might to some extent also be due to the countries geographic position which puts it far from the centre of the European Union.

In Model 2 the same socioeconomic variables are added as in the second model of Table 1.4. The above described significant positive effects of the economic household situation, higher education and language knowledge are visible in this model, too. However, if only Turkish migrants are included in the model, there are no significant negative effects of age or gender.

Finally, the last model includes all remaining independent variables. The previously described effects regarding the German and Romanian country dummies and the socioeconomic variables persist. However, in contrast to Model 3 of Table 1.4 there is no apparent effect of contacts in the CoR or third country contacts abroad. Nonetheless, there is a positive effect of the acquaintance with Turkish citizens abroad, as long as they are not living in Turkey itself.

Table 1.5. Logistic regression models for recent physical mobility of Turkish migrants within the European Union (unstandardised regression coefficients)

	M1	M2	M3
Turkish migrants in:			
(baseline: Turkish migrants in Denmark)			
Germany	-0.888***	-0.786***	-0.603**
Italy	0.521**	0.370	0.301
Romania	-2.241***	-2.522***	-2.135***
United Kingdom	-0.179	-0.395	-0.293
Current economic household situation		0.258**	0.213*
Education *(baseline: lower secondary education or less)*			
Intermediary secondary		0.774**	0.868**
Higher secondary		0.497**	0.630**
University		0.884***	0.961***
Knowledge of additional language/s		0.494***	0.255
Female		-0.185	-0.217
Age		0.00343	0.00951
Duration of stay in CoR		-0.00420	0.000688
Partner's origin			
(baseline: no partner or partner from CoO)			
CoR			0.0418
Other EU country			0.183
Third country			-0.418
Social contacts in CoR - Number of family members, in-laws and friends originally			
from CoO			-0.182
from CoR			-0.0190
from 3rd country			0.106
Social contacts abroad - Number of family members, in-laws and friends originally			
from CoO and living there			0.0168
from CoO living neither there nor in CoR			0.257*
from third country living in any country but CoR			0.231
Frequency of communication abroad via			
Telephone or VoIP (Skype etc.)			0.0849
Mail or e-mail			-0.0553
Social networking sites			0.0967
Consumption of TV content in a third language			0.117*
Constant	-0.0480	-1.557***	-2.379***
Cragg & Uhler R^2	0.193	0.271	0.321
N	1,250	1,190	1,136

*** p<0.001, ** p<0.01, * p<0.05

As in the previous regressions, the pseudo-R^2 values indicate that the explanatory power of model three (which combines cross-border variables, socioeconomic background and country dummies) is considerably higher than that of model one (which uses solely the country dummies as independent variables).

Conclusion

Using data from the current EUCROSS project, the presented analysis showed that Turkish citizens, residing as third country migrants in Europe are less mobile on an intra-EU level than Romanian citizens who migrated to the same countries. Nevertheless, a considerable proportion of Turks made use of what is otherwise considered one of the main accomplishments of the European unification. On average, four out of ten Turkish respondents visited another EU country at least once during the 24 months preceding the interview.

When considering international communication, it was argued that the respondents in four out of five surveyed countries regularly (i.e., at least once a week) cross international borders in a non-physical manner by talking directly to someone abroad. Therefore, it can be asserted that such transnational activities are a regular part of their daily lives. With regard to the extension of the respective personal networks, data showed a clear concentration both on Turkish citizens and on Turkey itself. However, for Romanian respondents contact to co-nationals in other countries and especially in their CoO is most common, too. A main factor in the explanation of this concentration is the EUCROSS survey design, which in its migrant related part, concentrated on individuals who were international movers and not naturalised in their CoR. A certain persistence of contacts to the country of origin is to be expected regarding this group. Nonetheless, nearly one quarter of all interviewed Turkish migrants has international third country contacts, too.

The presented data and regression analysis do not support the assumption that the surveyed Turkish nationals residing in Schengen countries are necessarily more likely to visit other EU states than those residing beyond the borders of the Schengen space. In fact, Turkish EUCROSS respondents who lived in the United Kingdom were more likely to have visited other EU countries than those who lived in Germany and therefore would not have needed additional permits to do so. Furthermore, the stated results suggest that other aspects, such as the individuals' personal networks, their education and economic situation are more relevant in this regard.

A positive effect of EU-citizenship on intra-EU mobility was found, yet it was not persistent when additional independent variables were introduced.

However, in this regard it has to be taken into consideration that Romanians, which were used as intra-EU migrants to contrast Turks as third country nationals did not enjoy full membership rights at the time of the survey. Therefore, further comparative analysis, for instance using data of EU-15 migrants, should be undertaken.

Acknowledgments

The author would like to thank Michael Braun for helpful comments on this chapter. This article is a reprint of a revised version of Poetzschke, S. (2015). Mobilities of Turkish Migrants in Europe. *Migration Letters*, Vol.12, No.3.

Chapter 2: Incentive to migrate and to return to home country: A comparison of Turkish, Moroccan and Egyptian cases

Yehudith Kahn and **Nir Billfeld**

Introduction

Most migration models assume that migration is an irreversible and permanent decision, however, this assumption is not appropriate in the Turkish, Moroccan and Egyptian cases. Some migrants return home either because they had decided before migration to remain abroad only temporarily, or because changing circumstances led them to reverse the previous decision to permanently migrate.

Since the 60s, emigration to the EU countries has become a major social phenomenon for all three case study countries: Turkey, Morocco and Egypt. From the beginning of this period, Turkish immigration has been a continuous reality for countries, such as Germany and France. In contrast, many Moroccan migrants have settled in Europe, with political instability and economic downturn at home leading to family reunification abroad and to large communities of Moroccans living permanently in Western Europe (De Haas, 2009). The top destination countries for the 85% of Moroccan migrants who live in Europe (De Haas, 2009) are France, Spain, Italy and the Netherlands (Ratha & Xu, 2008). Strong Moroccan emigration flow into Spain has taken place only during the last decade and is still relevant today, although the trend has somewhat decreased since 2006 (de Acre & Mahia, 2008). Historically for Egypt, migration flows have been largely directed to the Gulf countries; today there is a rising trend to migrate to neighboring European countries. During the oil boom in the 1970s, Egyptians migrated in large numbers to the Gulf States, however in the 1980s and 1990s Asian workers started to replace Arab workers in the Gulf. This change, together with the Gulf wars, put the brakes on Egyptian migration to the Gulf, and led to a new trend of migration to Europe. Moreover, as argued by Zohry (2007), migrants' demographic characteristics vary according to destination countries: While traditionally Egyptian migrants to Europe and North America were more educated than those to the Gulf, the increase of irregular migration to Europe has altered the balance, bringing large numbers of unskilled workers. In terms of the emigration experience, Egypt can be considered an exception. Over the last two decades, Egyptian emigrants in the EU represented only 0.1% of the Egyptian population. Saudi Arabia is the largest host country for Egyptian migrants (Schramm, 2005) and the minority of Egyptian migrants, who do remain permanently in Europe, reside mostly in Italy (Nassar, 2009; World Bank, 2008). This is in stark contrast to Turkey, which saw a slight decrease in emigration outflow, but annual emigration levels still remain high at 75,000 migrants per year, and Morocco, a country that today represents a growing trend of emigration (de Acre & Mahia, 2008).

In terms of migration and remittance patterns, the typical factors of migration differs among the three countries, as argued by van Dalen et al. (2005): in Turkey, a typical non-migrant with an intention to migrate is a man living in a rural household, where financial resources are currently perceived to be inadequate and where migrant household members have a relatively high level of education; in Morocco, the person who aspires to migrate is likely to be in a household with children and whose resources are perceived as insufficient.

Migration has traditionally been used as a survival strategy in times of high unemployment and financial crisis. Beyond mere short-term survival, migration can be seen as a deliberate choice to improve livelihoods (Bebbington, 1999) through accumulation of both financial and human capital. Consequently, economic factors are crucial for migration decision and the choice of destination country.

In Egypt, migrants are more highly educated than non-migrants, evidence of the 'brain drain' phenomenon, where the most highly educated migrate abroad in order to find improved job opportunities (Burns & Mohapatra, 2008).Education and brain drain is an important issue for Turkey as well: 5.8% of educated population migrated in 2010 and more than 2,000 migrant physicians in 2010 which makes 3.2% of the physicians' trained in the country (World Bank, 2011). Turkey is one of the top 10 countries whose students studying abroad, mostly in Germany, United States, France, and England, which make her the 7th highest ranking country of outflow students in 2004-2005. According to Gungor and Tansel (2014) economic instability discourages return intentions, and academic migrants are less likely to return.

Moroccan migrants also tend to leave their family for much longer than those from the other two countries, with an average duration of 10.3 years (compared to 4.5 years for Egyptian migrants and 5.6 years for Turkish migrants). Because migration from Morocco to Europe is more likely to be long-term or permanent, the relationship between the family at home and the migrant is usually that of parent-child. Push factors for Egyptian migrants are mostly economic, with high unemployment leading many young men to seek employment and better opportunities abroad. A field survey carried out in Egypt found that most potential migrants were currently unemployed, with 37% citing lack of job opportunities as motivation for migration (Zohry, 2007).

In Egypt, the most typical potential migrant is a man with a relatively high level of education and a paid job. The predominance of men among migrants fits in well with the social norms about migration that persist in Egypt- where migration is dominated by men who work abroad for a fixed period, and it is the social norm that the wife stays behind. According to Taylor et al. (2003), migration is a household decision with ramifications extending beyond the individual migrant, therefore, household surveys are ideally suited to data gathering in this field.

Despite marked national variations, there are common elements and trends in Turkey, Morocco, and Egypt: they are net exporters of labor, have a large number of unemployed citizens (in particular among the youth and women), underperforming education systems, oversized public sectors, and a very large informal economy (Martin, 2009). Also, all three countries are known to depend heavily on the inflow of remittances. Remittances sent back to migrant-sending regions have been shown to play a vital role in alleviating poverty and improving livelihoods (Adams et al., 2008; Shimada,2010) and often exceed amounts received in foreign aid (Ratha, 2005). Remittances comprise a higher percentage of GDP in lower income countries and can be seen as external funding for those countries (Ratha, 2005).

Therefore, for each country we consider two categories of explicative variables affecting the decision to firstly migrate and to return home: permanent characteristics of the migrants and changing personal and environmental conditions in destination countries. Permanent factors such as education, marital status before migration, diligence, the choice of the destination country, migrant age and changing factors such as the period of first migration, remittances received by households, length of stay, and the number of internal migrations before international migration should be considered as essential determinants of migration flows.

This paper is organized as follows: The second section describes data collection and the sample. In the third section, we describe our methodology. Descriptive statistics are presented in the fourth section and the results in a fifth section. The last section exposes conclusions.

Data and methods

Data was collected from the Netherlands Interdisciplinary Demographic Institute's (NIDI) database, which was commissioned by the EU's Statistical Bureau, Eurostat. The focus of the NIDI survey was to study the push and pull factors determining international migration flows in an attempt to understand direct and indirect causes of international migration to the European Union. Household surveys were conducted in Egypt and other countries between

May-October 1997 to capture individual, household, and contextual factors that influence people's decisions to move or stay.

The definitions of key concepts are as follows in the data: *Migrants* were defined as those who had lived in another country for at least a year, as defined by the UN Statistics Division (Ratha & Xu, 2008). Data for current migrants were obtained by a family member on their behalf.

Results

The present study first describes the psychological, demographic and financial characteristics of Turkish migrants compared to Moroccan and Egyptian migrants. Then, using a logit model, it identifies factors affecting the individual decision to migrate as well as the decision to return home after temporary migration. In addition, we use a multinomial logit model to explain the choice of migration's destination from different groups of countries, since Egyptian, Turkish and Moroccan migrate essentially to Europe and the Gulf countries. Each category is defined according to common economic and linguistic characteristics (oil-Arab countries, non-oil Arab countries, Western Europe and others).

This model predicts the choice of migration by type of destination country. Finally, according to migrant's characteristics, the paper makes a prediction of migrants' median length of stay using Weibull distribution survival analysis. The paper treats return migration separately from the decision to migrate. Thus, it enables us to understand the role played by various parameters in order to appraise the impact of different public policies on the migration flows.

Descriptive statistics

Descriptive statistics as presented in Table 2.1 show that the proportion of migrants is higher in Morocco (46.6%) compared to Egypt (27.9%) and Turkey (26.3%). The proportion of return migrants varies according to countries: in Egypt more than half of migrants (56.8%) come back home compared to 38.4% in Turkey and 15.1% in Morocco.

Table 2.1. Sample description according to status of migration

	Egypt	Morocco	Turkey
Non-migrants	4630	1913	3445
Current Migrants	776	1421	760
Return Migrants	1024	254	475
Nb of Observations	6430	3588	4680

For all countries, most migrants are married and better educated than non-migrants. We note that Moroccans and Egyptians in our sample are sensibly less educated than Turkish. Also, migrants receive more remittances than non-migrants. The proportion of migrants receiving remittances is the highest among Moroccan households (Table 2.2).

Table 2.2. Characteristics of migrants and non-migrants (%)

	Egypt		Morocco		Turkey	
	Non migrant	Migrant	Non migrant	Migrant	Non migrant	Migrant
Married	62.6	74.2	56.6	67.6	69.75	78
Divorced	1.7	1.22	1	1.97	0.7	1.5
Education:						
None	50.5	31.1	70.9	68.03	30.53	10.2
Primary	8.7	8.5	18.4	20.4	55.5	69.4
Secondary	29.2	34.4	7.7	7.4	10.7	16.9
Above	11.6	26.03	3.08	4.2	3.28	3.5
Remittances:						
Low	4.3	8.6	5.5	7.2	3.8	7.9
Medium	11.4	15.4	18.5	35.1	10.4	21.55
High	3.7	4.9	10.9	18.9	5.3	7.8

The first step was to determine factors having an impact on the incentive to migrate. We considered the following variables: marital status, different level of education, diligence measured as number of weekly work hours before migration and three different levels of remittances received by the household. We also performed the analysis according to migrants' destination countries.

As can be observed in Table 2.3, the same factors have a positive effect on the incentive to migrate for the three countries considered: Being married, education, diligence and remittances. However for Egypt and Morocco, high levels of education have a larger impact on the decision to migrate while in Turkey, secondary education is the most significant factor. Concerning remittances, we note that for Egypt and Turkey, low remittances have a larger impact on the decision to migrate than high levels of remittances. Indeed remittances seemed to act as a signal enhancing the willingness to migrate. In contrast, for Morocco migration is not proportional to the amount received by households.

Incentives to migrate vary slightly according to destination countries: For the Egyptian case, we note that married migrants tend to migrate to Arab oil countries, where the average households generally receive low and medium remittances, whereas divorced and highly educated migrants go to Western European countries (Table 2.4).

Table 2.3. Probit model of incentive to migrate (Marginal Effect)

	Egypt	Morocco	Turkey
Married	0.1470***	0.1717***	0.1178***
	(0.0000)	(0.0000)	(0.0000)
Divorced	0.0913	0.2334***	0.3090***
	(0.1177)	(0.0008)	(0.0003)
Primary	0.1202***	0.0753***	0.2060***
	(0.0000)	(0.0028)	(0.0000)
Secondary	0.1824***	0.1023***	0.3643***
	(0.0000)	(0.0044)	(0.0000)
Above	0.3194***	0.1025**	0.2617***
	(0.0000)	(0.0381)	(0.0000)
Diligence_hours	0.0008***	0.0030***	0.0013***
	(0.0002)	(0.0000)	(0.0000)
Remittances_low	0.1845***	0.2395***	0.2207***
	(0.0000)	(0.0000)	(0.0000)
Remittances_med	0.1066***	0.3123***	0.1940***
	(0.0000)	(0.0000)	(0.0000)
Remittances_high	0.0979***	0.2945***	0.1329***
	(0.0024)	(0.0000)	(0.0000)
Observations	6,392	3,426	4,381

*pval in parentheses, *** p<0.01, ** p<0.05, * p<0.1*
Control group: no education, no remittances.

In Morocco, education is affecting destination in an interesting way: migrants with primary education migrate to Western Europe, while secondary educated migrants move to non-oil Arab countries and the most educated tend to migrate to oil countries. Remittances have a higher impact for migrants to oil countries (Table 2.5).

In the Turkish case, migrants with secondary education tend to migrate to Europe and Oil countries, while those with primary education essentially migrate to non –oil Arab countries. Lower level of remittances increases the probability to migrate to Europe and to Oil countries (Table 2.6).

The second step was to determine factors having an impact on the incentive of migrants to return to home countries. We added to the previous variables the decade of migration, migrant age at first international migration and number of internal migrations before the first international migration. In this case, the control group is composed of migrants who moved before 1970, not receiving any remittances and without any formal education (Table 2.7).

For all countries, the decade of migration has a negative impact on the incentive to return home. We note that for all countries this effect is more significant for individuals who emigrated during the 90's, meaning that individuals who migrated later have a lower incentive to return home.

Moreover, migrant age at first migration have a positive but minor effect on the incentive to return. It is interesting to note that only in the Turkish case, the number of internal migrations before international migration positively affect their willingness to return home.

In Egypt and Turkey, married migrants tend to return more than others. Surprisingly, education does not seem to have any influence on the decision to return home for any country. Finally, in all countries, sending remittances reduce the probability to return home. Moreover, the higher the remittances, the less likely migrants are to return home.

Table 2.4. Probit model of incentive to migrate according to destination countries

Egypt

| | Destination Countries | | | |
	Oil Countries	Non-Oil (Arab)	West Europe	Others
Married	1.1501***	0.6479***	0.5654***	0.6089***
	(0.0000)	(0.0000)	(0.0027)	(0.0001)
Divorced	-0.2655	0.3597	1.6927***	0.3877
	(0.6579)	(0.3281)	(0.0004)	(0.4757)
Primary	0.4387***	0.5946***	2.0570***	0.5521*
	(0.0059)	(0.0001)	(0.0007)	(0.0547)
Secondary	0.7943***	0.6682***	3.3684***	1.0626***
	(0.0000)	(0.0000)	(0.0000)	(0.0000)
Above	0.8616***	1.2081***	4.2096***	2.3931***
	(0.0000)	(0.0000)	(0.0000)	(0.0000)
Diligence_hours	0.0090***	0.0093***	-0.0045	-0.0391***
	(0.0000)	(0.0000)	(0.2133)	(0.0000)
Remittances_low	0.9718***	1.0426***	0.2974	-0.1363
	(0.0000)	(0.0000)	(0.4624)	(0.6621)
Remittances _med	0.1668	0.9153***	0.8449***	-0.4730*
	(0.2168)	(0.0000)	(0.0003)	(0.0625)
Remittances _high	0.3766*	0.5629***	1.0644***	0.0422
	(0.0742)	(0.0037)	(0.0011)	(0.9015)
Constant	-3.4998***	-3.1784***	-6.8198***	-3.8007***
Observations	6,392	6,392	6,392	6,392

Control group are non-migrants, no education, no remittances.
Oil countries: Iraq, Kuwait, Bahrein, Qatar, Chad, Libya, Saudi Arabia and UAE.
Non-Oil Countries: Lebanon, Jordan, Morocco, Turkey, Yemen and Syria.
West Europe: Italy, Norway, Netherland, Greece, France, Germany, Denmark, Finland, Austria, UK, Spain, Switzerland, Sweden and Israel.
*pval in parentheses, *** p<0.01, ** p<0.05, * p<0.1*

Table 2.5. Probit model of incentive to migrate according to destination countries

Morocco

	Oil Countries	Non-Oil (Arab)	West Europe	Others
		Destination Countries		
Married	0.2344	0.0481	0.6469***	1.4129***
	(0.7302)	(0.9468)	(0.0000)	(0.0000)
Divorced	-14.7200	2.4158**	0.9199***	1.2849*
	(0.9971)	(0.0395)	(0.0047)	(0.0978)
Primary	0.1413	0.8981	0.2355**	0.9297***
	(0.8690)	(0.3460)	(0.0239)	(0.0001)
Secondary	-14.0035	2.9661***	0.2233	1.4950***
	(0.9926)	(0.0002)	(0.1475)	(0.0000)
Above	1.8280**	1.8727	0.2100	1.5151***
	(0.0287)	(0.1192)	(0.3233)	(0.0000)
Diligence_hours	0.0298***	0.0220**	0.0134***	-0.0050
	(0.0006)	(0.0397)	(0.0000)	(0.2468)
Remittances_low	2.4417***	1.1966	0.9756***	0.9585***
	(0.0098)	(0.2953)	(0.0000)	(0.0025)
Remittances_med	2.2214***	1.2548	1.3660***	0.4663**
	(0.0023)	(0.1096)	(0.0000)	(0.0437)
Remittances_high	-11.5791	1.7503**	1.3046***	0.4180
	(0.9826)	(0.0277)	(0.0000)	(0.1503)
Constant	-7.1152***	-7.3702***	-1.6367***	-4.2012***
Observations	3,426	3,426	3,426	3,426

Control group are non-migrants, no education, no remittances.
pval in parentheses, *** $p<0.01$, ** $p<0.05$, * $p<0.1$

The last step was to use factors determining the willingness to migrate and to return home, in order to predict the median length of stay for migrants. The longest predicted length of stay is observed for Egyptians living in destination countries, approximately 19 years compared to Moroccan (14) and Turkish migrants (12). The next step was to conduct a survival analysis using Weilbull distribution (Table 2.8), demonstrating that for Egyptian migrants, diligence and education have no effect on the length of stay. However, more educated migrants from Morocco and Turkey tend to stay less at the destination countries. We also found that younger migrants, in Egypt and Morocco, and married migrants, in Egypt and Turkey, are likely to stay longer at destination countries.

For all countries, remittances have a negative effect on the length of stay. Migrants who send remittances back home, probably left close family members behind and thus they tend to migrate back home. Moreover, the level of remittances also had an impact on the survival analysis: In Egypt, migrants sending higher remittances are staying longer abroad. Nevertheless, for

Moroccan and Turkish migrants low remittances reduce length of stay but from a certain amount the effect is reversed: Highest level of remittances increase the length of stay.

Table 2.6. Probit model of incentive to migrate according to destination countries

Turkey

	Destination Countries			
	Oil Countries	**Non-Oil (Arab)**	**West Europe**	**Others**
Married	15.0743	1.8925**	0.8185***	0.2925*
	(0.9817)	(0.0100)	(0.0000)	(0.0980)
Divorced	16.6191	-14.1353	1.3327***	1.3493**
	(0.9798)	(0.9983)	(0.0004)	(0.0180)
Primary	1.9711*	2.6601***	1.2860***	0.9964***
	(0.0584)	(0.0091)	(0.0000)	(0.0000)
Secondary	2.2970**	1.9165	1.8073***	0.9523***
	(0.0491)	(0.1199)	(0.0000)	(0.0018)
Above	-12.2394	-12.6078	1.1067***	1.4565***
	(0.9933)	(0.9946)	(0.0000)	(0.0001)
Diligence_hours	0.0232***	0.0299***	0.0064***	0.0079***
	(0.0012)	(0.0000)	(0.0000)	(0.0007)
Remittances_low	2.1204***	0.2663	1.0741***	0.8101***
	(0.0005)	(0.7970)	(0.0000)	(0.0069)
Remittances _med	0.3328	1.0211**	1.0268***	0.6062***
	(0.6673)	(0.0162)	(0.0000)	(0.0038)
Remittances _high	0.5173	0.5673	0.6921***	0.5690**
	(0.6235)	(0.4514)	(0.0000)	(0.0468)
Constant	-22.6903	-9.7663***	-3.4960***	-4.2296***
Observations	4,381	4,381	4,381	4,381

Control group are non-migrants, no education, no remittances.
*pval in parentheses, *** $p<0.01$, ** $p<0.05$, * $p<0.1$*

Table 2.7. Probit model of incentive to return (Marginal Effect)

	Egypt	Morocco	Turkey
Year1970	-0.1630	-0.1140***	-0.2120***
	(0.1802)	(0.0000)	(0.0002)
Year1980	-0.2479**	-0.2474***	-0.3796***
	(0.0318)	(0.0000)	(0.0000)
Year1990	-0.6299***	-0.2614***	-0.5474***
	(0.0000)	(0.0000)	(0.0000)
First_age	0.0009	0.0045***	0.0095***
	(0.6261)	(0.0000)	(0.0000)
Count_internal	0.0081	0.0226	0.0584***
	(0.5608)	(0.1355)	(0.0003)
Married	0.1122***	-0.0447	0.1182**
	(0.0032)	(0.1223)	(0.0121)
Divorced	0.0731	-0.0004	0.2246
	(0.5638)	(0.9952)	(0.1446)
Primary	0.0280	-0.0107	0.0222
	(0.6159)	(0.6649)	(0.6875)
Secondary	0.0216	-0.0404	-0.0055
	(0.5703)	(0.2395)	(0.9385)
Above	-0.0632	-0.0500	-0.0110
	(0.1052)	(0.1424)	(0.9185)
Diligence_hours	-0.0002	0.0008**	-0.0003
	(0.7742)	(0.0140)	(0.6308)
Remittances_low	-0.1630	-0.1140***	-0.2120***
	(0.1802)	(0.0000)	(0.0002)
Remittances_med	-0.2479**	-0.2474***	-0.3796***
	(0.0318)	(0.0000)	(0.0000)
Remittances_high	-0.6299***	-0.2614***	-0.5474***
	(0.0000)	(0.0000)	(0.0000)
Observations	1,601	1,534	986

Table 2.8. Survival Analysis using Weibull distribution: Length of Stay's Prediction

	Egypt	Morocco	Turkey
First_age	0.1097***	0.3992***	0.0099
	(0.0085)	(0.0000)	(0.6845)
Year1980	-7.5673***	-11.844***	-9.0066***
	(0.0000)	(0.0000)	(0.0000)
Year1990	22.8453***	-13.079***	-16.774***
	(0.0000)	(0.0000)	(0.0000)
Married	3.1142***	0.1337	2.2161***
	(0.0000)	(0.9363)	(0.0000)
Divorced	4.3224	5.6316	1.9640
	(0.2676)	(0.2736)	(0.2877)
Primary	1.0723	-3.0373*	-1.0868
	(0.3945)	(0.0650)	(0.1560)
Secondary	0.4181	-5.7529***	-1.5964**
	(0.5888)	(0.0001)	(0.0372)
Above	-0.0761	-6.8713***	-3.3969***
	(0.9220)	(0.0000)	(0.0000)
Diligence_hours	-0.0104	-0.0384	-0.0016
	(0.3480)	(0.1557)	(0.8094)
Remittances_low	-6.1510***	-4.4741**	-2.1551***
	(0.0000)	(0.0184)	(0.0000)
Remittances_med	-5.6773***	-5.9055***	-2.5567***
	(0.0000)	(0.0001)	(0.0000)
Remittances_high	-5.0333***	-5.2635***	-1.9694***
	(0.0000)	(0.0006)	(0.0008)
Observations	1,580	472	934

Control group: migrants before 1980.
pval in parentheses, *** p<0.01, ** p<0.05, * p<0.1

Conclusions

The present paper found that marital status, education, diligence and remittances positively affect the incentive to migrate from Egypt, Morocco and Turkey. The originality of our analysis is to differentiate migration incentives by country of destination. While in Egypt, married migrants tend to migrate to Arab oil countries, whereas divorced and highly educated migrants tend to migrate to Western Europe. Moroccan migrants who only have attended primary education migrate to Western Europe, while secondary educated migrants move to non-oil Arab countries and the most educated tend to migrate to oil countries. On the contrary, Turkish migrants with secondary education tend to migrate to Europe and Oil countries while those with primary education essentially migrate to non –oil Arab countries.

The present study identified new variables affecting incentives to return home: For all countries, the decade of migration has a negative impact on the incentive to return home. We note that for all countries this effect is more significant for individuals who emigrated during the 90's. This finding may be the result of more restrictive migration policies in host countries, such as Oil economies and Western Europe countries. We found that the number of internal migration before international migration positively affected the willingness to return home only for Turkish migrants. Moreover, in Egypt and Turkey, married migrants tend to return more than others. These findings are understandable, since migration from these countries is essentially composed of men leaving family members behind. On the contrary, many Moroccan migrants could benefit from family reunion policies, essentially from European countries. In all countries, as remittances are higher the less likely migrants are to return home. Therefore, remittances are not only a positive signal encouraging people to emigrate but also a reason to stay at the destination country. Remittances have a double effect on the migration decision. On one hand they act as a signal to enhance the first decision to migrate. On the other hand, they further indicate a strong tradition of migrant's commitment to the home community and therefore reduce the median predicted length of stay at destination countries.

Finally, incentives to migrate and to return were used in order to make predictions on the length of stay of migrants according to their individual characteristics. We found that individuals who migrated during the 80s tend to stay at destination countries less than later migrants in Egypt. However, in Morocco and Turkey, 90s migrants stay less at destination countries than migrants who moved in the 80s. Also, more educated Moroccan and Turkish tend to reduce their length of stay compared to less educated migrants. In a further research, we propose to refine the prediction by destination countries.

Chapter 3: Turkish refugees and their use of health and social services in London

Nilüfer Korkmaz Yaylagül, Suzan Yazıcı and George Leeson

Introduction

Following the Second World War, workforces in more developed countries needed labour to reconstruct and further drive their economies, and to satisfy this demand, labour was increasingly *imported* from less developed countries, and the phenomenon of "labour migration" was thus born. For the receiving countries, this was a simple way to meet a transitional demand for labour, and for the sending countries – one of which was Turkey – it was a way of easing off population and unemployment pressures as well as an opportunity for generating hard foreign currency for the economy. The migrant workers were expected to provide financial support to their families left behind and to invest in their home countries (see Akgunduz, 2013:195).

In the case of migration from Turkey to Europe, the whole migration process can be divided into three distinct periods with three distinct types of migrants. The first phase started with the bilateral labour force agreements with Germany in 1961 and this was followed by similar agreements with several other countries (Austria, Holland, and Belgium in 1964; France in 1965; and Sweden in 1967) and together these agreements facilitated mass labour migration from Turkey (Gokdere, 1978:275). Germany has been the main receiving country of Turkish migrants, but large scale labour migration has declined following the recent economic recession in Europe. The second phase occurred during the 1970s as those first waves of migrant workers gained permanent residency status which gave their families the opportunity to join them. Family reunion increased the number of Turkish migrants across Europe and changed the demographic structure of migration as women and children moved to join their migrant husbands/fathers. The third period of Turkish migration was the political migration sparked by the military coup in Turkey in 1980. The coup was followed by ethnic tensions during the 1990s, and as a result an increasing number of asylum seekers sought refuge within Europe (Toksoz, 2006: 4-6).

There is no labour force agreement in place between the United Kingdom (UK) and Turkey and thus there has been no mass migration similar to that between Turkey and Germany. However, there was migration of Turkish Cypriots to the UK after the Second World War, and there was further labour migration in the mid-1970s after the partitioning of the island. Since 1989, Turkish citizens have required a visa for entry to the UK. Migration from

Turkey to the UK continues, and even though the incentive for migration is often economic, migrants do seek asylum as this is regarded as an easier option. Furthermore, by various ways and means, rejected asylum seekers manage to remain in the country (Adiguzel, 2010).

The Turkish population resident in the UK is generally known as the *Turkish-speaking community* in the literature because the Turkish population as such is not a homogeneous group and includes various ethnic groups such as Turkish Cypriots, Turks and ethnic Kurds with Turkish citizenship (King et al., 2008a; Adiguzel, 2010).

The population of migrants originating from Turkey was 91,115 according to the 2011 population census (D'Angelo et al., 2013; Sirkeci & Esipova, 2013:6). Almost two thirds of them live in London, and approximately 71,000 live in the northern London boroughs of Hackney, Harringey and Enfield. This concentrated Turkish population has created its own new lifestyles. The target population of this research comprises Kurdish and Alevi migrants, who arrived as refugees towards the end of 1980s and in the early 1990s. They were typically middle-aged or at least did not begin to work in the UK until they were middle-aged as the application process was lengthy. Changing forms and structures of production which manifest itself as de-industrialisation in the UK after the 1980s resulted in an expansion of the baking and services sectors of the economy, with the consequence that the less-qualified migrants found it increasingly difficult to get a foothold in this new labour market. The situation of these migrant groups as they age is of particular interest because of their vulnerability.

This research aims therefore to consider the interaction between migration, ageing and health. Even though migration need not be directly related to health, the type of migration, life prior to migration and conditions in the host country can all impact on the individual ageing process, health and quality of life (Oca et al., 2011: 2).

Methods

This study adopts a life history and life course approach which is important in ageing studies as it deals with personal and historical time simultaneously, and because ageing is affected by social and individual life histories at the same time (Oca et al., 2011: 3). Ferraro and Shippee (2009) use the cumulative inequality conceptualisation about health in a life course perspective and according to this approach, the life of individuals is shaped by risks, accessibility of resources and personal choices. For example, health is affected by cumulative inequalities during the life course, and conditions in childhood as well as in adulthood impact on health outcomes which become more pronounced in old age. As far migration and health are concerned,

36

conditions prior to and after migration need to be evaluated (Ferraro & Shippee, 2009: 335).

Migration and ageing together are considered as multiple inequalities (Leeson, 1989; Torres, 2006: 240; Ahmed & Phillipson, 2006). Migration in later life creates disadvantages in language and orientation, with housing support to migrants creating gettho communities (Topal et al., 2012; Bilton, et al., 2003:165-166). Living conditions add to the problems of old age, thus reinforcing double societal disadvantages (Seedsman, 2014). Access to health and social services are affected by this disadvantaged situation. With old age, health, care and financial insecurity increase with the use of health and social services (Gundara and Jones, 1992; Warnes et al., 2004.

This research is the second part of a project about First Generation Turkish Migrants in Europe carried out at the Department of Gerontology, Akdeniz University. The first part of the research was completed in Denmark in 2011 in collaboration with the Centre for Healthy Ageing at the University of Copenhagen, while this second part investigated access to health and social services of older migrants and refugees living in London in 2012 with the cooperation of Oxford Institute of Population Ageing at the University of Oxford.

This qualitative research aims to evaluate the use of health and social services of older Turkish migrants living in London, taking into account life course, daily lives, social and physical environments and cultural conditions. Purposive sampling and snowballing were used to identify and reach the respondents, who were recruited by the native Turkish speaking researcher. Respondents have a Turkish background, are aged 50 or over and live in the London boroughs of Hackney and Haringey, where there is a large Turkish population with community centres, shops, social clubs and social centres (King et al., 2008a). Turkish Cypriots were excluded from the study because their migration process and history is different from that of refugees originating from Turkey. A total of 10 men and 10 women aged between 50 and 86 years were interviewed between August 2012 and January 2013. Most respondents had migrated to the UK at the end of the 1980s and the beginning of the 1990s. Of the 20 respondents, six were illiterate, 10 had only basic education, two had college education and two were university graduates. Seven of the respondents had worked in the UK for more than 20 years, four had worked for about 6 years, and the remainder had worked for only short periods or not at all.

The leaders of local Turkish social centres were informed about the research and the interviews, and they helped secure appointments with potential interviewees. Each interviewee was asked to identify other potential interviewees. Semi-structured interviews were carried out in Turkish in the community centres, in the interviewee's home or workplace, as preferred by the interviewee. Informed consent was obtained.

A number of potential interviewees refused to participate because of their refugee background or because of their wish to remain anonymous due to political conflicts in Turkey. Most of the completed interviews were voice recorded and subsequently transcribed for descriptive analysis, although a number of interviewees preferred the interviewer to take notes of the interview. Field notes were also gathered to record contextual information and where possible photographs were taken to add to this contextual information. Interviews lasted between 60 and 120 minutes.

Results

Migration and Life in the UK

There is a body of research which shows that the main reason for Turkish refugees to move to the UK is economic (for example, King et al., 2008b; Adiguzel, 2010), and this is supported by the results of this research. Even though most of the respondents applied officially for political asylum, it is clear from the interview material that economic reasons had determined their applications.

"We don't know why we came here. We don't understand politics. They have asked me why I came here. I have told them that I have applied as a refugee for being Kurdish and Alevi. If they ask me what a refugee is, I still don't know…" (Female, 68 years old).

Two of the respondents had moved to the UK to improve their childrens' opportunities to receive a better education. Most of the women interviewed (and their children) had entered the country illegally, but applied for asylum to gain residence.

Adaptation and settlement are some of the determinants of migration which are also important for health and access to health services (Papadopoulos, 2007; Davies et al., 2006). Most of the respondents still regard Turkey as their home country, and almost all of the respondents spend 1-3 months per year in Turkey. They described their lives in the UK as stressful. Originally, both the labour migrants and the refugees intended to remain in the UK only for a temporary period, hoping to return *"one day"*. This dream of a return ticket is found in other research in these groups (Leeson, 1989). The interviewees have only basic English language skills which limits their ability to communicate and access information about available health and social services. Furthermore, cultural differences between the Turkish population and the native population hindered the development of meaningful relationships between members of the two groups. As a result, they feel more confident and comfortable with social life in Turkey and therefore more isolated in the UK. However, being part of an established Turkish community in the UK and maintaining at the same time close relationships with relatives in Turkey makes them feel *at home*.

> *"We have created a small world and we live and move in that world"*
> *(Female, 77 years old).*

Interviewees have worked mostly in the food and textile sectors, and while some of them have been in work for up to 20 years in the UK, many have had to leave work for health reasons and others because of the lack of suitable work. However, those not in work have been supported by their children as they themselves grew up and started to work and the social benefits available have been a disincentive for many in terms of finding work.

While most of the interviewees complained about the cost of living and stated that these costs had been much less when they had first arrived in the country, some of them were content.

> *"...living is not difficult here. This country is unique, they don't leave you hungry..." (Male, 64 years old).*

Others feel simply that they have "just enough to survive".

Interestingly, given the labour force status of many of the interviewees, none of those still in work expects to retire, perhaps because of the lack of investments or pensions in Turkey, although those aged 60 years and over state that their social benefits have increased after turning 60. Generally, because of poor communication skills, access to social services is established with the help of their children or with assistance from a (Turkish) community association.

Health Status and Access to Health and Social Services

Among the interviewees, a number of diseases such as high cholesterol, diabetes, hypertension, back pain, and cancer were mentioned. Treatments for these were received mainly in the UK, mostly because health services are not free of charge for them in Turkey. For dental and ophthalmologic investigations and treatments which are not free in the UK, interviewees would typically seek assistance in Turkey. Overall, interviewees prefer to consult Turkish doctors, and given the choice, they would prefer to seek treatment in Turkey, where waiting times to see a specialist for serious diseases such as cancer are much shorter than in the UK. A number of interviewees had been to Turkey for check-upsand the like on several occasions. Most interviewees who had accessed health services stated that they had been treated much better in Turkey – as long as they had the money to pay for treatments. However, free access in the UK was appreciated.

Of course, they are able to access their GPs in the UK and they are all aware of the health system. As such, therefore, they do not have physical problems in respect of accessing health services, but they do complain of communication problems with the health care staff, of late appointments and of incompetent diagnosis.

"…the doctor told me to take off my shoes. I didn't want to do that as no one else took them off. I said that my feet would get dirty. A Turkish Cypriot came and told me that the doctor wanted to measure my height…" (Male, 82 years old).

Some of those interviewed ask their children or other family members for help and sometimes they aks for or are provided with professional translators, but this is not regarded as an effective form of communication.

"I tell the interpreter, he tells the doctor, the doctor tells the interpreter, he tells me, I tell one thing and forget two other things I want to tell in between. You can express yourself much better in your mother tonque…" (Female, 59 years old).

Cultural factors are also important determinants of the way in which the health system is used. Understanding medication can itself lead to unforeseen problems.

"…I used to wash dishes in restaurants. I got ill and itched all over. I went to many doctors, but nothing seemed to help. I didn't understand it that time, but at last I got it. I went to three different doctors and I used the different medications they had prescribed at the same time. It was the side effects…" (Male, 65 years old).

Even though this respondent had lived in the UK for many years, he lacked the awareness and knowledge that different medications prescribed by different doctors should not be used at the same time.

There are a number of reasons for not learning the language of the host country. As asylum seekers, they worked illegally and usually in workplaces owned by Turkish people. Once their families arrived, they only interacted and communicated with Turkish people in Turkish, and there was no perceived need to learn English. At the same time, literacy levels were low, and this made it difficult to learn a new language. Isolation and ghettoization prevented them from having contact with the native population, and the support of associations meant that they did not have to access public services personally.

Papadopoulos (2007) argues that the (torture and prison) experience of refugees in their home country has a negative impact on their health. The interviewees in this research are different, in as much as they came primarily for economic reasons, but their migration history and the insecurity during their asylum seeking period has clearly had an impact on their health. They believe that the long wait for family reunion and their loneliness and isolation have all had a negative impact on their health. The whole process of integration and the difficulties experienced during the asylum seeking process had simply *worn them out*. Many stated stress and migration-related problems and traumas as the reasons for their health problems.

"Stress made me like this. Almost everyone here is like me.They have diabetes, all from stress and worry..." (Male, 54 years old).

Research suggests that the climate and pace of life in Turkey had positive effects on health (Sahin-Hodoglugil & Polit, 2005), and some of the interviewees in this current did in fact relate their stress to the weather and the stress of life in the UK.

"... you feel better in Turkey. At least your bones get some sun. Here, this is a dark country. It is always raining....to see the sun in Turkey makes you feel great...." (Female, 72 years old).

Most of those interviewed have a sedentary lifestyle as a result of limited social and physical activities, which in turn are the result of economic constraints. Although they are eligible for free London Transport bus passes once they turn 60 years of age, and although they make use of these passes, this does not appear to increase their levels of physical activitiy. The interview material suggests that walking (or *wandering around*) is the only physical activity in which they engage.

Finally, most of the interviewees receive some kind of income support and/or housing benefits, and some receive unemployment benefits or food vouchers, so the services accessed most frequently are local authority social services and GPs. They may previously have used professional translation but currently they have to deal with it themselves.

Conclusion and discussion

The pre-migration and migration history of the interviewees in this research comprises micro and macro sociological factors which affect access to resources such as health and social services. Even though the underlying reason for the migration of the majority of the interviewees was not political, some had experienced torture and persecution which has subsequently affected their health. The long procedure and duration of asylum seeking with its attendant insecurities forced them to survive on a basic income and with limited housing opportunities. Some of the interviewees had lived alone for many years before being joined by their families and this too had a negative impact on their health.

The interviewees variously have a variety of chronic diseases which increases their need for health services. Stress is named as one of the reasons for ill health. Berry and Kim (1988) state that the level of stress increases with social and economic marginalisation and decreases with integration. The level of stress is closely related to mental and physical health (Papadopoulos, 2007).

This research found that the interviewees are able to access health and social services, which supports the work of Livingston et al (2002). However, while Livingstone et al (2002) found that migrants' access to social services (day care, non-medical health care, psychiatric services, informal care) and primary and secondary health care services in the UK was not different form that of the UK population, this current research reveals that this particular group are unable to use these services effectively as they are unable to access them directly. The difficulties in the adaptation to new conditions, issues in negotiating access to services and and poor command of the English language appear to be the main barriers to direct access, as reported elsewhere (King et al., 2008a; Davies et al., 2006).

Professional translators are not widely available because of the limited number of translators available, the contraction of voluntary sector services due to costs involved. Children accompanying the adults as translators especially in GP appointments, provided less social communication support as they grew older, had their own responsibilities and had less time to take care of their parents. Older refugees try to solve their problems themselves or seek help from associations and social support networks (King et al., 2008a). Social support networks consist of family, relatives, and community services. Even though these services are seen as a barrier to the integration of migrants, research among Polish migrants found that community centres in fact improved the ability of migrants to access services (Ryan, 2011).

The reason for migration, the time of migration and the migration history all affect the integration process of Turkish migrants in the UK. The migrants created a unique, cultural and economic way of life in the UK influenced in part at least by the UK migration policies. Migrants received readily information about services and they used community associations to enable their access to these services rather than doing so themselves. Access to health and social services of the migrants is therefore primarily indirect (through their children and community associations) and can be ineffective.

In order to reduce the inequalities of access, social and health policies need to engage with the existing social networks of these migrant groups while encouraging personal engagement.

Chapter 4: A Widening immigrant – native gap. Child income and poverty in Sweden among immigrants from Turkey and the surrounding region

Björn Gustafsson and Torun Österberg

Introduction

Sweden has received immigrants from Turkey for many years. As a consequence, in 2010 there were approximately 20,000 children with a Turkish migration background have living in Sweden. That is, they are born in Sweden having at least one parent born in Sweden or are themselves born in Turkey. How is this group faring in terms of income in the households they live in? How large is relative poverty among such children? We expect to find an income gap and ask if the gap has widened over a period of one generation, and if so, we try to understand the reasons underlying such a development.

Migrants have also arrived in Sweden from several countries situated close to Turkey. In 2010, Sweden was the home to approximately 48,000 children with a background from Iraq, 17,000 from Iran, 16,000 from the Lebanon, and 11,000 from Syria. There are also approximately 4,000 children with a backgrounds from Romania and about 3,000 children from Greece as well as from Hungary. This paper aims to investigate the economic living standards among such categories of children. As we will see in many respects, children from the above mentioned countries lived in similar conditions to children with a background from Turkey (2008-2010). This implies that they lived in families with lower income than the average native family and child poverty rates are much higher among the migrant population. Our study also shows that the situation was rather different during the years 1983 to 1985, and that much of the widening of the gap had already occurred during the 90s.

A number of studies have investigated the labor-market situation in Sweden for adult immigrants from the countries of focus in the present study.[1] Taken together they show a situation which is increasingly problematic for many such immigrants. This shows up in economic data as low employment high unemployment as well as in low earnings. There are many possible reasons for this situation. Many immigrants from the countries under investigation have shorter education than the native Swedes and such education often is not highly transferable to the Swedish labor market. Only exceptionally do immigrants from the region we study, master the Swedish

---

[1] See for example Rooth and Ekberg (2003), Bengtsson et al (2005), Gustafsson and Zheng (2006), and Lundborg (2013).

language when they arrive. A number of immigrants from the region have migrated to Sweden as refugees and have for this reason larger health problems than natives.[2]

Another explanation for the low participation rates of a majority of immigrants in the labor market is problems of finding a job even if the person is high skilled. This was less of a problem, when for example manufacturing and similar industries had a large demand for unqualified workers as knowledge of the Swedish language was often not required, some decades ago. However, due to structural change, most of such jobs have disappeared. Results from a number of recent field-experiments shows convincingly that Swedish employers tend not to invite job-applicants who, according to documents are as qualified as natives, but have attributes signaling Muslim or another non-western foreign background.[3] The structure of the Swedish labor market might also be one of the reasons why many immigrants from the regions concerned are not employed. Due to collective barganing, the effective minimum wages are relatively high in Sweden where inequality due to low wages is often perceived as a positive feature by trade unions because high minimum wages can displace lower paid jobs. However, it may be the case that this thereby contributes to the low employment rates among several migrant groups. Furthermore, the interplay between progressive income taxes and means tested benefits (social assistance, housing benefits) and income related fees for public funded child-care, might make the incentives to work low for families with many children. In addition, although Sweden uses many resources for programs aiming to integrate immigrants in the labor market not all are cost-efficient.

This study throws light on the situation of immigrants from Turkey and neighboring countries from a new perspective.[4] As we are interested in the well-being of children, disposable income in the households are used as a point of comparison. Unlike most labor market studies, we consider that households can also have income sources others than earning; public sector transfers, capital income and also that they pay income taxes. Furthermore, it was considered that people may live in households where they are assumed to pool incomes with other members. The paper is related to the study of child poverty among immigrants to Sweden, which has shown that immigrant

---

[2] See for example Wiking et al (2004)

[3] For a survey of the literature see Ahmed and Ekberg (2009).

[4] Previous studies of immigrants to Sweden from Turkey include National Board of Health and Welfare (1999), Westin (2003) and Bayram et al (2009).

children from low and middle income countries is substantially larger and more persistent than among native children.[5]

This study is based on register data and it covers all persons living in the country, not a sample. We concentrate on children who are themselves native born – the second generation immigrants. At the individual and household level we define income over a three year period in order to even out some year to year variations. We compared the situation for the three year periods 1983 – 1985, 1995 - 1997 and the three year period 2008 – 2010.

A major finding is the existence of a rapidly widening gap in income between Turkish children and other children with a background in the same region and native children. The same development is evident when inspecting child poverty rates, which during the period 2008 to 2010 are rather high for many immigrant children. Results from regression analyses show that changes across years in parental characteristics like education, age and location within Sweden do not contribute to explain the widening gap in income between immigrant and native children.

Immigrant children

Migration from Turkey to Sweden has occurred for several decades. The first immigrants from Turkey arrived during the 1960s and the first half of the 1970s as worker migrants. However, since then family unification and political factors have been the main determinants as to why migrants from Turkey have received a resident permit in Sweden. Immigrants with a Turkish background living in Sweden define themselves along different ethnicterms. Besides, the Turkish ethnic majority others belong to Turkey's Christian minority (Syriani/Assyrians) who mainly arrived during the 1970s, and were granted residence permit due to humanitarian reasons. Others, who arrived more recently belong to the Kurdish ethnic minority. Swedish registers document a person's country of birth, not his or her ethnicity or / and religion, therefore we are not able to distinguish between these ethnic groups.

Table 1 displays the number of children living in Sweden (2010) that have a Turkish background and the same information for children originating in each of the countries Greece, Hungary, Iran, Iraq, Lebanon, Syria and Romania. We distinguish between three categories: Children themselves born in the specific country of origin, children born in Sweden with both parents born in the specific country of origin and children born in Sweden with one

---

[5] See Galloway et al (2009) and Lindquist and Sjögren Lindquist (2012). For a cross country study of differences in poverty between on one hand immigrants and ethnic minorities and natives on the other hand see Smeeding et al (2009).

47

parent born in the specific country of origin. As can be seen, the largest country of origin is Iraq with 48 100 children. Second in size are those with a background in Turkey (20 400 children) and in third position, with a slightly smaller number, is shared by those having a background in Iran or Lebanon, followed by children with a background in the three EU countries Romania, Greece and Hungary. The present study will focus on children who belong to the second-generation group of migrants, the largest of the three subcategories. Exceptions are children with a background in Hungary and Greece among whom the largest category is those who have one Swedish born parent.

Table 4.1. The number of children living in Sweden 2010 with a background from Greece, Hungary, Iran, Iraq, Lebanon, Syria, Turkey and Romania (Hundreds of persons)

Country of background	Foreign-born	Born in Sweden with two parents born in the foreign country	Born in Sweden having one native born parent and one parent born in the foreign country.	Sum
Iraq	182	281	18	481
Turkey	11	138	55	204
Iran	13	117	47	167
Lebanon	7	131	27	165
Syria	8	88	13	109
Romania	7	18	14	39
Greece	3	7	19	29
Hungary	5	7	14	26

Source: Authors computations based on data from Statistics Sweden

Method

We use data from Statistics Sweden, originating from different registers: the Population register, the Education register and the Income and Tax register. The first mentioned refers to all persons (Swedish citizens as well as foreign citizens) who are registered as residing in Sweden and thus does not include asylum seekers. This is not a sample. For the children (persons aged under 18) and their parents we obtained information on demographic variables like year of birth, country of birth and year since immigration and place of domicile in Sweden from the Population Register. Information on parents' level of education used in the regression analysis originates from the Register of Education, which includes detailed administrative records of education completed in Sweden and information on education received outside Sweden obtained from questionnaires or validated certificates.

We have access to detailed income information from the Income and Tax register at Statistics Sweden, which in turn receives its information from the tax authority and various authorities paying transfers to the households. From this information we have computed disposable income per equivalent unit by applying an equivalent scale.[6] In order to even out short term fluctuations in income at the household level, the average household income over a three year period was calculated. The analysis for the first such period available was from 1983 to 1985, followed by the period 1995 to 1997 as well as the most recent period 2008 – 2010. Each person was assigned the value of the household income, and the analysis is then carried out with individuals as the unit of analysis, an analytic choice now standard in studies of the distribution of income. Comparisons across the three periods make it possible to map changes in income. Between the fist and third period there is approximately one generation. During those years, Sweden experienced several changes. For example, a change from low unemployment to a deep downturn in the beginning of the 90s, followed by a recovery. Another change is that the distribution of income became considerably more unequal.[7]

Results

The first results we can report refer to average household disposable income among second generation immigrant children in comparison to native children and are shown in Figure 4.1. For each country of background, there is one bar for the three year period 1983 to 85 a second for the period 1995 to 1997 and a third for the period 2008 to 10. The main impression from the Figure 4. 1 is that relative mean child income for all immigrant children have deteriorated rapidly. For the period 2008 to 2010, the negative gap for immigrant children from Turkey was as large as 37 percent compared to 11 percent in 1983 to 1985. Most of the changes in the relative income position of immigrant children had occurred in 1995-1997. For immigrant children with a background in Syria, Iraq and Lebanon, the gap in 2008 to 2010 was over 40 percent, at least two times as large as for the period 1983 to 1985. The income for immigrant children from the three EU countries was in 1983 to 1985 rather similar to the income of native children, but also deteriorated rapidly over the period studied. To what extent do differences in parental education, location and some other background variables contribute to explain

---

[6] For details on equivalence scale see the documentation for the LISA data base: http://www.scb.se/statistik/_publikationer/AM9901_1990I09_BR_AM76BR1104.pdf

[7] See for example Björklund and Jäntti (2013).

49

the gaps in income reported in Figure 4.1? To answer this question, we ran a linear regression model with logarithm of child income as the dependent variable and region in Sweden, mother and father's educational level, age of the child and parents, number of children in the family and dummies for country of background as explanatory variables. Separate estimates were made for each period under study.

Figure 4.1. Unadjustaded percentage difference to children with Swedish born parents three year disposable income - Second generation

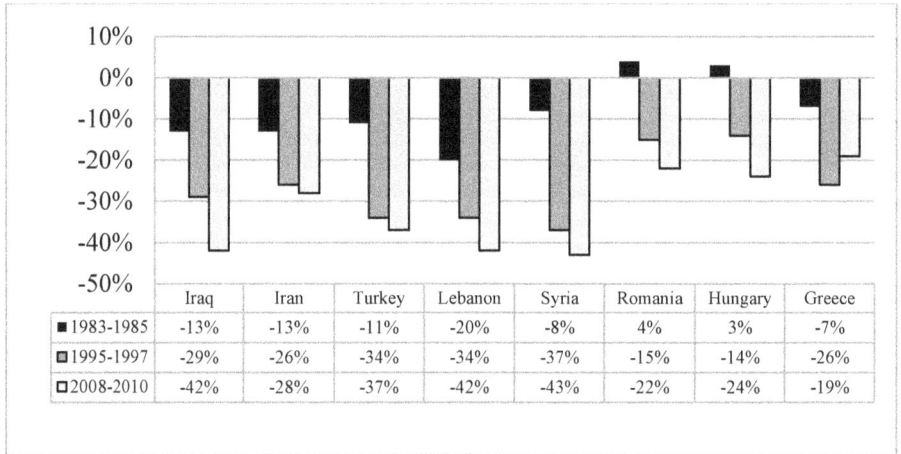

	Iraq	Iran	Turkey	Lebanon	Syria	Romania	Hungary	Greece
■1983-1985	-13%	-13%	-11%	-20%	-8%	4%	3%	-7%
▨1995-1997	-29%	-26%	-34%	-34%	-37%	-15%	-14%	-26%
☐2008-2010	-42%	-28%	-37%	-42%	-43%	-22%	-24%	-19%

Figure 4.2. Adjustaded percentage difference to children with Swedish born parents three year disposable income - Second generation

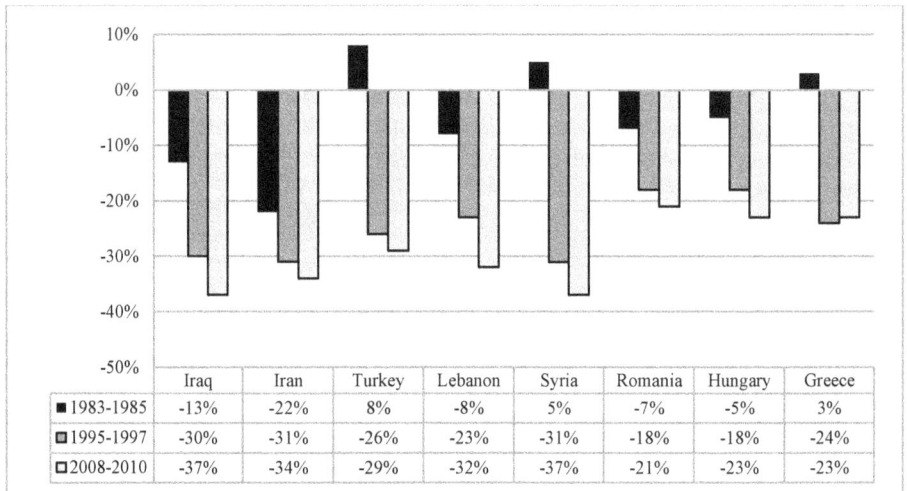

	Iraq	Iran	Turkey	Lebanon	Syria	Romania	Hungary	Greece
■1983-1985	-13%	-22%	8%	-8%	5%	-7%	-5%	3%
▨1995-1997	-30%	-31%	-26%	-23%	-31%	-18%	-18%	-24%
☐2008-2010	-37%	-34%	-29%	-32%	-37%	-21%	-23%	-23%

Figure 4.2 shows the estimates for the country of background dummies, the penalty of being an immigrant child, expressed as percentage difference to children with parents born in Sweden. We find that in 1983 to 1985, Turkish immigrant children lived in households that earned 8 percent more than expected from their parental education and other variables included in the model. However, in 2008 to 2010 an income penalty of 29 percent appeared. The change over time for the other countries of background was similar and the penalty is not much smaller than the "raw" income gaps reported in Figure 4.1.

Figure 4.3. Poverty rates three year median disposable income (60% poverty line) - second generation

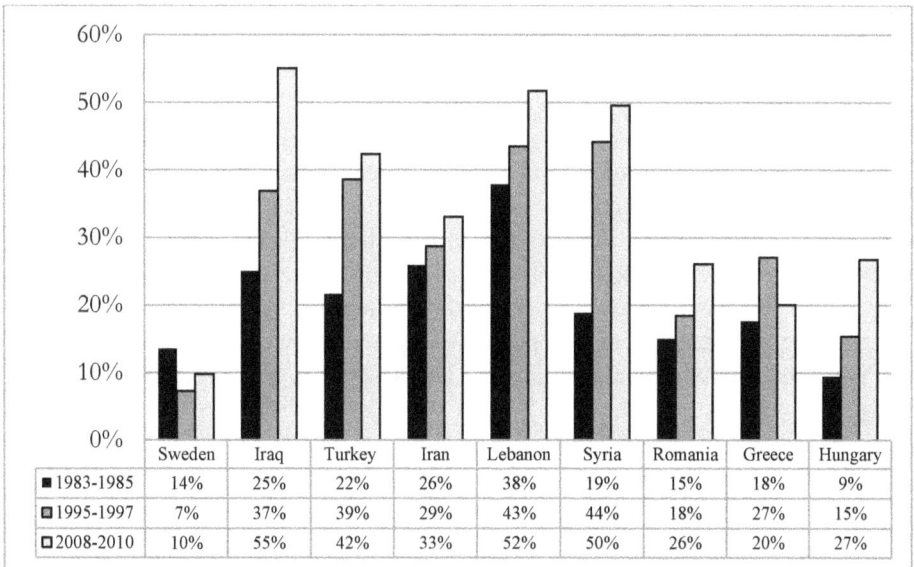

	Sweden	Iraq	Turkey	Iran	Lebanon	Syria	Romania	Greece	Hungary
■ 1983-1985	14%	25%	22%	26%	38%	19%	15%	18%	9%
▨ 1995-1997	7%	37%	39%	29%	43%	44%	18%	27%	15%
▢ 2008-2010	10%	55%	42%	33%	52%	50%	26%	20%	27%

While averages provides an overall picture in some circumstances of focus is on people at the lower end of the income distribution. Relative poverty rates among children are sometimes discussed in the public debate and for policy making. Figure 4.3 reports relative child poverty rates defined as living in a household with an income that is less than 60 percent of median income in the specified countries of background during the same period. Such relative poverty rates were around 10 percent for native children during all periods. However, among Turkish children the poverty rates were two times as high compared to natives during the first period. Thereafter they increased to become four times as large in the 90s, and remained at about the same level during the third period.

The figure also demonstrates that all categories of immigrant children experienced an increase in child poverty rates between the two periods, which is in contrast to the development among native children. In most cases, the increase in child poverty rates continued between the second and the third period. The development meant that during 2008 to 2009, a slight majority of children with a background in Iraq and Lebanon were classified as relatively poor, a fraction five times as large as among native children.

Conclusion

We have studied how children born in Sweden with parents from Turkey, Greece, Hungary, Iran, Iraq, Lebanon, Syria and Romania are faring in Sweden in terms of disposable income and have made comparison with native children. The time periods from 1983 to 1985, 1995 to 1997 as well as from 2008 to 2010 were investigated. The empirical basis consisted of data on the entire population, as opposed to samples.

Our results indicate an increasing gap in child income between the second generation children with Turkish parents compared to other countries in the same region and native children. This took place mainly during the first half of the 1980s to the second half of the 1990s, when the economy experienced negative economic growth and decreased levels of employment. Reasons for this development are probably several. The regression analysis conducted indicates that one possible explanation can be ruled out: A disfavourable development of parental characteristics like education, age and location within Sweden.

The deteriorating situation for immigrants from Turkey and other countries in the region also shows up in rapidly increased child poverty rates. The development has meant that in 2008 to 2010, poverty rates for children with a Turkish background are four times as high as for native children. Poverty rates for children living in Sweden with a background in countries located close to Turkey were also higher or much higher than for native children. In our view, this situation has not attracted the attention it deserves among the public and among policy makers. It calls for a wider discussion of what kind of policy measures that can be effectively applied in order to improve the economic situation of a substantial number of immigrant children.

Chapter 5: Alevis' transnational practices and the consolidation of Alevi identity in the United Kingdom

Ayşegül Akdemir

Introduction

Alevi[1] immigrants from Turkey who live in European countries have actively established associations for solidarity and for demanding democratic rights for Alevis back in Turkey. They do not only struggle for the official recognition of Alevi belief and places of worship in the host countries such as Germany, Netherlands, UK and France, where these demands can be accommodated through existing laws in the host countries, but they also strive for recognition in the host countries to set an example for desired improvements in Turkey itself and thereby transform Turkish society in such a way that Alevis' rights are improved. Consequently Alevi demands focus on obtaining recognition "as a distinct community in a particular, nonstigmatising way" (Sökefeld, 2008, p. 17). For Alevis being recognised means both the acceptance of the distinct qualities of their belief system and also being free from stigma and discrimination due to these differences. This is described as 'equal citizenship' (*eşit yurttaşlik*) by the leaders of the Alevi movement.

In this article, I look into Alevis in London, their identity and struggle for their rights in the "transnational social space", which is the "relatively stable, lasting and dense sets of ties reaching beyond and across the borders of sovereign states" (Faist, Fauser & Reisenauer, 2013: 13–14). I argue that the context of immigration facilitated Alevis to discover and/or act upon their religious and political identity. Analysing their transnational attachments on both vertical and horizontal levels, I find that Alevis employ a universalist, cosmopolitan and pluralist attitude especially in their vertical level transnational practices and they regard the universal human rights prevalent in the host society to be compatible with the elements in their belief system such as humanism, egalitarianism and democracy. Due to some institutional changes particularly in the recent period, the activities and identity manifestations of the community became more inclusive of other identities and became more pluralist.

---

[1] Alevis are the second largest belief community in Turkey and are estimated to be approximately 15-30 % of Turkey's population Vorhoff (2003:94). Alevi belief cross cuts ethnicities and there are Turkish and Kurdish Alevis as well as smaller groups such as Arab and Balkan Alevis.

This article is based on an ethnographic study of Alevis in London which I conducted from July 2012 to August 2013 mainly in London and partly in Istanbul[2]. During my fieldwork I conducted over 50 interviews, and engaged in participant observation, and collected documents from the community centres such as press releases and leaflets of the events they had organised.

The bulk of the Turkish migration to Britain started in the late1980s. Tthere are different estimates about the number of people from Turkey in the UK. Duvell estimates that "there are at least a quarter of a million Turks residing in the UK" (2010), while Israfil Erbil, the former chairman of England Alevi Culture Centre and Cemevi (EACC) the current chairman of Britain Alevi Federation (BAF), estimates that there are at least 300.000 people from Turkey in Britain[3], that nearly 80 % of this population lives in London and the majority of this population is Alevi.

The majority of Alevis in Britain are also of Kurdish ethnic origin claimeing asylum mainly through Kurdish identity[4]. Although not all these migrants necessarily had been involved in Kurdish politics when they were in Turkey, in the first years of migration the activities and homeland politics were organised mainly around their Kurdish identity (Wahlbeck, 1999: 158), rather than Alevi. There were people who joined the armed struggle after they had been influenced in the Kurdish community centres in London according to my research participants' accounts. The armed conflict between the Kurdish guerrillas and the Turkish armed forces affected the lives of many people in the region, including those who were not directly involved; therefore it was a justification for seeking asylum., In addition to providing "advice on welfare, housing and asylum issues, language and training courses as well as various social and cultural activities" to the immigrants from Turkey,community centres in London also promoted Kurdish identity in the 1980s and 1990s (Wahlbeck, 1999:156).

Although there was an Alevi presence in Britain since the 1980s, the organisation around Alevi identity in Britain began in the 1990s due to specific factors. First of all, the global trend of identity movements dominated class-based struggles and from 1960s and 70s onwards "conflicts have

---

[2] In Istanbul I interviewed only organisational elite in order to get a common sense of the Alevi identity in Turkey and their demands. In London I interviewed both the organisational elite and ordinary Alevi people from various backgrounds.

[3] The exact numbers are unknown. This generous estimate belongs to the former chairman of EACC, who was informed by the Turkish embassy about the number of immigrants from Turkey. This estimate is based on the belief that the number of Alevis predominate the number of Sunnis (from Turkey) in the UK.

[4] Few of my research participants expressed that they included discrimination due to being Alevi as a justification for their refugee application. The majority had fear of detention/ persecution due to being Kurdish and/ or being member to illegal political organizations.

developed in advanced Western societies that, in many respects, deviate from the welfare state pattern of institutionalized conflict over distribution" (Habermas, 1981:181). The so called new social movements became more sensitive to human rights, minorities' problems and environmental issues. Gradually identity began to be considered as a right (Soysal, 2000) and this turn influenced the demands of minorities and immigrant groups for their cultural rights. In this context Alevis, who had been experiencing migration, utilized their social networks and connections in the cities and an 'Alevi revival' emerged in Turkey and Western European countries with Alevi population (mainly Germany). As Zirh (2008:105) argues, this revival was not a spontaneous awakening but rather a reconstruction of identity on the basis of new opportunities enabled through migration; through these extensive social networks on a transnational scale Alevis aim to overcome the historically rooted marginality). This turn explains the need for a socio-political framework for identities to be manifested publicly. Although they were aware of being Alevi (especially the older generations who had knowledge on Alevi rituals in the villages) they were not actively defending their cultural rights or to express being Alevi until there was a legal / political and cultural framework that enabled it.

Finally in 1993 EACC was established in London and it embodied a framework for identification with Alevism and organised activities around it. Shortly after the foundation of EACC, an attack against Alevis took place in Sivas province of Turkey in 1993. A fundamentalist Islamist mob set a hotel on fire during an Alevi cultural festival, killing over 30 people. This affected the community deeply on a transnational level and intensified the need to organise. Alevi organisations, which began to appear in the late 1980s, accelerated after this critical event both in Turkey and in Europe. As the former chairman of EACC Israfil Erbil[5] explained during our interview, thousands participated in a large scale rally in London protesting the attack on Sivas and the membership to EACC increased rapidly. According to Sökefeld, after the Sivas massacre "in London (…) 10,000 people said to have joined in a protest march" (2008:122).

As the organisations' activities intensified, the Alevi identity became more visible. New branches of Alevi culture centres were opened in Britain as a parallel development to Turkey and other European countries. Through their local and transnational activism Alevi identity as a social category

---

[5] He was the chairman of London Alevi Culture Centre and Cemevi at the time of this research. Currently he is the chairman of Britain Alevi Federation.

became more visible in Britain. The activism of EACC strengthens the identity-awareness of the community[6].

Currently there are 10 Alevi culture centres dotted across Britain (in London, Coventry, Croydon, Sheffield, Doncaster, Nottingham, Glasgow and Hull) and these have recently united under the umbrella of the British Alevi Federation (BAF) in 2014. The federation also communicates with the Alevi Confederation which is a voluntary cooperation among various European countries' Alevi federations.

Understanding transnationalism

Transnationalism has been a significant analytical approach in understanding contemporary migration. The concept, which emerged as the result of the need for describing the empirical phenomena, looks into "how the migrants reconfigure space and live their lives in two or more places simultaneously" (Schiller et al., 1995). It is "a response to the fact that in a global economy contemporary migrants have found full incorporation in the countries within which they resettle either not possible or not desirable" (Schiller et al., 1995:52). Vertovec defines migrant transnationalism as "a broad category referring to a range of practices and institutions linking migrants, people and organisations in their homelands and or elsewhere in diaspora" (2009:13). Though not an entirely new phenomenon, contemporary transnationalism has novelties such as the transformation of the nation-state, normalisation of transnational activities, increased speed and frequency of contacts and transformative agency. In addition to international migrants, immobile residents also contribute to this social space (Faist, 2000:200).

Transnationalism, especially of persecuted diaspora groups, challenges the idea of the nation-state as the primary social space where identities are defined and manifested. While the nation-state is still powerful in controlling borders and migration, immigrants' dual loyalties and transnational activities promote identification and engagement with more than one locality. Transnational practices of immigrants have the potential of transforming the home country in favour of those persecuted ethnic or belief communities. My interest lies in those transnational activities of Alevis that have the potential and aim of social transformation regarding Alevi identity. While transnational practices such as personal communication or consuming Turkish media do not necessarily contribute to the improvement of Alevis' rights in Turkey,

---

[6] Here the Alevi 'community' should not be understood as a monolithic group due to the internal differences such as ethnicity as well as the way Alevism is conceptualised. Also members of the community identify with Alevism on a varying degree and not everybody has a strong sense of community.

other active engagements potentially do. For example events such as organising commemorations, panels and rallies, lobbying on the EU level or symbolic attachments with the Alevi identity in Turkey have the capacity for social transformation.

Transnationalism is a context-dependent phenomenon (Morawska, 2011:157); transnational activism does not occur at all times for all immigrants and it does not have to disappear some time after immigration. It plays roles in different parts of immigrants' lives; such as solidarity with co-ethnic and co-religious communities, economic improvement, maintaining family ties and struggling for social and political rights. Also, for the London Alevi community, transnational practices and identities are manifold. The community is not homogenous and is composed of mainly Kurdish Alevis, migrating from central-Eastern Anatolia, and partly of Turkish Alevis. When they arrived in Britain during the late 1980s and early 1990s as asylum seekers, the conflict between Turkish security forces and Kurdish guerrillas in the Southeast and Eastern Turkey was at its peak. The identification with Kurdishness was politically more relevant at the time, although many of these people had not been directly involved with armed conflict regarding the Kurdish issue.

Alevi identity politics also came into prominence in Turkey in the 1990s with the booming Alevi culture centres in Turkey and in Western Europe. 1990s was a critical time for the rise of Alevi movement because it was also the rise of other identity based movements; for instance the rise of political Islam was seen by Alevis as a threat, against which they needed to organise. In addition, the pressure put on political activity after the 1980 coup was less intense and some of my research participants stated that Turkish state promoted the foundation of cemevi in Turkey in order to coopt moderate Alevis and prevent them from supporting the Kurdish movement. Van Bruinessen also argues that "by the late 1980s, the growing influence of the PKK among Turkey's Kurds increasingly spread among Alevi Kurds, giving the authorities another incentive to allow and even stimulate the development of Alevism as an alternative "ethnic" identity" (van Bruinessen, 1996:8). In this time period Alevism was not officially recognised as a belief system yet its cultural aspects were acknowledged.

This visibility in Britain is often juxtaposed to the oppression in Turkey. My research participants often said they had to hide their Alevi identity from neighbours or even from their own children until they come to a certain age. Most of them had limited knowledge about Alevism: they knew they are Alevi yet few had information on the theology and rituals of Alevi belief. After immigration to Britain, they gained new opportunities and social networks through community centres and could express previously stigmatised

57

identities such as being Kurdish or Alevi. Indeed many of my research participants, even those who identify with Alevism only as cultural background, stated that when they fill out official forms, in the religion section they tick "other" option and write "Alevi". A rather extreme example is one of my Kurdish Alevi interviewees who migrated with his family at the age of 10. He says: *"Let me tell you openly, in Turkey I never knew if I was Alevi or Sunni. I mean I didn't experience anything like that. Because when I went to school, nobody asked me 'are you Alevi or Turk?' When I came to this country, in this country I found my identity"*[7]. Similarly one of the banners in a rally organized by EACC in Trafalgar Square for protesting the violation of Alevis' rights in Turkey and voicing the demands, was very telling: *"I found out I was Alevi at the age of 14"*[8].

UK Alevis' activism and transnational links for the purpose of gaining rights did not start as soon as they arrived in England, these developed as a response to a complex social political and economic context they settled and led their lives in. A vibrant identity movement in Turkey and critical events such as attacks against Alevis were transmitted to Alevis settling in Britain. Their socio-economic improvement [9] due to international migration also contributed to the funding of cultural and organisationsal activities. They benefitted from the liberal environment of the UK which seeks to accommodate minorities' demands as long as these are compatible with the liberal and democratic norms of the state (Taylor, 1997). Also as Portes (2003) argues, multiculturalism in the receiving country encourages immigrant transnationalism. These activities are mainly undertaken by a small group of people who have the necessary qualifications such as the mastery of Turkish and English languages and social networks. As Guarnizo et al (2003) argue a small group of people carry out these activities and a larger group of people take part occasionally. Also Faist et al argue that not all migrants involve in transnational activities and those who do take part, vary in their intensity (2013:43) and their activities may be comprehensive or selective. Alevis in Britain also carry out their activism through the leadership of a core group of volunteers and the rest of the society either participates occasionally or does not take part at all.

In my analysis of UK Alevis' transnational practices, I have used Morawska's categorisation of vertical and horizontal transnationalism, since

---

[7] Interview, London, 05.10.2012.

[8] Field notes, London, 16.02.2013.

[9] Although half of my interview partners and also many people I observed among the Alevi community receive benefits (either partially or entirely), there is an improvement in their overall living conditions after migration. Furthermore there are now business people and professionals among the Alevi community in London.

this model captures UK Alevis' transnational activism operating on different levels. As Morawska points out, the prefix trans- is interpreted in different ways in the literature: transnational practices referring to those that are *above* state/nation-level memberships are vertical and those that reach across nation-state borders are horizontal (2011:153–4). For instance the EU-level claims-making which nurture from global human rights discourse can be seen as vertical, while "plural civic-political memberships, economic involvements, social networks, and cultural identities" that cross borders are horizontal (Morawska, 2011:155). My analysis shows that the public identity presented on these two levels are not vastly different from each other; the values which are believed to be inherent in Alevi culture such as humanism, egalitarianism, culture of sharing are communicated through universal principles on both levels.

UK Alevis' vertical level transnationalism

Since Alevis are a persecuted and discriminated minority group in Turkey, Alevi organisations aim to make demands be heard in public. Living abroad and having more direct access to the European public and its political actors facilitates this aim. In Turkey Alevis' places of worship (called *cemevi*) still lack legal status and the violent attacks that they faced in history have not been recognised by the state. In order to gain rights and create awareness about their major demands, Euro-Alevis as well take part in activities to promote equal citizenship (*eşit yurttaşlik*) ideal of Alevis in Turkey. At this level they develop public relations with European politicians and use supranational institutions in order to promote their rights.

The EU is an important framework for Alevis since Turkey wishes to become an EU member and one of the many adjustments it has to undertake is to improve the conditions of minority groups. EU progress reports frequently mention the fact that Alevis' demands have not been met by the Turkish state and that physical attacks and discrimination in public and job market towards Alevis continue. Alevis in Europe express their demands in European public. For instance, British Alevis, along with their counterparts in member states, participated in a conference organized by the EU parliament on 20.02.2014 which gave them an opportunity for making their voices heard on supra-national stage. Alevi Federations of Britain, Belgium, Germany, France, Netherlands, Denmark, Sweden, Switzerland and Austria participated in this conference, hosted by Helen Slautre, Head of the Turkey-European Parliament Relations Joint Commission, and Maria Eleni Koppa, Vice Chair. Israfil Erbil shared his views on the meeting afterwards in the EACC's website:

"We expressed that from now on Alevis must be known with their Alevi identity, be valued, and that the European administers must recognise and describe us over this identity. Moreover we said we would like to be represented in the European administrative cadres proportionate to our population"[10].

Another critical issue in the recent transnational activism of UK Alevis concerns the Syrian conflict. Alevis are alarmed by the Turkish government's support for the Syrian opposition, which includes predominantly Sunni opposition and Islamist groups. The perception is that the Syrian War has prompted hostility to Alevis in Turkish dometic politics. Alevis in Turkey fear that the fall of the secular Assad regime would strengthen radical Islamist groups in the region and further sectarian violence (Phillips, 2012). In addition, Alevis' anti-war position has been misinterpreted by the Turkish Prime Minister Erdogan as Alevis' alleged support for the Assad regime due to sectarian affinity and this misinterpretation was used to demonise Alevis. Being concerned by these developments, UK Alevis took initiative and Britain Alevi Federation (BAF) sent an open letter to the United Nations Security Council on 17 Feb 2014 to ask for prosecutors to investigate Erdogan's support for the opposition. The letter reads:

"Alevis and all Alevi organisations residing in different countries around the world are witnessing the massacre and murder of Alevi people residing at the village of Maan, near the city of Hama in Syria in the hands of Islamic fundamentalists and Sharia supporting terrorists. Similar massacres were also carried out by these terrorists supporting jihad at Latakia Alevi villages previously. It is not a secret anymore that these jihad supporters are given all back up by Turkey." [11]

In this letter BAF also demanded that "action must be taken against the current government and its leader Recep Tayyip Erdogan on the basis of providing weapon and ammunition to Al-Qaeda and Al-Qaeda connected terrorist organisations in Syria." And they "request(ed) the United Nations Security Council attain prosecutors to begin the relevant investigations".

The framework of UN gives an opportunity for the oppressed groups to raise their demands from states when the nation-states are not responding sufficiently to their problems or when the nation-states are the very cause of the problems. In this document BAF refers to the specific laws that are binding for Turkey and they claim that action must be taken against the Turkish government. In a follow up interview in September 2014 I ask Erbil

---

[10] http://www.alevinet.org/
[11] http://www.alevinet.org/

what has happened after their letter to the UN; he explains that they did not achieve a satisfactory response yet:

"There was no reply, we had had an application there. Now for example these days NATO countries, leaders of 66 countries are coming to Newport, on 3-4-5 September we will go there and we will have a protest tent, we will camp there. There will be leaders of 66 countries including Erdogan and Obama. (...) Our claim is that now in the Middle East, Isis, Al Qida, Al Nusra which are massacring Alevis, are fed by these countries, have been used as gendarme for themselves."[12]

Alevis describe their faith as one that "looks at 72 nations with one gaze" which means seeing all humans as equal no matter what nationality they are and they promote equality of ethnic and national groups as well as other religions. Especially the politically involved Alevis often argue that true Alevism requires them to be in solidarity with all the other oppressed social groups. Such an interpretation of Alevism makes it possible to move from particularist views and become more involved in global issues. Lately a direct involvement of the EACC was the protest of the massacres of Islamic State against the Ezidi population. A platform "Democratic power unity, Britain" founded by many other community centres in London, including HTAs, political associations and Britain Alevi Federation, had a joint press release in EACC on 1 September 2014 and asked for support in order to help the Ezidi people. They condemned the massacres against Alevi, Kurdish, Turcoman, and Ezidi people and started a donation campaign in order to help the victims.

In this vertical activism and the discourse produced as a result of it, the framework is the supranational organisations and the discourse of universal human rights. This framework gives Alevis (either as individuals or as institutions) to base their demands on and struggle for their rights.

UK Alevis' horizontal level transnationalism

Activities such as raising awareness to the problems of Alevis in Turkey through rallies and public releases, sending remittances and helping Alevi organisations in Turkey are on the horizontal level. Among the several actions, I will explore two specific examples: the commemorations of Maras[13] massacre and the petition campaign concerning proposals for a newConstitution in Turkey introducing an executive presidency

In the late 1970s the Alevis in the region began to prosper economically, and the Sunni majority saw this as a threat to their economic well being in the

---

[12] Interview, London, 01.09.2014

[13] Maras is a town in south east of Central Anatolia which had a significant Alevi population until the massacre in 1978.

region. This hostility led to physicalattacks on Alevi shops and houses in Maras in December 1978. The security forces did not intervene to stop the events until the attacks escalated with eventually over 100 people killed and many more injured (Sinclair-Webb, 2003). After the attacks many people migrated to nearby cities and/or emigrated abroad.

The majority of Alevis in Britain come from various districts of Maras and although in the districts they did not experience the massacre directly, they were highly affected by the trauma. This sensitivity and symbolic attachment to home town encouraged their activism in order to support the commemoration rallies in Turkey. The commemorations are still prevented or restricted by the local administrations and the police force. In addition, more recent attacks that occurred after this are interpreted by the community as the consequences of not confronting with the past.

Before 2010 the local governors did not allow Alevi organisations to conducta peaceful, non-violent commemoration march in the Maras town centre to mourn the deceased and protest against the neglect of the state in protecting a proportion of its citizens. The protests were allowed only in Narlı, a remote district of Maras with a high concentration of Alevis. This meant that the protests would be invisible to the wider audience in Maras. EACC decided to take action, while simultaneously the local branch of another Alevi organisation, Pir Sultan Abdal Culture Associations, was working for the same cause. Eventually they managed to organise the protest in Maras town centre despite the attempts of the local governor and police forces to prevent it. Since 2010 the commemorations are carried out and EACC and local Alevi organisations show their support but the restrictions by the security forces continue.

The protest and the visitors from Maras were televised by YOL TV which is a satellite broadcasting TV channel established and run by the Germany Alevi Federation. This had the effect of highlighting and strengthening the EACC's confidence in their actions as these had an influence on Turkey. It is thus that we can suggest transnational practices may transform society on various levels; as Vertovec puts it "(w)hile not bringing about substantial societal transformations by themselves, patterns of cross-border exchange and relationship among migrants may contribute significantly to broadening, deepening or intensifying conjoined processes of transformation that are already ongoing" (2004:972). The actions of EACC and their cooperation with local organisations in Turkey enabled these protests not only to be enacted but to reach wider audiences. According to EACC organisers and their guests from Maras Alevi culture centres, this cooperation gave confidence to the Alevi population in Maras as they felt the international support for their cause. The chairman of the local Alevi culture centre in Maras explains thus:

"The commemorations sometimes appear from the outside: the local cooperationists and our friends who come from Europe or England, they are perceived as people who come from outside to spoil the game. Actually we are not separate/other than the associations in here (Britain), we are us. This might be an institution on an international level, founded on the basis of the laws in here but its reason of existence is our reason of existence there (in Turkey)."[14]

Another horizontal transnational practice was about the consultations for the proposed new Turkish Constitution. The 2010 referendum voted to change the1982 Constitution prepared and promulgated the military junta after the 1980 coup and amended several times since ('T.C. Anayasa Mahkemesi', 2013). London Alevis demanded that Alevis' views and opinions should be taken into account and their rights should be protected in the process of writing a new Constitution. London Alevis started a lengthy protest[15], where volunteers stayed in a tent day and night to raise awareness of Alevis' rights in Turkey and to demand that Alevis should be included in the decision making of the new Constitution in Turkey. More than 7000 petitions were collected and the chairman and some representatives of EACC presented the petitions to the Turkish parliament. Supported by the Member of Parliament Hüseyin Aygün from the main opposition party CHP, Israfil Erbil presented the petitions, addressing members of the parliament in a press conference. (*Aleviler, Anayasal Hak İçin TBMM'de*, 2013).

In his speech Erbil argued that even though Alevis are a tiny minority in the UK they have the freedom to open their institutions and gain rights on the basis of citizenship or residency. For example, the inclusion of the Alevi faith in the religious education curriculum of British schools (as a pilot project in a few schools in North London) was a big step for Alevis whose demands have been ignored in Turkey[16]. By carrying the demands of Alevi people from England to Turkey, EACC not only carries the documents that show a transnational link from the UK to Turkey but also uses the discourse of rights arising from citizenship. Later in an interview Israfil Erbil summarised his

---

[14] Interview, London, 06.06.2013.

[15] The tent protest took place in Manor House, London, from late April to end of May 2013 for 37 days in order to say no to a new Constitution which will neglect Alevis' demands.

[16] Since 2008 Alevi belief is included in the curriculum of religious education classes, which predominantly teach Sunni Islam. The way Alevi belief is taught is far from Alevis' demands and does not overlap with the Alevi experts' opinions that were taken in the preparation of the curriculum.

expectations from the new Constitution: *"Secular, social democrat, egalitarian, pluralist... we don't demand that the word 'Alevi' should be mentioned in the Constitution, we are not saying that*[17].

We see the development of a discourse which blends the particular elements of Alevi belief with universal rights. These include citizenship rights with the expectation that a secular state should be at equal distance to all religions. This can be seen as one of the core demands of the Alevi movement. More specifically they demand from the Turkish state the recognition of their belief system and *cemevi* as a place of ritual; the abolition of the Directorate of Religious Affairs (DIB); the abolition of mandatory religious instruction in schools; cessation of mandatory construction of mosques in Alevi villages; and the inclusion of Alevi culture in the mass media. These principles, however, are not only the result of international migration and coming into contact with Europe. Due to the importance education for Alevis and their involvement in leftist movements since the 1960s (Massicard, 2007, 2007; Okan, 2004) Alevis were already familiar with egalitarian ideals. What is novel is the identity politics aspect; having experienced the egalitarian and secular environment in the host country they are able to compare their new living standards withthose experienced in Turkey, use the social networks that they developed after immigration and place the values of their belief system and culture into the centre of their public discourse.

Conclusion

The public visibility of Alevis increased both in Turkey and in the European countries in which they live, since they began to organize to struggle for their demands from the Turkish state, which they describe as 'equal citizenship' (*eşit yurttaşlik*). Internal migration to urban and metropolitan areas of Turkey and emigration to mainly Western European countries gave them a new repertoire of social, political and cultural opportunities that facilitated mobilization for their identity. Also the liberal environment in the countries of migration made it easier to be able to identify with Alevism in public. For instance the first generation immigrants in Britain, who are now in their 40s or older, grew up in Turkey after internal migration and before the Alevi movement emerged. This generation could neither learn about traditional Alevism practiced in the villages nor () did they experience modern Alevism which is promoted by modern institutions such as associations and cemevi. In some contexts also the fear of persecution or discrimination in Turkey made it difficult to identify with Alevi belief.

---

[17] Interview, London, 22.07.2013.

Alevi cultural institutions and their transnational activism after immigration enabled individuals to maintain their symbolic attachment with Turkey and state their demands through demonstrations and campaigns. Such activism, particularly after 2008 when EACC's administration changed and adopted a more egalitarian public discourse, more people began to identify with Alevism. In this public discourse the focus on humanism and egalitarianism, which it is argued is inherent in the Alevi belief system, are blended with the Western democratic values and the liberal environment of the host country. The demands on the vertical transnational level relies on concepts such as universal human rights, Western democratic values and protection from massacre and discrimination, in addition to the official institutions that embody these principles. On the horizontal level, mainly citizenship rights and the core demands of the Alevi movement, "equal citizenship" (esit yurttaslik) guide UK Alevis' activism. As I demonstrated through the examples above, the horizontal and vertical levels of transnationalism are useful for analytical purposes however the two levels can also intersect. There is variation in the demands and discourses around the transnational activities on two levels, especially the universal human rights discourse and the institutions that enact these abstract principles make Alevis' claims stronger on the vertical level, yet these principles also influence the idea of "equal citizenship" and more particular demands on the horizontal level. Therefore it is necessary to see the two levels not as entirely distinct but as mutually influencing each other.

Chapter 6: Turkish teachers' views on European identity in Belgium

Ali Faruk Yaylacı

Introduction

Identity, as a theoretical and phenomenological notion, has long been a part of international migration studies (Coll and Falsafi, 2009; Vertovec, 2001). Immigrant identity and belonging has also been a part of the literature on immigrant integration because immigrants' perception of their own identity and that of the host society influence the processes of integration. Esser (as cited in Sahin, 2010) states that identity is an important dimension of social integration. It is related to an individual's sense of belonging to a place and a community. In this process, education also has a role to play. Formal education institutions are fundamental arenas for the construction of identity. Indeed, individuals are driven through a systematic process of identity formation at school as determined by the state. In fact, the learning itself is an experience of identity. This applies to immigrants as well.They gain their perceptions of being and identity in the society during their school years. These perceptions influence their integration. Many scholars have stressed that teachers' personal backgrounds, as well as their identities, impact on their views of teaching. Teachers bring themselves and their personalities into the classroom. The teachers' backgrounds influence what is taught, interpretations of classroom situations and students' behaviours, as well as pedagogical decisions (Koopmans, 1999; Mosselson, 2011; Wenger, 1998; Coll and Falsafi, 2009; Smith, 2000; White, Zion, and Kozleski, 2005). Therefore, it is critical to investigate the integration of Turkish immigrants in Europe in relation to the identity of teachers from Turkey. This study aims to shed some light on this process.

European Turks and European identity

According to official records, approximately four million Turks are settled in western European countries (MFA, 2014). Cooperating with the authorities in relevant countries, the Ministry of National Education of Turkey sends teachers to teach Turkish language as mother tongue and Turkish culture to ensure that Turkish students are provided with these classes in countries of their immigration. Currently, a total of 1730 Turkish teachers have been appointed to several countries abroad (approximately 70 in Belgium) to deliver Turkish mother tongue courses and courses on Turkish culture (MFA, 2014). As underlined by Koopmans (1999), in Germany, the students of immigrant origin are rarely exposed to teachers of foreign descent who could serve them as a role model. Turkish children in Europe are exposed to Turkish teachers in a different context. Turkish teachers who work in Europe spend some time with children of Turkish immigrants as part of the Turkish Language and Turkish culture courses. Volunteer teachers who have professional experience of five years and proficiency in a foreign language are selected through an official exam administered by the Ministry of National Education (MEB, 2014). These teachers, who are sent from Turkey to Europe for five years as part of their official duties, are expected to ensure that children of Turkish origin who live in Europe learn Turkish and keep Turkish culture alive. These teachers are also expected to help the children with their integration process (MEB, 2006). Even if they engage in the educational process for a relatively short period of time, the teachers coming from Turkey have an impact on the perceptions of students of Turkish origin with regard to their Turkish and European identities.

The integration of immigrants of Turkish origin in Europe is examined occasionally in terms of assimilation. However, as underlined by Kaya (2008), Turkish immigrants are not well assimilated in many European countries, but this does not mean that they are not integrated at all. Turkish perceptions about Europe and a strong perception about their own Turkish identity may create an obstacle to the expectations related to assimilation. Another study regarding the example of Germany concluded that the level of maintaining the Turkish culture, adopting the Turkish identity, and communicating with Turks are considerably high among Turkish immigrants (Sahin, 2010). This is also supported by Yaylaci (2012b) who found that Turkish people living in Belgium define themselves not as Belgians or Europeans, but as Turks and Muslims. Yet another study focusing on France revealed that the majority of interviewees define themselves as Turkish-European or European-Turkish, in other words with a *dash of Turkish (?)* and multiple identities (Kaya, 2004). These findings may be indicative of the fact that the Turkish identities and European identities of Turkish people, who have been living in Europe for a long time and thus have somewhat settled do not always overlap.

Turkish people who live in Europe are likely to suffer a dilemma between two "worlds," two cultures, and even two languages, thus develop a problematic identity (Manco, 2002). Regarding the issue of learning Turkish as maintaining culture and identity (Goktuna Yaylaci, 2012) is effective in this process. Turkish courses, as well as the Turkish language training in Belgium, are crucial in protecting the identity of Turkish young people who live in Europe and developing their language skills (Yagmur, 2010). These courses are provided by teachers who are appointed from Turkey by the Republic of Turkey for approximately five years. These courses conform to the curriculum in Turkey. The curriculum back in the homeland dictates that the main purpose of the courses is to give students some basic skills like using Turkish properly, critical thinking, communication, problem solving, and some values like patriotism, tolerance, respect for diversity, peace, and cultural awareness (TTK, 2009). These courses, organized in some Belgium schools and some associations, are recognized by The Turkish Embassy, and are open to all children of the parents from Turkey, regardless of their ethnicity and religious or cultural backgrounds, in elective status. In fact, the number of students attending these courses is quite limited. Of 40,000 students who have Turkish origin are known to live in Belgium, only approximately 6,000 students attend these courses (Cemiloglu and Sen, 2012; MEB, 2006). The largest group of students benefitting from Turkish courses attends primary schools (Manco, 2002). Nevertheless, Turkish courses is a source of concerns for many. Yagmur (2010), for example, state that such courses cannot be transferred to younger generations by inexperienced and unequipped organizations and institutions and that they may do more harm than good for Turkish education in the hands of NGOs, whose objectives and activities are outside the scope of education. The views of teachers, who give Turkish courses, on European identity, are likely to affect the integration processes of students.

Method

This study was configured as part of a case study, which is one of the qualitative research methods. Data was collected by a semi-structured interview form prepared by the researcher. The interview form consists of nine open-ended questions eliciting demographic information, views on the self-definition of identity, European identity, as well as integration in terms of European and Turkish identities. The study group was formed by using the criteria sampling method, which is a means of purposeful sampling. The sample consisted of 20 teachers who had worked in Belgium giving Turkish and Turkish culture courses and returned to Turkey after the completion of five-year duty. Codes indicating the participant number, age, and sex were used at the end of direct quotes from the interviewees (example: P35 M; a 35-year-old male participant). The data were analyzed using the descriptive analysis method and evaluated in the light of literature.

Results

The study group consists of 20 teachers, 14 male and 6 female. Three participants are under 30; while 12 of them are 31-39 years old, five of them are over 40. All of the participants lived in Belgium for five years.

Self-Definition of Identity

An analysis of participants' self-definition of identity (Table 6.1) shows that they define themselves using the concepts of being a Turk and Muslim. For example, two interviewees' self-definition in terms of citizenship, nationality, and religion involved concepts such as *Muslim-Turk* (P39, F) and *Turkish Citizen* (P35, M). An interviewee who defines himself as a Muslim says that religion has no political meaning to him:

I'm a Muslim, but I'm not following the religious rituals, because I believe that it's exploited by religious functionaries and politicians. (P35, M)

Table 6.1. Self-Definition

	Female	Male	Total
Turkish	2	5	7
Muslim Turk	3	3	6
Muslim	1	3	4
Turkish Citizen	-	2	2
Human	-	1	1

An interviewee who defines himself as a Turk says that his definition does not exclude other identities:

I would define (myself) as a Turk, but it doesn't mean excluding other identities. I would rather define myself with a more universal identity which covers all of these values. (P42, M)

An interviewee defines himself only as a human, indicating his view as follows:

I define (myself) as a human. I could have been born and brought up in a different country. (P33, M)

Views on European Identity

The interviewees' responses to the item about their definition of Europeans in the country where they live are threefold (Table 6.2). The interviewees are of the opinion that the majority of Belgians define themselves as Flemish or Walloon. While 15 interviewees agree with each other, two interviewees said that Belgians define themselves as Belgian, and three of them said that Belgians define themselves as European. An interviewee clarifying this issue underlines that being a European has nothing to do with homogeneity:

European people don't display a homogeneous picture, either. It's a little bit difficult to evaluate both Europe and Europeans in such heterogeneity. (P42, M)

Table 6.2. How the Host Community Defines Itself

	Female	Male	Total
European	1	2	3
Belgian	1	1	2
Flemish/Walloon	4	11	15

According to some interviewees, some Belgians define themselves as Flemish or Walloon because their ethnical or national origins get ahead of their European and Belgian identities:

There are two societies called the French or Flemish in Belgium. The latent and clear conflicts between them and current interests are keeping them together. (P30, F)

In my opinion, being a human overshadows their nationalist identities, but they are open to cooperation to protect their own races or beliefs, when necessary. They insist on defining themselves through their national identities. If they could, they would establish the Flemish National Republic. (P41, M)

They define themselves as a Flemish or Walloon, not as a Belgian or European. I think Europeanness is like a historical and geographical symbol, rather than identity. (P35, F)

The interviewees' views on the basic dynamics of identity, as far as they experienced this in Belgian society, offer clues about the criteria by which the European identity is perceived (Table 6.3). Interviewees maintain that 14 dynamics constitute the identity of the host society. The interviewees reported the identity of the host society in terms of five dynamics, among which the economic *welfare* is mentioned the most often. It is followed by *individualism, freedom, religion* and *Europeanness,* and marginalization and *xenophobia.*

Table 6.3. Dynamics Establishing the Identity of Host Society

	Female	Male	Total
Economic Welfare	5	13	18
Individualism	4	12	16
Freedom	3	10	13
Religion	3	8	11
Europeanness	3	7	10
Marginalization	2	7	9
Xenophobia	2	4	8
Ethnicity	2	4	6
Nationalism	2	4	6
Multi-culturalism	2	4	6
Culture	2	3	5
Language	1	4	5
History	1	3	4
Geography	1	2	3

The majority of interviewees report that economic welfare, social state understanding, individualism and marginalization are the basic dynamics of European identity in terms of common life standards:

Awareness of Europeanness, human rights, equality between men and women, religious freedom, individual freedom of thought (P33, F).

Economic welfare, individualist life style, cultural Christianity and negative thoughts about the other (P39, F)

In my opinion, if the biggest dynamics and current order of the social states changed negatively, their points of view would totally change (P36, M).

The interviewees mostly reported that a common European identity is out of question, and the structure which emerges as economic welfare, individualism, and marginalization is not likely to refer to a common identity, saying that the European identity is in the process of formation:

To be more precise, there is a common life standard and overall rules rather than a common European identity. It might be establishing the identity. (P42, M)

The European system of thought supports multiculturalism, and thus when we talk about identity, we cannot mention a single identity, but there is an ongoing process of establishing the European identity. (P29, M).

I guess there is not and there has never been a common European identity throughout history. The EU is trying to establish this identity, but they are indecisively stuck between a definition based on national origins, historical heritage and Christianity and a more universalistic definition on the basis of modern, advanced civilization and human rights. (P39, F)

The interviewees gave two-dimensional answers to the question of whether there has been a change in their image of Europe before and after serving in Belgium. The majority of them said that their image of Europe had been positive before their life in Belgium, but that it changed negatively after working in Belgium:

The image of Europe was too different in my mind before I worked in Belgium, but it dramatically changed after doing this. (P42, M)

There was a considerably different image. There was an image of Europe which has gone beyond nationalist and traditional boundaries belonging to the past thanks to modernity, and progressiveness. I have seen that it was not the case in Turkey. (P39 F)

Some interviewees, on the other hand, reported that their image of Europe was not different before and after their lives in Belgium, saying that this situation was caused by such reasons as their previous experiences about Europe or the impact of communication technologies:

As I was born in Germany and returned to Turkey at the age of 14, I wasn't puzzled. (P30, F)

In my opinion, there is no difference. Nothing is a secret in our era, when the communication is this much strong. (P40, M).

Views on Harmony between European and Turkish Identities

It was also found out that half of the interviewees had negative views on the harmony between Turkish and European identities specific to Belgium, reporting that there could not be any harmonization between these identities. One fourth of the interviewees reported that harmony could be ensured, while only three participants said that the harmony is a difficult process (Table 6.4).

Table 6.4. Harmony between European and Turkish Identities

	Female	Male	Total
They could be harmonious	2	4	6
They could not be harmonious	3	8	11
Harmonization is possible, but it's a difficult process	1	2	3

All of the interviewees are of the opinion that Europeans, specifically Belgians, have negative views on different identities in particular the Turks, and this negative approach hinders Turks' integration within the host society. This situation was mentioned by an interviewee as follows:

The Turkish identity is negatively perceived, it's considered as violent culture and it's thought that the Turkish women are exposed to violence. As they think that we don't have a universal culture and we are an introvert society, some people are even incapable of establishing communication with Turks. (P40, M)

Moreover, an interviewee explained the negative perspectives in terms of religious beliefs:

Belgian people think that the Turkish identity is incompatible with Europe. They have some prejudices resulting from the religious and historical past. (P39, F)

Some interviewees highlighted that the Belgians and Turks excluded each other mutually. An interviewee elaborated on this as follows:

The identities which exclude each other cannot be compatible. There is mutual exclusion both in Turkey and Europe. Turks move away from Europeanness due to the contemptuous and exclusionist manner and double standards that they experience in Europe. (P39 F)

An interviewee attributes this to the fact that the teachers working in Belgium individually fail to exert efforts which are aimed at harmonization:

I believe that all of the people could and should live together and cooperate. My colleagues, whose five-year duty period in Belgium ends without even having a cup of coffee with a European citizen and participating in a social activity with Europeans, cannot help forming prejudices, and eventually fail to make any contribution to the European Turkish identity. (P38, M).

The interviewees who argue that there could be harmonization among the identities expressed their views based on the cultural characteristics of Turkish society, as well as humanitarian values;

The Turkish society adapts itself to the places they visit and also maintains its own culture. (P33, M)

Of course the harmonization could be mentioned. We are all human. Those who cannot talk about harmonization think that (national and religious) economic values are more important than humanitarian values. (P41, M)

Conclusion

The present study, which intends to analyze the views of teachers coming from Turkey and working in Belgium about their harmonization with the European and Turkish identity, revealed that the teachers define themselves primarily as Turks and Muslims. This finding is similar to definitions of identity which are made by the immigrants of Turkish origin who live in Belgium or other European countries. These findings disagree with those of Kaya (2004) which claims that Turks prefer to define themselves as a French-Turk or European-Turk. The views of teachers from Turkey regarding their identities agree with Goktuna Yaylaci's (2013) findings that the Turkish people living in Belgium define themselves as Turks or Muslims.

The views on European identity seem to reflect the ongoing discussions about European identity to a great extent. Naturally it is not easy to define what Europe is and who the Europeans are. The focus has been on the issue of whether a European identity has gradually emerged as a result of some efforts and initiatives such as a common currency and common constitution since the Maastricht Treaty. Those who argue that there is not a European identity claim that there is so much diversity in Europe, and the shared values, laws and administrative organizations are out of the question in the entire Europe. Those who disagree claim that there is a shared historical heritage, as well as social, cultural and political values throughout Europe, despite the diversity in Europe. A great many different definitions of Europe could be made today. In their definition of Europe, the conservatives rather underline Christianity and homogeneity and reject the cultural mix. On the other hand, the thought of Europe developed by social democrats and liberals are based on such principles as diversity, cultural difference, a common future, democracy, human rights, and secularism (Dinc, 2011; Kaya, 2004; Cinpoes, 2008). The participants are usually of the opinion that a common European identity is impossible. What's more, particularly in Belgium, they put forward their ethnic-national identities, rather than a common European identity and they define themselves as a Flemish or Walloon, not a European. Furthermore, some findings supported the perception that Europe is not a 'Christian Club' and Christianity is a 'supra-identity' only in terms of 'other' civilizations (Senay, 2002). According to interviewees, the European identity emerges on the basis of such dynamics as economic welfare, individualism, and freedom. The teachers considerably agree that the cement which brings together the Europeans is not a shared identity, but the shared projects and objectives (Dinc, 2011).

It is also interesting to note the views of teachers who work in Turkey and Belgium differ with regard to European countries. According to the European values in school project EU teacher information research, the majority of teachers in Turkey have more positive perspectives about the European Union countries. Indeed, Europeanness is associated with respect for environment and nature, human rights, equality and justice, freedom of the press, free life, and democracy (European values in school project, 2014).

The interviewees generally think that the harmonization between Turkish identity and European identity is impossible or quite difficult. That is why the teachers teaching Turkish and Turkish culture are appointed to ensure that they contribute to Turks' process of harmonization. As indicated by Manco (2004), the majority of teachers coming from Turkey and living in Belgium for five years fail to learn and speak the language of the country where they work and also fail to adapt to the Belgian educational system. This situation is further evidence to the difficulty of harmonization between Turkish and European identities.

This study, which was conducted specifically with regard to teachers who teach Turkish and Turkish culture and who come from Turkey to Belgium for a five-year duty, revealed no positive change in the views of the incoming teachers on the European identity. The teachers' worldviews are likely to create an impact on their perspectives about identity. Moreover, it is interesting to note that, after their five-year experiences in Belgium, teachers think that a healthy harmonization process between Turkish and European identities will be impossible or quite difficult to attain particularly because of religious reasons, as well as perceptions about identity. Further research needs to be conducted to analyze the Turkish teachers' views on a healthy development of the harmonization processes of Turks who live in Europe. Training the teachers who are appointed to teaching positions in Europe about such issues as international immigration, intercultural communication, national and transnational identities, integration and assimilation would make great sense. It would positively influence students' perceptions of their own identities, as well as about the identity of the host societies.

Chapter 7: Turkish women in Alsace: Language maintenance and shift in negotiating integration

Feray J. Baskin

Introduction

European political themes in the 21st century are overwhelmingly dominated by concerns about the nature of national identity, the role of Islam in democratic society, and the impact of immigrants and their descendants on the perceived cultural homogeneity among the majority of EU countries (Modood, 2013; Meer & Modood 2013; Joppke, 2007; Crul et al., 2012; Akgönül, 2009). The immigration policies of the European Union have been critical towards immigrant populations in the sense that policies have been inconsistent and heavily focused on assimilationist processes.

French immigration policies are dictated by the assumption that full citizenship and inclusion in the French state is only achieved through proficiency in the French language and culture. While such a model of national identification is not unique to France, French immigration policies have upheld the assimilationist model vehemently, often excluding recent immigrant newcomers, such as Turkish communities. Furthermore, it is difficult to make a clear-cut generational distinction with the immigrants who arrive to European countries through marriage. What should one call these new grooms and brides? Is this a repetition of the first generation? In contrast to the largest immigrant ethnic group in France, i.e. the North African, the Turkish community, despite sharing the same religion with Algerians, Moroccans and Tunisians, they have a different migration background. The Turkish community is described as being the least integrated in France. According to a 1994 survey by l'INED, the Turkish case is described as: *"aucun group d'immigrés ne comporte les signes d'un repli identitaire aussi nets et répétés que celui de Turquie"... les femmes "sont presque totalement coupées de la société."* (Bozarslan, 1996: 14)

On their homepage, the Migration Policy Institute defines immigrant integration as: *"the process of economic mobility and social inclusion for newcomers and their children."* There are four important domains where integration can be measured: work, education, social inclusion and active civic rights, which are all intertwined and attained through language.

Research questions

The four major research questions are: (1) What varieties of Turkish and French culture are transferred between the generations? (2) What role does media, in particular Turkish television play in language maintenance and language shift? (3) What are the perceptions about the uses of different linguistics tools (French, Turkish, "immigrant Turkish, code-switching) in order to communicate among the different generations within the ethnic community as well as the local French community? (4) How is integration understood and evaluated between and within generations? However, in this paper, which is part of a larger project, I address the question of integration by conducting discourse analysis of interview extracts with two participants. The interviews took place in the living room of the participant's house. I did a semi-structured interview, which lasted two hours and was recorded with a digital recorder. The focus of the extracts below is on language and identity and the preservation of culture through language in Turkish community in Alsace.

Migration policies in Europe

In the media as well as in academia, assimilation, integration and multiculturalism are sometimes not properly understood and used interchangeably. This is especially the case for the terms assimilation and integration. Also, the notion of multiculturalism is representative of the American context, and therefore, should be used with caution in the European context. Assimilationist policies *"require ethnic minorities to become essentially undifferentiable from the host population, embracing its culture and identity along with its language, customs and traditions."* (Hale-Williams, 2013:22-3) The goal of this model is "sameness and unity" in terms of homogeneity. Integration can be defined as representing *"an inclusive state strategy whereby host societies provide clear legal and procedural channels for immigrant incorporation without requiring that they set aside all differentiating cultural manifestations of their native culture."* (Hale-Williams, 2013:2). In contrast *"multiculturalism attempts to celebrate diversity while promoting harmonious coexistence."* (Hale-Williams, 2013:2) These three definitions can be represented on a continuum with assimilation and multiculturalism on each end and integration somewhere in the middle with different degrees of integration embraced by immigrants throughout time in the host society.

Turkish Migration in Europe: France

After War World II, Western European countries needed cheap labor in order to rebuild their economies. Therefore, West Germany, France and other European countries signed bilateral agreements (starting in the early 1960s) with Turkey. These agreements made it possible for over 600,000 Turkish citizens to migrate to Western Europe in the search of work between 1961 and 1971. In 1973, France allowed *"family reunification"* for its immigrants. This was done in order to promote the integration of migrants into the host society. And, as a result, the influx of Turkish women occured between 1974 and 1990.

There are currently about half a million Turkish immigrants residing in France. In the French media, one hears negative discourses on immigrants: Turkish immigrants and their poor assimilation of French values (Bozarslan, 1996), especially women who are portrayed as insulated within their own ethnic communities and unmotivated to learn the French language (Aksaz, 2006).

Language and Integration

Caught between the standard and prestigious forms of both French and Turkish (Turkish media), Turkish immigrant women in France are pressured to understand and use both languages. Can one assume that there is a continuum between the two linguistic codes? My research will demonstrate whether or not there is a continuum and how these women are developing their own ways of speaking, including code-switching and/or *"immigrant Turkish"* (Backus, 2005).

In France, Turkish women negotiate the use of their linguistics varieties, i.e. French and Turkish and their variants within their social networks (e.g. family, friends) and national institutions (e.g. public spaces, government agencies). This helps them build their monolingual and bilingual communities, and it allows, to some extent, language maintenance across generations. It also facilitates or hinders their integration into French society. France is known for having used an assimilationist model of integration, in which immigrants are asked to become fully integrated into the French society by setting aside their own culture and language and embracing French language and culture. What is unique in the French situation is that culture is prescribed through linguistic competence. Although the assimilationist model seems to have come to and end in France (Tribalat, 2013), does it mean that the French government should give up on integrating its immigrants altogether? How and to what extent should France expect them to acquire French language and culture? What are some of the viable alternatives to assimilationism and how can that be measured? What are the consequences of these policies for the everyday existence of immigrants in France? In my study, I will address these questions and will specifically investigate the role of language and language attitudes in this process. I will examine the sentiment that if one does not speak 'proper' French, or have an exotic name one is à priori not considered French even if one is French by jus soli.

Measuring Integration

How can integration be measured? 'Immigrant integration' is defined, by the Migration Policy Institute, as: "*the process of economic mobility and social inclusion for newcomers and their children.*" (Migration Policy Institute, 2014). Even this definition is not accurate in the sense that it applies to newcomers and not necessarily to those who migrated in the 1960s and 1970s for instance. There are four important domains where integration can be measured, which are: work, education, social inclusion and active civic rights. These domains are all intertwined and attained through language. This way of measuring integration may vary within the European countries. In France, for instance, integration is defined as language mastery and that it is measured in work, education, and social inclusion. As Yağmur and Akıncı (2003) highlight, "[*the mastery of the French language is] seen as the most fundamental aspect of the acculturation process because language is considered to the overarching value to achieve social cohesion and national unity in France.*"

The Venue

The research was carried out in Wissembourg, France. The area is geographically advantageous as it is a border town between France and Germany. The town has a population of less than eight thousand inhabitants of which five hundred are of Turkish descent. In Wissembourg, national (French) and regional (Alsatian) identities and values are reinforced by the locals. Immigrants as well as locals are crossing '*linguistic borders*' (France-Germany) to go run errands on a weekly basis. Three of my participants, shop owners, expressed the importance of knowing German in order to do business with the German tourists when they visit the region. The linguistic market (Bourdieu, 1991) is very well defined for these female entrepreneurs in order to enable economic growth and make tourism attractive. These intrinsic identity and linguistic negotiations in Wissembourg are key to the study and examination of Turkish women's practices, attitudes and what they can tell us about immigrant integration in Europe, more specifically in France.

The bulk of my data collection comes from a generational sample of 38 adult Turkish women living in Alsace, France. However, for this paper my sample consists of 16 female members of generation 1.5 (born in Turkey but raised in France) and members of the 2nd and 3rd generations (born and raised in France). I met with each of these women and conducted semi-structured interviews in their homes. The language of the interview was only French, only Turkish, or a mix of French and Turkish. I also conducted participant observation in public spheres such as the workplace. Each participant was asked to complete a questionnaire either in French or in Turkish. In the semi-structured interviews the following modules were introduced: basic demographic information, language proficiency evaluated through a scaling method, language choices and uses in different settings with different interlocutors, identity and integration, importance of cultural activities and connections with Turkey. The question on language proficiency was measured on a 5-point scale where participants were asked: *"How would you rate your speaking, reading, listening, and writing in Turkish and French?"*

The interviews enabled me to gather data about participants' uses of their language, for instance: *"Which languages do you use with your siblings, your parents, your grandparents, your peers? Which languages do you use at work?"* It also enabled me to elicit information that I was not be able to observe during participant observations. Having conduced participant observation in the household has enabled me to describe and investigate the importance of media, especially TV, in language maintenance or loss. This is a project that I have started for another paper. It is worth noting that television, in most Turkish households is regularly on. The programs are all in the Turkish language and diffused through a satellite dish, effectively bringing Turkey into Turkish households all across Europe since the late 1990s.

Preserving culture through language

Studies in the literature on gender and language demonstrate the relationship between gender roles and language change in different migration contexts. Gal's bilingualism study (1978) on Oberwart, a small town in Eastern Austria, where German and Hungarian are spoken showed that women were leading language shift by moving away from using Hungarian because of its association with 'peasantness' (hence the rejection of that identity) to German, which was associated with job opportunities, better life as a spouse, i.e. socially prescribed modernity. Another study in which social mobility and prestige is demonstrated through language shift is in McDonald (1995) in which Breton women associated their language with *"the peasant lifestyle and the French language with finery and a city life."(55)*.

Cavanaugh (2006) also demonstrated the prestige of the standard language versus the dialect. She studied the language shift of the vernacular of Bergamo, a small town in Northern Italy, to standard Italian. She stated that women are not maintaining the vernacular-on the contrary; they are encouraging and facilitating the use of standard Italian within the household and elsewhere. In fact, women are blamed, in a social context, when using the vernacular with their children because *"they are responsible for their children's linguistic habits and abilities, just as they are held responsible for their socioeconomic futures through their education"* (Cavanaugh 2006: 200), which is in standard Italian and not in their regional dialect. This is an expectation from within a female community to see pressure to speak standard Italian, to their children early on, so that *"they will not endure the linguistics difficulties and social humiliation their parents and grandparents suffered in school as they struggled to learn Italian."* (Cavanaugh 2004 cited in Cavanaugh, 2006:201). If standard Italian is associated with women and social prestige, the dialect of Bergamasco is associated with a particular type of blue-collared man, either isolated shepherds or manual unskilled labor, and thus with a low social economic status.

Furthermore, there is a stigma attached to bilingualism in this community among the teachers who describe the situation as follows: *"[children] arrive at school speaking a localized Italian, with numerous Bergamasco features. Children who speak in this way are often judged to speak incorrectly in general and deemed rough and uneducated."* (Cavanaugh, 2006:202) For these reasons women do not maintain the (ethnic) vernacular language because of its association with 'non-modernity.' In all three studies, upward cultural and economic mobility is associated with the language of the host society at large. Is this a universal generalization? Are all women leaders of language shift? Do they all decide to speak the dominant and more prestigious language rather than their ethnic language? Is there a correlation between language shift and loss of culture? These are questions that are best answerable through ethnographic fieldwork.

In my own research one of my 2nd generation informants' brother made the point by saying that he and his siblings were required to speak Turkish until their 15th birthday. The reason being that it was in order to preserve the Turkish culture. The interesting part in his utterance is when he switches to Turkish (line 13.3) to refer to the Turkish culture.

13.1   parce qu'on avait
         because we had

         pour pas qu'on oublie le turc
         so that we don't forget Turkish

13.3   kendi kültürümüzü falan unutmayalım diye
         so that we don't forget our own culture
                              (Extract from interview-Baskin 2014)

Later in the same conversation I asked about whether losing one's own language means losing the culture (line 14). For my female participant, the response was partly affirmative (line 15), because only a part of the culture will be lost if language is not preserved, whereas dining practices may still be observed.

Nevertheless, she thinks that the transmission of the culture occurs through language. In contrast, her brother strongly believes that if the language is forgotten, everything is forgotten (line 18). The utterance *"on oublie tout"* (line 18) refers not only to culture, but also to the identity of the individual.

14.FB :   ok
ok
alors est-ce que oublier la langue c'est oublier la culture
so does forgetting the language mean forgetting the culture

15. Z :   une partie quand même
some of it though

16.   FB : comment ça
how so

17. Z :   ben pour comprendre la culture faut quand même avoir des connaissances en langue
so in order to understand the culture you must at least have some knowledge of the language
enfin j'ai pas
well I don't know

18. B :   chez nous on a un proverbe si on oublie la langue on oublie tout
(here) we have a saying if one forgets the language one forgets everything

(Extract from interview-Baskin 2014)

This phenomenon, of culture being maintained through language in ethnic communities, has been accounted for in the literature (Mukherjee, 2003; Zuercher, 2009). For instance, in Malaysia, Bengali immigrant women with a close network use the Bengali language more than those who have a diffused network (Mukherjee, 2003). Furthermore, in order to preserve their culture through language, the elderly women in the community advocate for brides from India, because they are more valued than the young women born into the Bengali Malay community in preserving the language (Mukherjee, 2003). Thus, women in the community are involved in different activities to preserve their ethnic language, and consciously decide to use Bengali as an identity marker (Mukherjee, 2003) as well as a form of loyalty toward their culture. In comparison, the younger generation chooses to speak English primarily for economic reasons.

In essence, through linguistic practices, i.e. speaking the minority language in the household, the ethnic culture is preserved and passed on to the future generations. In contrast to the Bergamasco case, in some cultures, such as Turkish for instance, women are perceived as bearers of tradition and culture specifically through their choice of language. However, there are reasons to think that language contact will result in language shift and that women are the primary leaders of this process. Nonetheless, this is not universal, as women are also the gatekeepers of their culture through language (Mukherjee, 2003).

Discussion

Studies of (regional) bilingualism have examined choices and uses of different varieties of languages by women and their significance for the community as well as for the larger society. Since in many cultures the mother is the primary caretaker of the infant (Cavanaugh, 2006) she decides what language to speak to her children. For this reason, when it comes to the preservation of the ethnic language, women are either conservative, and use the ethnic language as the main linguistic tool within the household and with their friends, or they are un-concerned with the preservation of their ethnic language and encourage the use of the host country's language within the household (Cavanaugh, 2006; Khemlani, 2003). In Wissembourg, France the Turkish language of the immigrants is still alive within the household and the ethnic community.

The intergenerational transmission issue reveals that it is much more complicated and complex than it appears, especially among the younger generations. Generations 1.5, 2 and 3 maintain their parents' dialectal Turkish language to some degree, within the household and in the communities, while they may speak French with their friends; and they may even mix both languages when talking to a peer, as some of my participants have noted *"whatever is the easiest."* In addition to parental use of Turkish, Akinci (1996) argued for the role of TV in the maintenance of the language among children in Turkish immigrant families in France, however, there was no data or references to what should be considered, as 'Good Turkish' and what should not.

In a sociolinguistic study, about the future of the Turkish language in France, conducted among participants from Lyon, Akinci (2003) concluded that there is a generational difference. The first generation did not see a future for their ancestral language; on the other hand, the younger generation believed that *"the Turkish language is going to obtain a strong status in the future."* (Akinci, 2003a:140) Why this disconnect from what the youth believe and what adult predicts? Who is right? Are both groups right in a way?

Chapter 8: From retreating to resisting: How Austrian-Turkish women deal with experiences of racism

Katharina Hametner

Introduction

Recent European discourse on integration (e.g. debates about integration tests or national cultural values) focuses more and more on a societal model which understands integration not as societal participation and equality of opportunities (Alexander, 2013; Hess and Moser, 2009; Kaya, 2012) but as cultural assimilation. The markers of difference used in this hegemonial integration discourse work particularly along the axis of cultural difference, a characteristic of a (new) form of racism called "neo-racism" (Balibar, 1991) or "differential racism" (Taguieff, 2000) which focuses on cultural difference instead of biological aspects.[1] Neo-racist arguments are based on the assumption that "cultural groups" are incompatible and xenophobia is a quasi-natural attempt to protect one's "own culture" (Balibar, 1991; Çinar, 1999; Terkessidis, 1998). Thus social categories as culture are naturalized by referring to an underlying essence – a process of psychological essentialism – and "merging different groups" appears as dangerous (Holtz & Wagner, 2009).

In Germany and Austria, discourses of assimilative integration are highly concentrated on Turkish migrants and their descendants – who are identified as particularly problematic and exposed to a variety of stereotyping ascriptions (for a critical perspective see, e.g., Çelik, 2006; Weber, 2007). Underlying images often derive from an orientalist discourse described and criticised by Saïd (1978). Saïd reconstructs a constitutive conjunction between the production of a (post)colonialist "Western" identity and the imagination of the "Orient" as its negative counterpart; while "Western" societies are perceived as modern, democratic and egalitarian, "Oriental" ones are seen as traditional and patriarchal. Based on this knowledge, migrants of alleged "Oriental" origin are perceived and treated as constitutional "others". The Austrian discourse, which frames the study presented in this paper, is structured by a special historical constellation – the Austro-Turkish war and the siege of Vienna by troops of the Ottoman Empire in the year 1683. It influences the construction of Austrian identity and creates a special form of

---

[1] The shift to new forms of racism more focused on cultural than on biological representations are also discussed within the field of social psychology (Augoustinos, 2009). At the same time, the problem of essentialism and reproducing race in psychological research cannot be neglected (Hametner, 2012; Howarth, 2009).

frontier orientalism in Austria (Gingrich 2003). Stereotypical perceptions of Turks as invasive and hostile inform current Austrian discourse about Turkey and people of "Turkish origin" (Girstmair *et al.*, 2011, 2012). People of "Turkish origin" – through a labelling process – are permanently marked as others not belonging "here". This labelling takes place on a very concrete everyday level – e.g. through continued questions like "Where are you from?" or "How come you speak such good German?" (Terkessidis, 2004) – and is based on an ascribed orientation towards tradition, religion and patriarchy and an assumed unwillingness to integrate (see, critically, Çelik, 2006; Weber, 2007). Thus, people of "Turkish origin" are turned into a "group" which, culturally, does not fit into the Austrian context. These discursive surroundings coincide with narrowed subject positions: men with a "Turkish migration background" are reduced to traditional, often violent patriarchs (Ha, 2004; Scheibelhofer, 2007); women, by contrast, are perceived as oppressed victims barely speaking any German, lacking education and needing the support of the majority society (cf. Shooman, 2011). These ascriptions not only have discursive meaning, but are real experiences of *othering*. In one way or another, people of "Turkish origin" have to deal with these experiences of racism on a daily basis (Mecheril, 1997).[2] Following these considerations, this paper explores how the described discursive ascriptions and everyday experiences structure the *habitus* (Bourdieu 1987) of young Austrian-Turkish women,[3] their ways of dealing with everyday experiences of racism and – especially – their practices of resistance.[4] After briefly introducing the methodical framework of reconstructive biographical research, the article presents an empirical reconstructed typology of ways in which Austrian-Turkish women deal with neo-racist interpellations.

Reconstructive biographical research

As the paper focuses on incorporated forms of dealing with racializing experiences, it is concerned with structures of habitual practice which cannot be accessed by asking directly, but have to be reconstructed from accounts that refer to the lived experience of the everyday (Przyborski & Slunecko,

---

[2] For studies which investigate the implications of everyday racism and the experiences of "racialized" people see, *inter alia*, Howarth (2004), Mecheril (1997), Räthzel (2006), Terkessidis (2004).

[3] In the rest of the article, women who migrated to Austria themselves or whose parents came from Turkey will be named "Austrian-Turkish" women. The quotation marks indicate the construction of the national categories used and their problematic essentializing components.

[4] Regarding the importance of focussing social psychological research on the strategies of resistance, see, for example, Howarth (2006, 2009).

2009). According to the reconstructive paradigm (Bohnsack 2007; Przyborski & Wohlrab-Sahr, 2008), access to these implicit biographical structures is possible via "process- and sequence-analytical reconstruction of practices of action" (Bohnsack, 1997: 196, my translation). Reconstructive methodology understands the social world as structured by the interpretations of the subjects (Schütz, 1962). The social researcher deals with an already interpreted world and, as such, has to *reconstruct* the constructions of the researched (Bohnsack, 1997). Following this approach, I gathered twenty biographical narratives from Austrian-Turkish women between the ages of twenty and thirty using narrative interview technique (Schütze, 1983) and analysed these according to the *documentary method* (Bohnsack, 1997, 2007; Nohl, 2006; Przyborski, 2004). The documentary method differentiates between two levels of meaning, reflecting the difference between reflexive and practical knowledge:[5] *manifest* and *document meaning*. Manifest meaning describes the development and structure of the content; it consists of what is literally said. Document meaning, by contrast, refers to what a text or an action shows through its performative composition and form (diction, pauses, intonation, elisions, etc.). Reconstructing the document meaning allows the identification of different types of experiencing (Przyborski, 2004), coping with and resisting orientalist neo-racism.

Retreating and reducing ambitions

Several of my respondents reacted to experiences of racism (e.g. othering, degradation, exclusion) by retreating either in a concrete spatial sense (e.g. leaving the room, wishing to re-migrate to Turkey) or in a more imaginary sense of the term (e.g. retreating to another ethnicity or abstract ethics). They often couple this reaction with a reduction of their claims and ambitions.

Sequences of Meral's[6] narrative function as examples for this first modus. Meral comes from a so-called "guestworker family", is twenty years old and lives in a small Austrian town. Having left school, she is now participating in an apprenticeship in care work. Already in school, but more explicitly in her practical training, she experiences situations of discriminating degradation.

... a:nd I some- don't know somehow that's always such a problem wherever I go:: (1) many I've tried somehow (.) ((Breathing)) (.) to tell

---

[5] Reflexive knowledge refers to knowledge that can be accessed directly; practical knowledge is understood as implicit in everyday actions and cannot be requested directly (Przyborski & Slunecko, 2009).

[6] All names are pseudonyms.

(.) I am Turkish okay: my parents come from Turkey: but I want to do that job; so far there were only some who said hey you are good for interpreting; (.) no one said you are good for caring °somehow;° (.) every time I am there for translating: or for helping out or (1) somehow; that way; ...[7]

By using her as an interpreter, she is reduced to her parents' Turkish origins and her skills as a nurse are not valued. In different episodes of her narrative it becomes evident that she experiences Austrian majority society as perceiving "Turkish" people not as individuals but as stereotypical representatives of an already classified group. But it is not only an experience of being stereotyped but one of degradation:

... there is a young woman who comes from Turkey, already pregnant (.) and she came for economic reasons because her husband couldn't leave his job here, (.) ((Breathing)) they've said äh (1) right next to me: so we were three in the office and then she said to me (1) ah the Turkish women are coming, (.) and I would be surprised, if now t- if the baby now gets the Austrian citizenship; that's an impudence; so to speak; ((breathing)) and they ranted and cursed next to me wherever possible about the Turks I was giving my @infusions@ and went away I ignored it, ...

Meral responds to such experiences in her everyday practice with a resigned stance. If she is attacked directly she tries to ignore the racist insults by continuing to carry out her tasks or by leaving the room. She also reduces her spare-time activities in public:

... a:nd I am very active, @(1)@ I also go to concerts, to theatre productions, I used to be even more active in matters of education I would always go to (.) German something theatre or such integration things and (.) I've had enough of it @I don't want to go there any more@ no matter where I am, ((Breathing)) (.) I receive critique and I'm fed up with it; now I'm not listening anymore I'm doing well now, I'm proud of what I've done ...

---

[7] The signs should be read in the following manner (.) = hiatus less than one second; (1), (2) = hiatus of one, two, etc. seconds; underlined word = emphasis; **bold word** = loud voice; °word° = low voice; ( ) = incomprehensible; (no) = uncertainty in transcription; ((coughing)) = nonverbal incident; wor- = stopping in the word; wo::rd:: = prolongation; word=word = slurring; @ = laughing; , = slightly ascending intonation; ? = highly ascending intonation; ; = slightly falling intonation; . = highly falling intonation, there are no punctuation marks.

After continuous experiences of racialised discrimination, she stops investing in her education and participating in "integration things" and retreats to her private sphere. Apparently those integration projects which are currently offered cause even more negative experiences rather than supportive collectivity – an important resource in dealing with racism (Howarth, 2006). The reduction of standards as the second element of this mode of (re)action to racializing discriminations can be found in Meral's narrative as well. For example, at the end of her narrative she refers to three important things which she wants to achieve: her diploma, a driving license and holidays with her boyfriend. Not only does it express a more privately orientated lifestyle, but also her pragmatic reduction of standards to smaller but, despite her discriminating experiences, still hopefully achievable, goals.

Trivializing racist experiences and assimilating to the majority society

Other interviewees reacted to an orientalist sphere by assimilating with hegemonic interpellations. This included renouncing values perceived as Turkish and adopting the perspective of the majority society. The Turkish community is presented negatively, whereas the Austrian society is idealised. Accordingly, racist experiences are marginally brought up or, if they are brought up, are trivialized.

Leyla's biographical narrative is characteristic of this way of dealing with experiences of racism. Leyla also comes from a "guestworker *milieu*", is twenty years old and lives in the small Austrian town where she was born. Leyla is the first in her family to study. She never explicitly mentioned racism in her narrative, but experiences of racism were implicit. Asked directly about these insinuations, she first claims not to remember such things exactly. As she afterwards, nonetheless, talks about her experiences of refusal or exclusion as a "Turkish" girl (e.g. by teachers in school), she frames these narratives as misinterpretation or finds the reason to be her lack of popularity. Her modus of coping with the situation is one of minimizing or reframing the experienced. Simultaneously she is trying to strengthen her own social position by joking about "Turks":

Ahm (1) @(.)@ so I am until this day, still that way that=I: (.) ahm (1) @tell@ a whole bunch of jokes about Turks, @(1)@ and (.) well that doesn't really matter, yes; bec- I am a Turk myself; but (.) somehow they then thought, it was really funny; again and again, (1) and ahm (.), yes they thought this kind of (.) °g-° they thought this (.) they thought that all this (.) was cool that I now, (.) me: (.) that I talk so openly about it, and that I joke about it so openly, and such, ...

Via such practices, she distances herself from "Turkishness" – a hegemonic interpellation – and adopts the majority perspective. Moreover, she seeks to assimilate with the "standards" of Austrian mainstream society and wants to live "like the girls (.) who live here", who she identifies as being modern and "free of constraints". Thus, she seeks the subject-position of the discursively constructed "good migrant" who incorporates the idea of assimilation (Capdevila and Callaghan 2008). In this way, she reacts to experiences of racism not only by denial but by turning away from "Turkishness" and assimilating into an imagined Austrian lifestyle (for an example in the British context, see Andreouli 2013). Insights into her relationship with her strict and even violent father render visible the deeper significance of this demarcation:

... a:nd (1) yea ahm (.) (ah) my childhood I actually can't remember many things, so (.) ähm (.) it is sad that I have to say that but actually only (.) one thing, and that was the experience with my father, ((Breathing)) (.) ah:m (.) so @(.)@ @ one knows@ that Turkish fathers are somehow more strict; I think that's known everywhere ...

By applying the category "Turkish" to her father, his behaviour becomes comprehensible to her as a *cultural* orientation. This modus of culturalization helps her to make a difficult familial situation understandable and provides her with an apparent solution: cultural assimilation. If her father – as she requests – assimilated into an imagined "Austrian culture", maybe his behaviour towards her would also change.

Naming the facts and aiming to improve the situation through communication

A third form of (re)acting in the field of racializing experiences can be described as naming racist experiences and communicatively explaining cultural aspects of and differentiating perspectives on a "Turkish community". Central to this orientation is the attempt to play an active part in the discourse. The role of clarifying pioneer also enables the person to maintain this position in his or her social surroundings.

Examples of this coping strategy can be found in Ipek's biographical narrative. Ipek was born in Vienna, is now twenty-one years old and is a student. In the first lines of her narrative, we can observe an important aspect of Ipek's experiences of and coping with discrimination – focusing on being special:

... a:nd my parents are from Turkey, they were born there, (.) raised:, and with (.) about twenty-three years they came here, (.) and that not for: economic reasons so=for financial reasons but (.) they were ahm (.) sent by the state (.) here, (.) namely as imams ...

By emphasising that her parents did not come to Austria for economic reasons, Ipek distances herself from the "guestworker *milieu*". She further highlights the distinctiveness of her family when she mentions that her parents were "sent" to Austria to take up a position in society as religious advisors. Likewise, by focusing on her success in the educational field and her ability to successfully support other young women in their educational ambitions, she distances herself from the mainstream and finds her own *special* position in the social arrangement. She is not no one but a role model. Still, her being special is continuously contested:

*... ah the **teachers** (.) ((Swallowing)) were as mentioned before n- not as nice as the teachers (.) in the Hauptschule (secondary modern school) I think because (.) they were also a bit racist °not a° bit but really @racist@ I have ex- experienced, (.) for example some cases, (.) wh:at I never for- forget [...] the pupils were anyway always (.) yes exactly I was completely different @(.)@ I was completely differ- I was there with=the head scarf, ... a:nd y- ähm (1) yes sometimes they for example asked questions (.) concerning my religion and (.) yes: (1) in the history lesson it was really very very bad because (.) every time we were speaking of the siege of the Turks °@(.)@° @(.)@ yes really (.) then she began so yes: and the fourth siege of the Turks @is already now@ ...*

Through her experiences of discrimination and othering, her feeling of being special – as educated woman *and* a Muslim wearing the head scarf – is turned into negatively connoted otherness. The continuous questioning about Islam indicates that her teachers regard this religion as dubious; when they refer to her religious background in the context of the siege of the Turks, they construct her religiousness as something dangerous. As she explicitly characterizes her experiences as racism, she is taking an active and denominating position. Here the importance of being able to put into words the racism she experiences becomes evident. This active modus of coping is expressed throughout the interview in two ways: one of critique and one of pedagogy. In the modus of critique, she explicitly describes her experiences as racism and defends her position by criticizing devaluating generalizations and explaining her point of view – especially in respect to religion, e.g. by presenting better knowledge about Islam. In this context, she slips into

91

pedagogical mode. By teaching others to have a better and more educated understanding of Islam or "Turkish culture" she recovers an active, knowledgeable and, once again, special position.

... they never considered that from the positive point of view I think not really I never saw w- where, where we I would for example as teacher ((Swallowing)) organize a day on which (.) for example everyone from home bake (.) a speciality from home or so (.) and have a a national- well a day of nationalities or (.) a multicultural day [...] so that they (.) so that they also yes get to know each other better and also mh:: yes (.) but for us it was totally (.) so a the different @case@ (.) ah in fact (.) we were always as- we were always isolated ...

Her description displays a strong belief in the power of communicative learning. This goes side by side with her orientation towards education in general, people knowing each other and each other's practices as a consequence of education; in this way, problems could be avoided. In Ipek's mode of active critique and educated-communicative pedagogical activities, the image of the suppressed Muslim woman is rejected. By taking a stance in which being a Muslim and a critical and educated woman is not a contradiction, she resists the discursive categorization (Andreouli, 2013.)

Delegitimizing and transcending racist stereotypes through the use of irony

The fourth reconstructed modus is a form of delegitimizing racist stereotypes and responding to them with amusement and irony. In reaction to stereotyping interpellations, the interviewees refer to situations in which definite categorizations become impossible or absurd.

As an example, two extracts from Ferda's narrative are presented below. Ferda was born in Germany while her parents were students there. She was brought up in Turkey and came to Vienna for her own studies. At the time of the interview she was in her late twenties and was working as a researcher. In an episode about her life in a student hall of residence in Vienna, she refers to a neighbour of "Arab" origins:

... but I had an [Iraqi:] so a neighbour, (.) coming (.) from [Iraq] ah:: ((Breathing/Clicking her tongue)) so he was over forty; he w- he was funny; °and (.) @(.)@° (1) he was named Osama and @back then that was yet@ @(1)@ ((the following words spoken with a smile)) and as I had a fish: s=äh=I had: two fish in an aquarium back then; (.) have: left with hi:m ((Breathing)) well my fish became (   ). so @(.)@ he almost

@killed my fish Osama@ @(2)@ ((Breathing) but out of <u>love</u> because he fed much @(.)@ mh::: yes ...

In her presentation she refers ironically to stereotypes about people with "oriental" names or origins. Playfully, and with amusement, she turns the stereotype on its head. Where, in hegemonic discourse, the name "Osama" is a symbol of danger, here the "threat" is too much love. By emphasizing his excessive love, the image of a threat becomes *ad absurdum* and the orientalist ascription is delegitimized. In a similar mode, she ridicules stereotypical ideas of the lives of Turkish women:

... ah: (.) I moved (.) in with a (2) so an Austrian friend, (1) a:nd (.) that were almost so <u>two</u> years too, (.) <u>back then</u> it was for me ahm (2) ah: (.) so (.) <u>me</u> funnily enough everyone here=w wondered; you are from <u>Turkey</u> and (1) your par- parents allow you, without being married to relo(.)°cate and to move in and° ...

Her description of her experience classifies the ascriptions as baseless; simultaneously her narrative implies the possibility of transcending the ascriptions by marking them as strange. Thus she is creating space in which to break orientalist dichotomies. As she categorizes herself as a "Cosmopolitan", she opposes definite cultural categorizations in general.

Conclusion

The aim of this article was to look at the different ways in which young Austrian-Turkish women deal with and resist experiences of racism. These women are subjected to similar neo-racist discursive topoi as well as to concrete discriminating incidents and all have to deal with these in their everyday lives. In reconstructing four very different *modi* of (re)acting in a neo-racist structured sphere, the article demonstrated not only that the ways of handling the experience differ considerably but also that there are many examples of women actively resisting or transgressing such experiences. All women have to (re)act within a discourse of racializing othering. However, only some forms of dealing with this experience remain largely "inside" this discursive framework, as becomes apparent from the way of retreating or of assimilating, while other forms actively try to intervene in and change the discursive ascriptions by communicatively differentiating or ironically transcending the neo-racist orientalist gaze. These findings show that the women are not simply subjected to racist experiences but also defend their position as active individuals. Emphasizing this perspective helps to criticise and hopefully overcome the victimization of migrants (e.g. Reuter & Villa,

2010) – especially of women of Turkish origin (e.g. Shooman, 2011) – as is often found in migration studies and integration policies. In addition, the findings could be of interest for anti-racist intervention, as supporting the women in their fight demands a clear understanding of existing coping strategies and possibilities of resistance. The examples of the four women, on the one hand, give insights into the problematic effects of one-sided categorizations and the interpellation of assimilation. On the other hand, they show the need for an approach to integration which avoids racializing othering and implies anti-racist strategies, and demonstrate the importance of supporting the efforts of the women to name the experience and to find ways of transgressing dichotomous categorizations.

Chapter 9: Social communication among Turkish immigrants in Belgium

Filiz Göktuna Yaylacı

Introduction

Turkey signed its first immigration and labour force exchange agreement with Germany in 1961, followed by similar agreements signed with the Netherlands, Belgium, Denmark, Austria, France and Sweden. Belgium has been one of the destinations for Turkish immigrants. According to the Turkish Embassy in Brussels a total of approximately 180,000 Turkish people live in Belgium (Turkish Embassy in Brussels, 2014). Similar to Germany, the Netherlands and France where a large volume of Turkish immigration was allowed, distinctive characteristics of Turkish immigration evident in Belgium. Turks arrived and settled in certain parts of Belgium due to family ties and networks. Half of Turkish people in Belgium live in the Dutch-speaking Flemish Region, 25 % in Brussels and 25% in the French-speaking Valloon Region (Kanmaz, 2003; Aydın and Manço, 2002).

Social communication and migration

Communication has an impact on individuals who define themselves through communication with others (Neuliep, 2006: 9). There is not a single commonly accepted definition in the field of social communication. Terms such as social communication, social interaction, face-to-face interaction and interaction in daily life refer to things that people have to do when interacting with others. Often definitions of these concepts overlap with each other (Leeds-Hurwitz, 1992: XV).

The communication and transportation networks between the host country and the country of origin are important in creation and preservation of diasporic identity among transnational communities. The modern mobility networks connect diasporic subjects both to their homelands and to the rest of the world (Kaya and Kentel, 2005:24-25). According to Georgiou and Silverstone (2007), diasporic daily life refers to neighbours in the settled country, friends and relatives where diasporic networks cover, as well as the family and friends left behind in the homeland. Communication flows are through phone calls or journeys in primary forms (social interaction) and advanced technologies such as radio, TV and Internet (Smets et al. 2009, 274). The media, as part of a social process, strongly affects the construction of identities, sociability and ability to establish a group or community. While people shape their daily communication around themes and representations shared through media consumption, the media makes their existence in the public settled (Georgiou, 2006: 29).

According to Kim's (1977: 28-29) findings, interpersonal interaction and organizational participation within the ethnic group are stronger than those of the host society, and participation in organizations in the host country, as well as participation in ethnic organizations increases in the course of time – increases with the duration of stay. While the circle of friends is dominated by co-ethnics in initial years, it gets diversified in due time and elderly people communicate more within the ethnic community compared to young people. Satisfaction with living in the host country among immigrants is closely related to their level of engagement with inter-ethnic communication, rather than intra-ethnic communication.

This study focuses on specifically Turkish people who are originally from Emirdağ and Posof districts who live in Belgium. The study aims at exploring the social communication processes and practices of Turkish people living in Belgium in terms of defining the self, daily language preferences, communication with friends and neighbours and the consumption of media.

This study adopts the cultural analysis model using a qualitative paradigm. The interviewed sample (55 persons) consisted of individuals selected by a purposeful-stratified sampling method among the Turkish people from Emirdağ and Posof living in Flanders and Brussels regions in Belgium. Interviews were conducted with two groups concentrated in certain towns or neighbourhoods. Both groups display the characteristics of a closed society with original qualities. They mainly describe themselves based on Turkish nationality and Muslim identity. Although there is no official data, according to mangers of migrant associations, Turks from Emirdağ (a town in Afyon Province in Western Turkey) and Posof (a town in Ardahan Province in Eastern Turkey) constitute more than half of the Turkish population living in Belgium. Those from Emirdağ is the largest group of Turks who originally come from a single town in Turkey living in Belgium. These people from Emirdağ and Posof cluster in certain locations and display characteristics of a close group which fits to the study design. It is important because this allows us to discuss Turkish immigrant group in comparison to other smaller closed societies. We have used in-depth interviews in collecting data on individual experiences and views, whereas participatory observation techniques were used for collecting data on the use of social environment.

Respondents interviewed in the study Included 28 men and 27 women. 32 of them were first generation immigrants, while there were 23 second generation Turks. Respondents were aged from 21 to 62 (Table 9.1). 33 interviewees were from Emirdağ, and 20 interviewees from Posof. There were two more interviewees from other parts of Turkey. Most of the sample group were married and educational attainment levels were quite low as there were almost no university graduates among the respondents. Approximately 40 percent of the interviewees were waged workers and 20 percent were unemployed. 33 interviewees reported to speak good or very good Flemish.

Table 9.1. Demographic profile of respondents

Education	Elementary	Secondary	High School		University	
f	9	34	8		4	
Marital Status	Married	Single	Divorced			
f	48	4	3			
Home Town	Emirdağ	Posof	Other			
f	33	20	2			
Occupation	Housewife	Jobless	Retired		Worker	Shop Owner
f	6	12	1		32	4
Duration in Belgium	-5year	5-10 years	10-20 years		+20 years	+30 years
f	1	3	13		7	28
Age	-20	20-30	30-40	40-50	50-60	60+
f	-	7	28	18	2	-

Sense of belonging among Turkish minority in Flanders and Brussels

Only one of the 55 interviewees was self-described as Belgian-Turk, and another ''in between'' Turkish and Belgian identities. Four interviewees described themselves firstly as Muslim and then Turkish. 46 interviewees defined themselves as Turkish. It can be said that the Turkish identity for these interviewees is very strong, but they are still confused about their sense of belonging. Two interviewees from the 2nd generation who define themselves as Turk stated that:

As I grew up here, I know the culture here and besides, hmm, I believe I also know the Turkish culture very well, but our circle of friends started to consist of Turks after a certain age, and therefore I feel rather Turkish. (45, M-2nd Generation)

I have nothing to do with the Flemish society. In other words, I don't like those atmospheres. I don't feel comfortable. I prefer playing around and hanging out with Turks. I don't have any real Flemish friend, either. I only had colleagues (36, M-2nd Generation)

Hayal describes herself as 'in between' in terms of being a Turk or Flemish and expresses her views as follows:

I'm in between, because one becomes a stranger here and people give us an evil eye. When we visit Turkey, people consider us German-Turkish and unfortunately this situation hurts me so bad, because every year we have a discussion there. People complain about us, saying that German-Turks are here again, prices increased, etc. but why do they consider us guilty? There were times, when I cried really so much in Turkey, because they don't allow us fit in here, and when they do the same there, it gets too hard for us. (36, F-2nd Generation)

Identifying herself mainly with her religious characteristics, Zekiye justifies this as follows:

No, mine is Muslim identity. There is no Turkish one. I mingle with people with my Muslim identity. Being Turkish isn't important. Of course, we are Turkish and we are proud of being one, but the important thing is being a Muslim. (46, F-1st Generation)

Ahu identifies herself with Belgium, underlining that her Turkish identity has turned into a discursive one:

Why I love Belgium? Because I live and work here, where the circumstances are better than those of Turkey. So, we are Turks and we should love Turkey. It's OK, but I don't feel that I belong to Turkey. On the other hand, there is no Turkey here anymore. Everyone says that we are Turkish and Muslim, but they do not know the Turkish history, the ancient name of Istanbul or the names of caliphates or the birthday of Prophet Mohammad. Turks here are not Turks anymore. (22, F-2nd Generation)

About the daily language

An analysis of the interviewees' responses to the question about what language is spoken by them and their children in their daily lives, shows that all of the interviewees spoke Turkish with their families and friends. They spoke Flemish only at work, if necessary, but their children spoke more Flemish than their parents. Some of the interviewees indicated that they consider speaking Turkish at home as a requirement of their Turkish and Muslim identities. However, most of them stated that they use Turkish in their daily interactions for they live in Turkish districts and have no proper contact with the Flemish people. Thus, they use Flemish in the workplace for compulsory reasons. It was also stated that Turkish children mostly use Flemish language because of their education:

Always we speak Turkish because we all live in Turkish neighbourhood. (46, M-1st Generation)

I speak Turkish anyway I have no Flemish friends. (39, M-2nd Generation)

We speak Flemish at work. Children speak Turkish at home and they speak Turkish with their Turkish friends but Flemish with Flemish friends. (47, M-1st Generation)

As stated by Göktuna Yaylacı (2012b), another language related feature among Turkish families in Belgium is that they switch to Flemish, when they get angry with their children. For example, when they want their children stop doing something and no to do something they say it in Flemish: "Nee! Dat mag niet! No, this cannot happen – Don't do that." The reason was that children follow warning in Flemish and behave, but they don't consider it highly and as obediently when it is said in Turkish.

Communication with friends and neighbours

In terms of becoming friends with others and neighbours, the interviewees were asked to reveal the persons whom they meet most frequently throughout a week in their lives outside business or shopping. All interviewees said that they exclusively met Turkish friends and relatives. Only a few interviewees have said they have some Belgian friends but they do not meet them as frequently as they do meet Turkish friends. Meltem, a second generation migrant, mentions the feeling of comfort provided by meeting with other Turks:

I feel more comfortable. I can become myself, I mean, of course I can become myself. I feel better, when I'm with Turks. Nevertheless, I was born and grew up here (33, F-2nd Generation)

The interviewees were asked to mention the places where they meet with their friends or relatives. Almost all of the interviewees said that they met at each other's houses, whereas the other occasions mentioned include wedding ceremonies, festivals and funerals:

I meet my relatives usually during home visits, and as I said, I meet friends usually at cafés or other places such as associations. But this is something related with some stuff such as relatives and friends, or in some case there is something related to funerals. I don't know how it is in Turkey, but this is the least common denominator, which brings all of us together here, and as we are Turks, once we hear that the deceased is a Turk, no matter who he is, we immediately go there. (41, M-2nd Generation)

Generally home as a family, but for example when we meet with friends, we, namely, the young generation, can go out. In other words, dinners, coffee or breakfasts are easier with young people outside. (24, F-1st Generation)

My family lives in Turkey and I already meet with my elder sisters online. I'm unable to meet with my relatives so often. I meet with my aunt's daughter once a week, either at his house or at my house. So we phone and meet each other. We talk to each other on the phone every day. (38, F-2nd Generation)

The interviewees reported that the most important criteria to choose friends is Turkish origin. Characteristics such as honesty, similar opinions and attitudes, and reliability come further down the list. . The last they look at the qualities such having a good character, avoiding gossip , as well as being humorous, sophisticated, and being a fellowman or a relative. The interviewees reported that they do not attach much importance to nationality. Arzu, one of the interviewees, says that she does not care about being Turkish or Belgian in her choice of friends, whereas Hayal says language and reliability are important:

I wouldn't distinguish, but I usually prefer a Turk to befriend. But of course it happens at schools, I had some foreign friends. (25, F-1st Generation)

Oh, in terms of language, and reliability, I guess a Turk is more reliable, I don't know, but reliable… (36, F-2nd Generation)

The interviewees were asked to mention where, why and how often they meet with their friends. The majority of interviewees reported that they meet with their friends at least once a week, saying that they mostly come together at mosques, associations, cafés and wedding ceremonies:

At social surroundings, coffee houses, mosques, associations, I mean, at such places… (45, M-1st Generation)

I especially meet my friends. I mean we go to a place, have breakfast in the morning and after school (after taking the children to school at 9). Hmmm, otherwise we go to shopping center. Of course, we don't have to buy anything, but we do this out of boredom, we just try to have some fun. (31, F-2nd Generation)

Honestly, let me tell you that it is generally on the level of friends or relatives here. And we meet with the people who are good friends from our town at the mosques, clubhouses or Turkish coffee houses. Sometimes sports activities like football are organized, and we meet each other this way. So we meet there, and also at weddings, God forbid, at such situations as funerals, I mean, we come together in these cases. (36, M-1st Generation)

In terms of their views on establishing good friendships with Belgians, nearly half of the interviewees reported that it is difficult to communicate with Belgians, and the remaining said that it is easy, whereas a small group said it is can be both easy and difficult:

Why wouldn't I want to make friends with Belgians? I'd like to do that, but it usually becomes unilateral. They want us to change and lead their lives as they have done before. They don't involve our life style, in other words, our religion and culture into such things. For example, they go to coffee houses after work. I go there with them in order not to be broken away. They usually compel us to do this or do that, I mean to do something. (35, M-2nd Generation)

It's hard, so hard. They don't trust much. They are harder than us. They don't trust very much. As we are more Turkish, we can trust more and in a shorter time, but they would not, and they get scared very much. Once the terms Islam and religious are mentioned, they get very scared. (36, F-2nd Generation)

It would be very difficult for a person who has no idea about the Belgian culture, because they do not know how to act in a society, and it would not make a difference to the others. Everything is so open, in terms of the words and stuff. And they usually use slang, except the governmental correspondence... It is not easy, because a guy sometimes shamelessly says that his wife is seeing somebody, he drinks alcohol, sleeps on the street, shouts and he was taken by a police. The culture is very important. (39, M-2nd Generation)

The interviewees were asked to talk about the communities with whom they establish relationships the most among other immigrant groups such as Moroccan and Polish people. The majority of interviewees said that they established such relationships with Turks, whereas some of them reported that they did this with different groups:

Obviously [we do this] with the Turks, because the neighbourly relations are very important and developed in the Turkish society. What's more, he/she is a neighbour in good and bad times. The neighbourly relations with other groups are quite poor. And such relations are poor among themselves, too. That's why we establish neighbourly relations with Turks. (47, M-1st Generation)

There is something more important than Belgians, in other words, there is actually discrimination about something among the nationals living here. People have more friendly or neighbourly relations with the citizens coming from Morocco. There is something about it, I mean, something common with them, namely, both those people and Turks are all Muslims here. (41, M-2nd Generation)

I have never had a neighbour. The people living next to me are Polish or Romanian, but I don't want to meet them, because I am a little bit suspicious about them, because normally two people live in that house, but 10 people leave home at the same time, do you understand what I mean? Therefore I kept some distance from them. Furthermore, the other reason is security. I live alone until late hours, even if they are Moroccan, I would say hi to them, I mean, I would talk to them. (35, F-2nd Generation)

[I would do this with] with Flemish, because they are polite, they always say 'hello' to you, if they see you. They do not say anything about your life style, your children's behaviours, etc. (22, F-2nd Generation)

Throughout the field research, it was observed that the Turks make friendships with their townsmen in most instances, followed by befriending with other Turks. There was no close relations or family gatherings with non-Turkish groups such as Flemish or Moroccans. For example, over a twelve month period, a Turk's home seen only one Flemish person has visiting while the reason for the visit was that their children were friends at school. And yet, this visit took place because the Flemish woman (mother of the child who befriended the child of family from Emirdag) insisted in doing so.

TV, newspaper, radio and Internet preferences

The interviewees were asked about their preferred TV channels, newspapers, radio stations and the Internet. Nearly half of the interviewees do watch Turkish channels and the remaining who are both Turkish and Belgian citizens said they watch only Belgian TV channels. Interviewees also reported that they watch Flemish television channels only for news and Turkish channels to improve their children's language skills:

I turn it on to watch the news as a requirement. I watch the Flemish channel. And also for my child, I open the cartoon channel, but I turn on the 'Yumurcak' channel on Turkish TV, because I want them to speak Turkish very well. In addition, they teach it there very well. I also watch the sports shows on Turkish TV channels. I really like it. In addition, I especially like discussion programs on Haber Türk and I'm very careful about it. For example, I watch everything on every issue, it if it appeals to me. (34, F-2nd Generation)

There are a lot of things. I mean, Turkish channels display the family too much. I mean obviously not all of them… I mean there are many shows which would disturb families or break up a home. I don't know how to say it, but there are some shows which would cause us to lose our identity. There are many programs and TV series which might lose our Islamic identity. And this situation disturbs us. (46, F-1st Generation)

They watch the Belgian channels. It depends on the children's age. My daughter is still young; she's 12, but considering recent years, they have been watching them from 5-6 years of age to 12, some educational programs aimed at the children in primary school age or they watch the things they see at school or among their friends on TV and talk to each other about them. (41, M-2nd Generation)

One third of the interviewees reported that they read newspapers online, while some others follow news in social environments such as coffee houses, mosques and various associations. Some respondents read newspapers at their work places. Besides some are subscribed to newspaper, and some others do not buy print newspapers at all:

Honestly, the children read it online or we do this at a coffee house or in the morning, if we can. We buy newspaper on Saturdays and Sundays. In general we read it at coffee houses every day. (45, M-1st Generation)

I read both Turkish and Flemish newspapers, I don't buy it, but I read online and there is Gazet Van Antwerpen. (22, F-2nd Generation)

Nearly one third of the interviewees do not listen to the radio. Some interviewees said that they listen only to Turkish radio stations, whereas some others indicated that they listen to Turkish radio channels at home and Belgian channels in their cars:

We can't listen to the radio here, we have no time but we do it in Turkey for one month. (36, F-2nd Generation)

I love listening to Radio TRT. I love each subject on TRT. Now I follow it through the satellite, but we have previously bought radios for 300 Euros corresponding to today's currency. We used to follow it. Now we mostly do this through satellite and we watch the TV less. (45, M-1st Generation)

According to the field research observations, most of the participants watch Turkish TV channels. It was evident in all home visits conducted during the field research that Turkish TV channels were watched continuously by household members and conversations about TV programs were mostly about shows broadcasted on Turkish TV channels. Possibly due to the influence of their peers at school, Turkish school-age children mostly watch cartoons broadcasted on Belgian TV channels. During the nine-month period of research, it was striking that no participant with whom the researcher travelled in his/her car lent an ear to any Belgian radio station but listened to music CDs in Turkish.

The interviewees were asked to mention whether they use the Internet or not, and the reasons for their usage or non-usage. Nearly one third of the interviewees reported that they don't use the Internet, whereas the remaining two thirds said that they use the Internet. Those who do not use the Internet said that they thought the Internet was harmful for their children. Some Internet users reported that they use it in order to stay connected with their relatives in Turkey. Besides, some interviewees said that they used the Internet for various reasons such as getting information, doing research, advertising or benefiting from it with regards to religious issues:

Honestly, I do not have time for them and clearly I would never watch them, but our children use them. There is one thing that I do not like and that I find annoying and that makes me depressed recently, in other words, if I become the prime minister of a country, I would destroy the creature called the Internet, because it is used but not for useful purposes.(48, M-1st Generation).

Oh, I do not know why people necessarily get involved in online chat. As it kills time, I could not use it much and I did not want it. I do not think that it is useful for my daughter, either, because she gets lost in games and I don't want her eyesight to deteriorate or fall behind at school. (25, F-1st Generation)

I do not search the MSN or Google with friends here or family in Turkey. Hmmm, I sometimes listen to a few songs. That is it. I do not like surfing the Google or listening to this and that. (31, F-2nd Generation)

Concluding remarks on communication preferences and integration

It can be said that social communication practices of Turkish people in Belgium is largely shaped by their Turkish identity and cultural perceptions and opinions. Thus, Turkish people in Belgium prefer to live mostly in Turkish neighbourhoods; they speak Turkish in their daily lives and they do not become neighbours or friends with the Flemish or other non-Turkish people. They also often think that Flemish people are not willing to befriend them and interact with them.

In terms of perception of identity and sense of belonging, the Belgian Turks interviewed in this study define themselves primarily as "Turks". This study shows that Turks in Belgium do not define themselves as "Belgian Turks" although such definition is evident among a small minority of younger generations. It is reported frequently that defining himself or herself as a Turk is required to protect their culture and existence in Belgium without compromising their own culture. The second and third generations though, only relatively define themselves as Turks, which could be interpreted in a way that those who are born and raised in Belgium do not exhibit same attitude of cultural protectionism and resistance to the host society culture.

Such attitudes are described as "language as nationalism" by Jandt (2010: 140), where a particular interest in speaking Turkish both in daily life and at home is evident. The survival of the mother tongue is defined as the most important instrument for sustaining cultural belonging and existence. This deliberate effort regarding protecting the language is linked to ethnic identity. The language preference in daily life is formed by both the perception of identity and the way of their lives are organised. The individuals living mostly in the neighbourhoods which are predominantly inhabited by Turks do maintain face-to-face communication with other Turks. This causes distance from the host society (or isolation), and thus it means distance to the language(s) of the host country. As underlined by Bavelas and Gerwing (2007: 283-284), the language is social and the primary location of language is face-to-face communication. The majority of daily social exchanges are through face-to-face communication. As a result, face-to-face communication is centrally important in terms of social communication. Among the Turks in Belgium, this is very limited with the members of the host society but very frequent with other Turks.

Cultural differences are considered an obstacle to communicational interaction. In this study, we have seen in a sense, there was an understanding of keeping a distance from the host society as much as possible, in order to preserve the original cultural values of the homeland. Those who think that it is easy to communicate with Belgian people and tried to do so have reported that the barrier to the communication was insufficient language skills and the fact that they live in Turkish neighbourhoods. However, besides such self-criticism, many more Turks think that the Belgian people are distant, cold, xenophobic and even racist and these are obstacles to communication. Ethnic social communication among those immigrants from Emirdağ and Posof in Belgium largely take place at certain locations: Mosques, associations and coffee houses are prominent venues. Visits to relatives, engagement and wedding ceremonies as well as funerals offer important communicational occasions bringing relatives and those from same hometowns in Turkey together. Also many Turks in Belgium find space to communicate with each other in markets, small convenience shops, coffee shops, bakeries, and restaurants run by Turks in Belgium.

Turkish people in Belgium mostly watch Turkish televisions via satellite, but they do watch the news on Flemish television channels, whilst their children mostly watch Flemish televisions, especially children programs.

A study conducted in Germany found that Turkish identification is characterised by following Turkish media, while consumption of German media was limited (Öztürk and Sevim, 2009: 242). A similar pattern was evident in our study in Belgium. Watching Turkish TV appears to be a natural reflection of Turkish migrants' identity and it has a vital importance in their daily lives. Improvements in communication technologies and spread of internet have contributed greatly to strengthening this pattern. Watching television reflecting once identity, thus, became easier with satellite television and recently with internet technologies.

Turkish people living in Belgium see Turkish TV channels as a necessity to preserve their mother tongue and their ties to homeland. They continue to watch them even though they criticize their broadcasting quality. The Turkish channels are preferably watched also because they are unable to find "themselves" on Belgian television channels. As indicated by many interviewees, immigrants do barely appear on Belgian television channels, and when they appear, they are often portrayed negatively.

People from Emirdağ and Posof in Belgium watch Turkish television channels closely and read Turkish newspapers as if they live in Turkey. Only a few people listen to the radio channels. Print media is followed by a very small minority. However, print media is important in terms of participation in ethnic social communication practices as it enhances ethnic consciousness through the literature.

Furthermore, the use of Internet is becoming gradually more commonly available among the people from Emirdağ and Posof in Belgium but at the time of the study, access to internet was relatively low. The younger generations use the Internet, especially to follow the news and to communicate with their friends. Moreover, the use of Internet plays an important role in the formation of ethnic consciousness and belonging to the hometown cultures (i.e. hemsericilik in Turkish) which even survives in the second and third generations.

Findings of this study can be discussed in terms of the system and social integration approach proposed by Esser (2006) where social communication processes are considered vital for social integration. It can be said that social communication practices of Turkish people in Belgium have not had any important impact on their system integration but possibly have negative effects on their social integration processes and relations with the Flemish society. This is because their social communication practices are mainly shaped by Turkish culture, language and media. However, this is not an outcome of Turkish community's preferences in Belgium. The attitudes of the host society and the Flemish people as perceived by the respondents of this study also play an important role in forming the social communication experiences of Turkish people. Communication is a two-way process, and in this case, it is a result of interaction, symbolic exchanges and interplay between Turkish immigrant community and Flemish host society. In other words, the Turkish community and the Flemish society do produce the above-mentioned communication processes jointly; thus the onus of integration is not only on the former.

Acknowledgement:
This study consists of some part of a doctoral dissertation by Filiz Göktuna Yaylaci entitled "Understandings of Particularism and Social Communication Processes of Turkish People Living in Belgium: A Research on Turkish People Who Have Emirdağ and Posof Origins".

Chapter 10: Tiryaki Kukla – Smoking cessation and tobacco prevention among migrants from Turkey in Switzerland

Corina Salis Gross, Claudia Arnold and **Michael Schaub**

Introduction

As seen in other countries (e.g. for the USA see Baluja et al., 2003), some migrant populations in Switzerland show higher smoking rates than the average population. Recent results from a Swiss survey among the migrant population[1] show significantly higher smoking prevalence rates for Turkish-speaking migrants (male: 55.2% and female: 29.5%) than the Swiss population aged 14–65 years (male: 21.7% and female: 19.5%; GMM II, Guggisberg et al., 2011). Additionally, male migrants from Turkey show the highest smoking prevalence rates among the migrant population in Switzerland (ibid.). Turkish-speaking migrants are often also among the highest smoking prevalence groups in other European countries (e.g., Nierkens et al., 2006; Reese et al., 2005). Behavioral therapies in groups (Stead & Lancaster, 2005) or single sessions (Lancaster & Stead, 2005) as well as nicotine replacement therapy (NRT; Stead et al., 2008) have been effective for smoking cessation treatment. In Switzerland, such therapies are offered by several providers (e.g., Cancer League, Lung League), but according to the statements of these providers and of other experts of the Swiss tobacco prevention that we interviewed, they are not able to reach the migrant population effectively. Studies from other countries also refer to problems in reaching migrant populations and show the importance of financial access and language barriers (Burns & Fenton, 2006). Another study highlights the importance of cultural aspects (e.g., norms of the religious leaders) when offering smoking cessation treatment for Turkish migrants (Nierkens et al., 2005).

However, there is a lack of adapted intervention programs for migrants who wish to quit smoking in Switzerland, and the Swiss Federal Office for Public Health emphasizes the need to lower the barriers of access to health and prevention programs for the migrant population (FOPH, 2007). From this perspective we designed a pilot project (Schnoz et al., 2011) aimed at

---

[1] This special survey included people from the biggest groups of migrants living in Switzerland (Portugese, Turks/Kurds, People from Serbia, and Kosovo), who are not speaking one of the official languages (French, German, Italian), and therefore are not already included within the general survey "Swiss Addiction Monitoring" (Gmel, Kündig et al., 2014). Additionaly specific groups of Asylumseekers (Tamils and people from Somalia) were also investigated through the special survey.

developing an efficient and sensitive "Tailored Smoking Cessation Program" (TSCP) that would be well-accepted by the migrants from Turkey in Switzerland. A parallel project, offering "Tobacco Prevention Events" (TPEs) within the local settings of the communities, aimed to raise the awareness of the target population concerning the dangers of smoking and of passive smoking, and was used for the recruitment of participants for the TSCPs.

The present article describes the acceptance and the main results of the effectiveness evaluation of TSCP (which in 2010 has been integrated into the Swiss National Smoking Cessation Program[2]) and of the accompanying tobacco prevention events (TPEs), which are both offered in Turkish language.

Method

The intervention consists of a TSCP and a TPE named "Tiryaki Kukla" (TPE hereafter). A male and a female Turkish-speaking migrant were recruited and received training as smoking cessation coaches (SCC).

The TSCP consisted of eight weekly group-counseling sessions. This design was based on the behavioral therapy model used by Cancer League Zurich. The program was aimed mainly at smoking cessation and enhancing the readiness to quit smoking before actually attempting to quit. We defined the guidelines of smoking cessation as they relate to counseling and behavioral therapies according to Fiore et al. (2000, p. iv): *"Provision of practical counseling (problem solving/skills training), provision of social support as part of treatment (intra-treatment social support); and help in securing social support outside of treatment (extra-treatment social support)."*

The SCC cautiously explained the use of NRT and recommended a combination of NRT and TSCP in accordance with Laniado-Laborín (2010). Quitting was usually prompted collectively on the day of the fourth group session. This adapted procedure resulted in a stronger emphasis on the collective decision of the migrant group compared with the standard cessation therapy for autochtone Swiss citizens. In brief, the TSCP sessions of our adapted program for the group of migrants were structured as shown in Table 10.1.

Public health strategies in Switzerland (FOPH, 2007) focus primarily on improving functional health literacy of the migrant population, because access to information and services are strongly dependent on these factors. However, interactive health literacy was also important for our intervention. Therefore,

---

[2] http://www.at-schweiz.ch/en/stop-smoking-activities-in-switzerland/national-stop-smoking-program.html, available on 5.1.2015

we implemented self-responsibility as a fundamental element in the mode of interaction between the participants and the SCC. Since the learning style of most participants was based on a traditional passive-receptive method, we emphasized the training of an active self-responsive way of learning for the participants instead. Other aspects, such as language barriers, knowledge about processes within the body, social and economic constraints, etc., were also reflected in our intervention. In our adaptation of the course, we kept the basic structure of the standard course as offered by the Cancer League Zurich. This course includes a phase of preparation followed by the (usually individual) smoking cessation program and a reflection on one's own behavior and relapse prevention. Our adaptations for the migrant population focused on the didactic form that relied on their reference systems (e.g., language and modes of interaction and learning, use of metaphoric explanation about biomedical processes, and explaining biomedical concepts of anatomy, use of the play "Tiryaki Kukla" for Turkish-speaking migrants that shows the dangers of smoking [see Stevens et al., 2002], use of cartoons in the manual drawn by a migrant from Turkey, collective and ritualized quit day, and celebration (see www.tiryakikukla.ch)).

Table 10.1: Structure of the adapted TSCP

Session 1: Introductions and administration
Filling out pre-questionnaire t1 for the quantitative evaluation of the intervention, etc.

Session 2: Information brokering
Delivering information about the effects of nicotine ("know your enemy"), NRT, and biomedical processes that are influenced by smoking (often using metaphors and images to meet the educational level of the participants). Handing out and explaining a smoking diary.

Session 3: Preparations for smoking cessation
Detailed explanation of NRT and of the harmful effects of smoking on the human body as well as explanation and discussion regarding possible craving symptoms of smoking cessation and of alternative actions for smoking.

Session 4: Quit day
Ritual of collective smoking cessation, enhancing the positive connotation of cessation (not a loss, but a gain of health and life quality), basic relapse prevention (hotline where SCC could be reached, NRT, etc.).

Session 5: First experiences as a nonsmoker
Exchanging experiences of smoking cessation, enhancement of the quitters, and discussing and assessing alternative actions for smoking.

Tobacco prevention events "Tiryaki Kukla" (TPE)

The tobacco prevention activities consist of informative events on the subjects of smoking, passive smoking, smoking cessation and situational prevention. These events take place in settings like migrant self-organisations, religious institutions, kin groups or informal groups. They pursue the objectives of sensitization of the target population to smoking related hazards and also the recruitment of participants for TSCP. Turkish and Kurdish media and conventional information channels of standard care were used to promote the events. Information on tobacco prevention and smoking cessation were disseminated via Turkish and Kurdish newspapers, journals, radio, internet and TV.

As no sampling frames for migrants from Turkey in Switzerland were available, we combined personal and advertising recruitment activities to achieve a diverse sample for TSCP and TPE: Key-persons enabled access and Turkish-speaking migrants were personally recruited at a variety of events surrounding the Turkish and Kurdish communities in Switzerland (i.e., clubhouses, etc.) with posters, flyers, and presentations. In addition, advertisements were spread via local newspapers and Turkish/Kurdish broadcasts at local radio stations. Outreach activities and peer effects, i.e. strong ties[3] among the participants turned out to be key elements for recruitment: Participants in 27 out of 37 therapy groups were recruited through outreach events within the communities.

The evaluation included quantitative methods for the TSCP (t1/t2, 12 month follow-up by telephone, weekly CO-analysis) and quantitative methods for the TPE (t1/t2). Effects of the therapy (TSCP) were assessed through a battery of questions including sociodemographic and socioeconomic items, the Hooked on Nicotine Checklist (HONC; DiFranza

---

[3] 'Strong ties' refers to the combination of time, emotional intensity, intimacy, and reciprocity that characterizes the social relationship among the group participants (see Granovetter, 1973). For similar effects of close and reciprocal social relationships on smoking cessation see also the studies of Christakis & Fowler (2008).

et al., 2002), the Fagerström test for Nicotine Dependence (Fagerström & Schneider, 1989), questions assessing smoking career and behavior, smoking among peers, attitude toward smoking and readiness to quit. The t1 was delivered at the beginning of the therapy, and the t2 was delivered approximately four months after. At every weekly group session, the carbon monoxide (CO) in the breath of every participant was analyzed with the PiCO smokerlyzer (Bedfont Scientific Ltd.) and documented by the SCC. Participants were asked about their use of NRT for treatment of smoking addiction and, finally, about the subjective perceived efficacy and the acceptance of TSCP. About 12 months after the quit day, a follow-up was conducted during which the participants were asked via telephone about their smoking status.

The programme and events (TPE) designed to reduce the level of smoking were also evaluated. Participants of the first 21 events were asked to complete a pre-questionnaire t1 before the event and a post-questionnaire t2 approximately 1 year later. Participants were asked about sociodemographic and socioeconomic aspects, their attitude toward smoking, knowledge about the hazards of smoking, smoking behavior and smoking among peers.

Results and Discussion

TSCP: From 2010 until 2013, 37 TSCP group sessions were conducted, mainly in the German speaking part of Switzerland (35), and 2 in the French speaking part. A total of 236 persons took part in the TSCP (133 female, 103 male).

65.7% of the 108 participants in 2012/2013 made at least one attempt to stop smoking until the end of the program. At t2 66.2% of the 228 participants (TSCP 2010-2013) were smoke-free, ranging from 58.1% (2013) to 72.7% (2011). Participants who continued smoking significantly reduced their tobacco consumption (on average 4.5 cigarettes less per day).

Furthermore, 58.4% of the 197 participants (TSCP 2010-2012) were smoke-free at the 12-month follow-up. Using NRT during the therapy was positively associated with successful cessation. Relying on peer effects of "strong ties" (reciprocal relationships between participants) was highly supportive and the sensitivity of the program to socio-cultural, socioeconomic, and migration-specific issues showed high acceptance and compliance-rates: Only 9 participants dropped out, while 96.2% of the participants completed the program between 2010 and 2013. Additionally, 84.1% of the participants found the TSCP useful in helping them to quit smoking and 96.2% would certainly recommend the course to others. The fact that the TSCP was free of charge was very important since many of the participants live on social welfare or belong to the group of lower income workers.

TPE: From 2010 until 2013, 75 information events were realized in 18 cantons of Switzerland. These events aimed to increase knowledge about the hazards of smoking, to encourage situational prevention (i.e. in clubhouses), to strengthen the intention to stop smoking, to change the smoking behavior at home and to promote smoking cessation. A total of 2799 person took part, the number of participants in an event ranged from 7 to 350 persons.

About 500 participants at the first 21 events were tested before and 1 year after the event. Their knowledge about the hazards of smoking and their critical attitude toward smoking increased significantly. Most of them already knew about the hazards of passive smoking. At home the smoking places changed: The participants reported that they increasingly smoked on the balcony and stopped smoking in the living room or in the kitchen. The number of persons in the family or circle of friends who smoked decreased significantly from t1 to t2. Among the participants the proportion of smokers fell from 50.1% (t1) to 40.3% (t2).

We therefore suggest that the tobacco prevention events contributed to a normative change in the Turkish and Kurdish communities. In addition, they were essential for recruiting the participants in the TSCP. Participants in 27 out of 37 TSCPs, were recruited through these outreach-events within the communities.

TSCP: The success rate of the sample at the final follow-up stage was surprisingly high. This result is particularly remarkable because our sample was characterized by strong disadvantage and psychosocial vulnerability (e.g., because of prior political persecution, incarceration, torture, invalidity, low socioeconomic status etc.) as well as a high mean number of cigarettes smoked per day.

TPE: The TPEs, effective in increasing knowledge and a critical attitude towards smoking, were also crucial for recruiting participants in the TSCP. Therefore the two interventions (TSCP and TPE) should be combined.

Overall, the present study results lead to the conclusion that, although vulnerable groups in the migrant population in Switzerland seem to be difficult to reach and treat, the outreach strategy for recruitment and integration of social, cultural, socioeconomic and migration-specific aspects into the smoking cessation programs and prevention activities produce effective results. Thus, combined interventions are planned to being introduced to other migrant groups.

Chapter 11: "Rewriting" Turkish-German cinema from the bottom-up: Turkish emigration cinema

Ömer Alkin

Introduction

Films from Germany dealing with any aspect of Turkish-German migration, such as the box-office successes *Fack Ju Göhte* (2014) and *Almanya – Welcome to Germany* (2011) are often considered as *"Turkish-German cinema"*. Nevertheless, what first comes to mind with this problematic term of "transnationalism" in the field of film (Higbee & Hwee, 2010) are the internationally celebrated films *Head On* (2004) and *Edge of Heaven* (2007) by Turkish-German director Fatih Akin. However, the term is to be questioned. Which parameters determine the belonging of a film to Turkish-German cinema? Is a film by a German director with Turkish migration background already a Turkish-German film due to the transcultural biographical reference of the director, even if the film does not contain any references to the social reality of Turkish migration, as it is the case in the Hollywood mystery film *Premonition* (2007) by director Mennan Yapo – which would be an essentialist and biologistic understanding of national cinema? For a discussion of the term it is crucial to analyse comprehensively the historical context. The fact that this does not happen becomes apparent in the marginal position of the Turkish films in the discourse regarding Turkish-German cinema. The Turkish films about emigration from the 1970's and 80's by Turkish directors like Serif Gören or Yavuz Figenli are not considered as a part of this transnational film history. But 'Turkish-German film' history has already attracted a considerable amount of academic interest (e. g. Burns, 2006, 2007, 2013, Göktürk, 2000a, 2000b, Ezli, 2009, 2010, Halft, 2011, Hake & Mennel, 2012) without really considering what the term actually refers to. I want to critique such writing because I will argue that it reproduces Eurocentrism and an epistemological one-sided-ness. Before giving arguments for a more comprehensive understanding of Turkish-German cinema, which includes Turkish emigration cinema, it is useful to understand the discussions surrounding the academic writing of the history of Turkish-German cinema first. It offers an insight into film history that can be read as a two-stage process of the appropriate representations of Turkish emigrants in Germany.

Precursors of Turkish-German cinema? Fassbinder's *"enlightened victimology"*

Several decades have passed since Turkey and Germany signed a labour recruitment treaty and the first Turkish emigrants arrived in Germany. Nevertheless, even after the fourth generation of emigrants growing up in Germany the relation between Turkish migrants and the German population is characterised by constructions of alterity with which cultural differences still persist (Beck-Gernsheim, 2007). This problem of perceiving people with Turkish migration background as 'foreigners' or 'others' due to differences in religion, language and visuality (headscarf and ethnic differences like black, dark-brown hair etc.) characterises the thematical orientation of Turkish-German cinema in its beginnings. The films focused on the problematisation of the economic and social situation of the emigrants – but also on the difference between Turkish and German culture. One of the first directors dealing with such issues of otherness was Rainer Werner Fassbinder. *Katzelmacher* (1969) and *Ali: Fear Eats Soul* (1974) were the first films, which addressed labour migration to Germany. In both films Fassbinder refuses what Özkan Ezli identifies as *"the logic of representation"* for later Turkish-German films: a strategy to present characters of the films as representatives of the specific cultural and national belonging through film-aesthetical and narrative means (Ezli, 2009: 213). *Katzelmacher* tells the story of four Bavarian pairs that project their sexual, social and psychological fears onto the Greek migrant worker Jorgos and Fassbinder's reknowned film *Ali: Fear Eats Soul* confronts the viewer with the duble tabooed and socially ostracised love between the old German widow *Emmi* and the black Moroccan labour migrant *Ali*. The inventive constellation of the relations between the characters unveil an interest in the processes of contructions of otherness and not in a presentation of *the* social reality. Fassbinder reflects the stereotyping and racialisation of the presented migrants – e.g. Fassbinder changed the national background of the protagonist in his *Ali: Fear Eats Soul* from a Turkish emigrant to a Moroccan one, as this prevents general prospositions about Turkish social reality in Germany that could derive or be received by the viewer.

The concept *"logic of representation"* helps to understand the constructivist feature of filmic strategies. It hints at the dangerous understanding of film makers and spectators to perceive films as media which mirror social reality. Such understanding is insofar dangerous as that it neglects the "contructivist" (cf. Hall, p. 25) and performative feature of media. Films as images do not only represent a given social and cultural reality, but as *"acteurs within the social field"* (cf. Holert, 2005: 234) they co-construct it.

116

Fassbinder focusses on *"fragile characters from the social periphery, whose social fragility (a widow, a Greek labour migrant, a black Moroccan migrant) and multipositionality still shows contact to the social centrum. This avoids that the characters are positioned as victims"* (cf. Ezli, 2012: 94). And this refusal to show his characters as pure victims refuses to insist in a presentation of social reality which could reproduce the victimisation of these outsiders not only on a level of fictional representation, but – due to the effect of representations to have impact on and to create social realities (cf. Schaffer: 77) – on a level of social reality.

Yet, the later films dealing with the issue of Turkish-German emigration walk right into this trap of the *"logic of representation"* and present migrants as almost mute victims.

First stage of Turkish-German cinema: The *"logic of representation"*

As one of the first directors, Helma Sanders-Brahms tells the story of a Turkish emigrant: *Shirin's Wedding* (1976) is about a woman of the same name, who flees from her village in Turkey to Cologne, after her family married her off against her own will to a custodian. Shirin's aim is to find her childhood love Mahmut in Cologne and to marry him. However, tragic events, e.g. the loss of her employment in the factory and rape, force her right into the arms of a pimp. Helma Sanders-Brahms feminist film presents a narration which characterises the work of several other Turkish-German films of the next ten years and further: the emigrant is a victim, suffering from his situation in a foreign land, kept in between two incommensurable cultures, of which the German one is modern and enlightened whereas the other is patriarchic, traditional and archaic. In the mid-1980s, Turkish director Tevfik Baser filmed *40 Square Meters of Germany* (1985) which illustrates what Özkan Ezli called the *"logic of representation"*. The protagonists of the film are the newly married Turkish couple Turna and Dursun. After their marriage in Turkey, Dursun takes his wife Turna who has only lived in her Anatolian village to Germany. What Turna does not realise is that Dursun will not let her leave their 40 square meters apartment there. He fears that the naive Turna could be spoiled in the German city. He considers to be permeated by sexual and other temptations threatening Turna and thus his honour and cultural identity. In one of the most important scenes of the film, Turna notices that Dursun forgot to lock the door. Turna ventures to leave the apartment and goes downstairs in her gaudy clothes. When she is confronted with a German couple at the stairs, she is terrified and tries to go back to her 40 square meters. More neighbors come out of their apartments, all of them old and looking strangely at Turna. The film demonstrates a *"logic of representation"* by the

117

extreme contrast of the gray-brown clothes of all of the German neighbours and Turna's garish clothes, the organisation of the characters in the filmic space, which divides their bodies and their gazes, but also through the positioning of the viewer due to the camera strategy. The film refuses vehemently to take over a subjective position, which would mean an identification with Turna and her subjectivity, but keeps the viewer in distance to the characters, a distance that does not offer a query into the cultural constructions being shown. Such space and *"costume dramaturgy"* (Ezli, 2009: 212) and other filmic strategies which phase visible elements of characters with their cultural or ethnical belonging offer a reading of the film with which Turna and the neighbours are contructed as representatives of the culture they are identified with.

Such culturalistic view that focuses on the insisted differences of Turkish culture as a foreign culture of the minority can also be found in films like Hark Bohm's *Yasemin* (1988) and Tevfik Baser's second film *Farewell to False Paradise* (1989), to name the ones that appear continuously in academical discussion about Turkish-German cinema (e.g. Göktürk, 2000a; Ezli, 2009; Halft, 2010; 2012; Yaren, 2013; Burns, 2006; 2007; 2013). In all of the films mentioned above there is a position of pity held ready for the viewer by the depiction of mostly female emigrants as mute and exploited victims who try to cope with their precarious situation in the patriarchal Turkish system they are born into. As modernity is associated with German culture and archaic tradition with Turkey, the narration often tells the salvation of these mute victims from the patriarchal Turkish social and familial structure as an act of emancipation of the oppressed subjects supported by the German lover. This is also the case in the films *Yara* (1998), *When We Leave (2010)*, *Aufbrüche* (1987) and *Dügün* (1992), which could be added to the group of films mentioned above. Especially the more recent production date of the films *Yara* and *When We Leave* show that the narrations about migrants as victims cannot be ascribed to the early era of Turkish-German cinema as topical academic discussions suggested. In fact they continue if not persist as the *"logic of representation"*.

Rob Burns sums up films that depict the emigrant as a victim not only of a patriarchal culture, but as ones of the economic system, with the term *"Cinema of the Affected"*. He derives it from the term *"Literature of the Affected"/"Betroffenheitsliteratur"* (Burns, 2007: 375) which was used for guest-worker literature that also dealt with the economic, social, cultural and psychological difficulties for the first emigrants and their families in Germany. The problem which is identified with this kind of representation of Turkish emigrants is that the images deriving from these films produce and reproduce the stereotype in social imagination and manifest the social positions of the represented. The 'pitier' (in the case of the films, the German viewer) strengthens his own hegemonic position as pity can only be developed from a position of superiority and at the same time s/he ascribes and manifests the minoritarian position of the pitied (which is that of the Turkish):

> "*In return, Germanness is produced as modern, enlightened, urban, and especially anti-sexist or as a scope for girls and women. [...] The results of the examination of the genre of 'female migrant drama' demonstrate the possibility that even affirmative images of minoritarian subject positions reproduce their minoritisation.*" *(Schaffer, 2008, pp. 66, 71)*

Second stage and a neverending story: "transcultural cinema", "pleasures of hybridity", "cinéma du métissage"

In later years, some Turkish filmmakers, mainly from Germany, started to tell different stories about people with a Turkish migration background in Germany. What was fascinating about some of these films from the late 1980s and the 90s is the implicitness of the depicted lives of the migrants and the playfulness with issues of cultural identity and belonging. The narration in films like *Aprilkinder* (1998), *Karamuk* (2003), *Anam* (2001), and *Almanya* (2011) did not depict the Turkish migrant kept in between two cultures and struggling for social recognition and fighting against processes of alienation in a foreign land, as it was in the earlier films. The migrant becomes a self-confident personality for whom issues of home and national identity as well as cultural identity are not a restrictive issue any more, but rather an open and positive question or what Rob Burns calls according to Homi K. Bhabha, negotiations through a "*third space*" (Burns 2012: 371): The third space is a space of outsourcing which is the necessity for a negotiation for ongoing and neverending processes of identification (cf. Rutherford, 2003: 211).

Deniz Göktürk identifies the film *Berlin in Berlin* (1993) by Turkish director Sinan Cetin as one of the earliest examples for the change of the representations of Turkish-German migrants in cinema (Göktürk, 2000a: 337-339). What Göktürk analyses in the film is the character of performativity which has the merit of the ironic way of dealing with issues of Turkish-German integration: by showing the efforts of a German photographer to integrate into a Turkish family in Germany, the film reverts the gaze possibilities for the viewer and makes it harder for the audience to consider characters of the movie and situations as representations of social reality.

> "*[...]* Berlin in Berlin *shows more potential in exploring the pleasures of hybridity than previous attempts to portray German-Turkish encounters. The reversal of the asylum situation and the resulting symbiosis open up possibilities of mutual humor and reflection, of traffic in both directions*

- aspects which seemed to be absent from earlier examples of a 'cinema of duty'." (Göktürk, 2000b, para. 5)

Rob Burns considers Thomas Arslan's trilogy *Brothers and Sisters* (1997), *Dealer* (1999) and *A Fine Day* (2001) also as undermining such former representations, which portray the emigrants as static and victimised individuals (Burns, 2013: 75-84). The first film tells the story of two Turkish brothers and a sister who try to cope with their everyday problems and situations in Berlin, whereas the second film depicts a Turkish young man's indecisiveness in leaving his old life behind as a drug dealer. *"A Fine Day follows one day in Deniz's life, a day that begins with her decision to break off the unsatisfactory liasion with her boyfriend, Jan"* (Burns 2013, p. 82). Referring to the aesthetic and reflective dealing with stereotypical characters Burns identifies a break with the *"Cinema of the Affected"* and calls these films of the third generation of emigrants *"Cinema du Métissage"*, a "cinema of in-between". Burns attributes Arslan's films with the capability to reject stereotype allocation of social characters and environments by aesthetic strategies (Burns, 2013, p. 79). In all of the three films, we see one minute tracking shots following the Turkish young protagonists without much story relevant action. Although the protagonist in *Brothers and Sisters* and in *Dealer* is a criminal Turkish young man who could be treated as the stereotypical Turkish small-time crook, Burns insists that such aestheticand reflected dealing with the created and filmed reality destroys a naturalistic realism, which is fundamental for the pity of the viewer as is the case with the *"Cinema of the Affected"*. On the contrary, the long shots, following the protagonist for almost more than a minute in all of the films, would create a distance for the viewer that disturbed the production of stereotypes or an emotional relation to the filmed characters (Burns, 2013: 81).

These two examples (Burns and Göktürk) of the defining of a change in Turkish-German cinema can be extended by more academic discussions. What all these observations have in common is that stereotypes of the mute migrant image is finally overcome by the time of the millennium, and that essentialistic concepts of cultural and ethnic identities are undermined by current Turkish-German cinema.

"Gone were the exploited guestworkers and their suffering wives and oppressed daughters. [...] The films offer self-confident responses to lived experiences often in conflict with the parent generation and open to other minoritarian positionalities be they other immigrant or refuge groups or gays and transgender people. In the process, they leave behind old dogmas of privileging politics over aesthetics, realism over fantasy, suffering over pleasure, and aesthetic of estrangement over emotional engagement." (Hake & Mennel, 2012, 6-7)

Özkan Ezli moves further with such evaluation as he considers Fatih Akin's cinema "*[...] disengaged from its Turkish-German connex and has to be treated as an international and global cinema. Cultural competence which does not tell Turkish-German stories, but at the same time transnational and transcultural ones, takes the place of intercultural competence*" (Ezli 2009, p. 211).

As will be shown in conclusions that celebrate overcoming the "*Cinema of the Affected*" can be overhasty, Eurocentric and at the same time epistemologically one-sided.

Turkish emigration cinema

Movies that deal with Turkish emigration and that were produced in Turkey mainly with Turkish resources by Turkish directors and Turkish production companies are considered as Turkish Emigration Cinema (Turkish: *Türk Dış Göç Sineması*) (Makal, 1994; Piskin, 2010; Anik, 2012). They do not form a coherent genre, but there are a remarkable amount of films from the 1960s to the present that deal with emigration to Germany or other European countries as the main or sub-plot.

The discourse about these films emphasises external migration within the context of internal migration in 20th century Turkey in general, which began from the 1950s onwards. Partly due to the US Marshall Plan that was introduced in Turkey after World War II, there was a spurt in urban industrialisation, and strong growth of the market economy in the rural areas. As agriculture was the main resource of income in rural Anatolian, the consequence of this rapid development was farm mechanization which displaced rural labour and encouraged urban migration seeking a better life. Entire families migrated to the newly industrialisuing cities in search of jobs and other opportunities (Icduygu et al., 1998). The consequences of these enormous migrations were extensively dealt within the Turkish cinema of the time (Piskin, 2010: 51-52). One of the best known examples is Halit Refig's *Gurbet Kuslari* (1962), which depicts the migration of a family from Anatolian Kahramanmaras to Istanbul and their social and cultural problems between their affiliation to Anatolian tradition and the modernity in the cities with which they are confronted. A more epic involvement was realised in Ömer Lütfi Akad's trilogy *Gelin* (1973), *Düğün* (1973), *Diyet* (1974). These three melodramatic films, each standing alone in terms of their narration, thematise the downfall of an Anatolian family as a result of life in the challenging modern metropolis Istanbul, which is constructed as a cultural counter-space to their Anatolian home.

A second figuration: External migration to Germany

 The October 1961 labour agreement between Turkey and Germany offered a multiplicity of economic migration possibilities to the Turkish population. These motives for emigration were used in Turkish cinema for the construction of further narrative figurations as an instrument of dramatisation (Kayaoglu, 2012: 86). Due to the reduction of sales taxes for film makers (Arslan, 2009: 64) a rapid growth of Turkish cinema took place. This period which is labelled as the Yesilcam era (English: *Green Pine*), named after an eponymic street in the district Beyoglu, Istanbul's leisure and shopping district, lead to the production of a volume of popular films, which were developed for a national Turkish audience. With over 300 films per year it was one of the most productive studio systems of its time, although it was not an organised, institutionalised and centrally controlled studio system, but rather a specific style of production with a coherent group of actors, character roles and staff (Arslan, 2009: 232-233). The open-air cinemas were established in rural parts of the country and were responsible for most of the income of the films doing the national circuit (Arslan, 2009: 107). Because of this, the producers had to rely on specific thematic choices. The quick and cheap production of films, mainly in popular genres such as melodrama, comedy and action, was dependant on the conflictual character of the narration and the social reality of emigration offered it. Thus, besides internal migration from rural areas to the urban cities, emigration often became a fundamental element in the fictional productions of Yesilcam cinema. These constellations of migration were a well-known issue, which incorporated the viewers emotionally and affectively into the narrations as the viewers were involved in such processes of "*deplacement*" and "*belonging*" themselves or were concerned indirectly (cf. Kayaoglu, 2012: 86). Generally, migration often became an integral part in a majority of the productions.

The event of emigration as narrative dramatisation in Yeşilçam cinema

One of the earliest films about Turkish-German emigration which dates back to 1966 is Hulki Saner's comedy *Turist Ömer Almanya'da* (1966). The film is one episode of the "Turist Ömer" series that shows the adventures of the tramp Ömer and orients itself indubitably by the Dean Martin and Jerry Lewis comedies of the 1940s and 50s. Although the film is considered to be lost, the narration is known as that Ömer migrates to Germany to work there and falls in love with German woman Helga (Kayaoğlu 2012:84). In later years, a more sociocritical perspective was established in the films that advised the consequences of migration for the migrants in society and which were centered around "the Seventh Man", a term shaped by the empirical fact that Jean Mohr and John Berger mentioned in their illustrated book *Labour Emigrants* (Berger & Mohr, 1976): every seventh worker in Germany and Great Britain is an emigrant (Göktürk, 2000a: 330). The most famous representatives of these sociocritical films were Şerif Gören's *Almanya Acı Vatan* (1978) and *Polizei* (1988), Tunç Okan's films *Otobüs* (1974) and *Mercedes Mon Amour* (1987). However, even in this period of sociocritical cinema, comedies, love films and melodramas (e.g. *Almanyalı Yarim* (1974) and *Almanyada Bir Türk Kızı* (1974)) were produced extensively as the involved filmmakers from Yeşilçam relied on the emotional and dramaturgic power of the event of emigration. *Bir Umut Uğruna* (1991) and *Deliler Almanya'da* (1980), just to name two, can be considered as two less known examples. The first, an Arabesque melodrama, shows the sufferings of an emigrant Turkish father who marries a German woman in Germany and recognises the incommensurability of the Turkish culture of his own and the German culture of his wife. The second example is a comedy produced in Germany about a singer and his double, who get involved into turbulent adventures with Turkish mafia in Germany.

One has to consider other films in which emigration is not a central topic, but a periphery part of the narration. Most of these films were produced in the wake of Yeşilçam: in *Yıkılış* (1978) by Natuk Baytan a Turkish family, which travels back to Turkey after having lived there for years, is terrorised by a violent motorbike gang. In Yilmaz Güney's *Baba* (1971) a family father desires to migrate to Germany to save his family from economical ruin. However, he is discharged so that rape, prostitution and drug trade destroys his family. Halit Refiğ's *Acı Zafer* (1974) presents the bloody revenge of an emigrant homecomer on Turkish villagers, which rape his German wife. In *El Kapısı* (1974) the wife of a farmer is forced to travel to Germany to secure the money for the leg operation of her husband whose injury is the result of an intrigue of the landlord who has fallen in love with the wife. However, the image of the emigrant shifts between such stereotypes to more complex representations.

Shift of representations in Turkish emigration cinema: a poorly investigated phenomenon

Yavrularım (1984) tells the story of a Turkish mother of a family of seven who develops lung cancer after the definite return from Germany to Turkey. The film does not refer to the repertoires of stereotypical representations of emigrants as it focusses on the fate of the family and uses the issue of homecoming for the production of a complex atmosphere of hopelessness. Another example of a more complex strategy of representation is *Amansız Yol*

(1985). The road movie refers casually to the issue of emigration. The protagonist is a truck driver from Germany who returns to Turkey and gets involved into the intrigues of his former friend who married his childhood love. In contrast to former films the fact of emigration does not turn the emigrant into a visually different person as it was in a lot of other Turkish emigration films before. By contrast, films like Ertem Egilmez's *Banker Bilo* (1980) or Temel Gürsu's *Baldız* (1975), made the emigrants visible through things, which could be characterized as visual agents of modernity: a hat with a feather, a radio, ties, wristwatches and German cars. The number of films referring to this visual stereotype is high (*Dönüş* (1973), *Davaro* (1981), *Gurbetçi Şaban* (1985) etc.). It becomes obvious that the Turkish emigration films as ensembles draw their own history of representation whose analysis is a desideratum to this day. Such analysis would work out that the emigrant is socio-visually constructed as reality by the images the films produced.

Crisis in Turkish film history: the dissolution of Turkish emigration cinema

A crisis was identified in Turkish cinema in the late 1980s and early 1990s (Behlil, 2010: 2). Furthermorethere are no film historical analyses on the issue of emigration in Turkish films of these years so far. The research is problematic as the crisis of Turkish cinema is caused by political events, as the military coup d'état of 1980 and the political repression which followed, and the media technical development of TV broadcasting. Television was introduced rather belatedly into Turkey in the late 1960s and really took off from the mid-1970s. The rise of the number of TVs in households led to the declining function and popularity of the once popular open-air cinemas and thus the market for films in general. Despite the large amount of TV films that can be found in the archives of television broadcasters, if at all possible, the object of analysis had to extend its area of research from cinema films to TV films. Such research is still outstanding to this day. The most successful attempt of the film industry aiming to overcome the crisis of Turkish cinema is Yavuz Turgul's blockbuster *Eşkıya – The Bandit* (1996) (Behlil, 2010: 3).

"[Surprisingly] the intense production environment brought about by the proliferation of private television channels in the 1990s laid the foundations for this brisk activity in the Turkish film industry" (ebd., p. 3). Since then [after Eşkiya was released] 34 local films have sold over a million tickets. While the market share of Turkish films does fluctuate, there has been a steady overall increase since 2002. More importantly, the overall number for movie-going audiences showed an increase of over 50%" (ebd. p. 3).

As can be seen, television did not only take part in the crisis of Turkish cinema, but contributed to its *"renaissance"* (Behlil, p. 3). In the wake of this renaissance some films showed interest in the issue of emigration. *Made in Europe* (2007) by İnan Temelkuran is an episodic film that shows four more or less common, but different situations of emigrants, which occur around the same time in four different cities in Europe, but are not connected from the logic of happenings. The film intends to present four differentiated experiences of emigrants and highlights the globalised moment of emigration due to the unity of time of the actions that take place (Alkin, 2013).

A more stereotypical construction of an emigrant is the comedy *Berlin Kaplanı* (2012). The protagonist of the mainstream comedy is Ayhan Kaplan, a Turkish boxer living in Germany who is involved in the Turkish mafia and tries to save himself and his trainer from them by selling his uncle's landed property in Turkey. Ersel Kayaoğlu considers the Turkish-German protagonist as *"a character which does not have any problems with his positiong within German society any more"* (cf. Kayaoğlu, 2012: 99). One further Turkish film about emigration in 2012 is Ali Levent Üngör's *Mevsim Çiçek Açtı* (2012). The narration turns its concentration on Turkish womenhood in Germany and draws from a narration, which we know from the German "Cinema of the Affected" very well: the oppression of a Turkish woman by Turkish patriarchy.

Eurocentrism in the discourse about Turkish-German cinema

The ascription of the victim position for female emigrants in the *"Cinema of the Affected"* was realised in a Turkish film in 2012. From this constellation, it is obvious that what was considered to be issues of feminity and individual oppression is not a German, but rather a modern question which does not lose its fascination for narrative figurations in both Turkey and in Germany.

Young woman Mevsim and her daughter Cicek are in the centre of Ali Levent Üngör's *Mevsim Çiçek Açtı* (2012). Mevsim's alcoholic husband Nazmi beats her almost to death. This was surely not the life Mevsim imagined when he brought her from Turkey to Germany. She and her daughter Cicek see themselves forced to leave him and to flee to a women's refuge. There she meets new friends, e. g. fun-loving flatmate Esra, taxi driver Asaf, and his mentor Musa who take care of the women and spend time with them amicably, though Asaf displays affection for Mevsim. Mevsim's father-in-law renounces his violent son and, as a believing Muslim, tries to find his daughter-in-law and his granddaughter in order to take care of them. The film tells Mevsim's fate as an anthology film view into the lives of the presented characters. Social spaces of masculinity, e. g. clubs and bars of the men which

Nazmi is surrounded by, are counteracted by images of a social peaceful living together of the women and both women-friendly men, Musa and Asaf. Thus, the film constructs different images of men in different social constellations and spaces and weaves scenes around the main plot of Mevsim which characterise the different male characters.

Feo Aladags honour killing drama *When We Leave* (2010) is inspired by the honour killing of the Kurdish woman Hatun Sürücü in Berlin. The film tells the story of Umay who grew up in Germany and lives in Turkey together with her son, her husband and his family. She decides to return to her family in Germany as she cannot bear her husband's violence and the life there. When Umay arrives in Germany her family however wants to send her back as all of her family members consider the honour of the family as being in danger due to Umay's emancipatory aims, to study and not to return to her husband: a married woman living separated from her husband is a threat to social order as she can commit fornication. When Umay's father Kader and both of her brothers try to send her to Turkey by force Umay flees with her son Cem to a women's refuge. *When We Leave* gets in line with other films of the *"Cinema of the Affected"*. On the level of content the film ist kept in a culturalistic view (Yaren, 2010), but for David Gramling it stands out from these films by a complex semiotic potential and strategies which lead to a mythological meaning of the film in a Barthesian sense. For Gramling the film must be considered in the Turkish-German cinema's bi-polarity between a *"Cinema of the Affected"* and the "pleasures of hybridity" as a *"struggle between hybridities and mythologies, a struggle in which* When We Leave *has staked an unequivocal claim"* (Gramling, 2012: 43).

Images of men in *"Mevsim Çiçek Açtı"* (2012) and *"When We Leave"* (2010): epistemological one-sided-ness

Whereas *Mevsim Çiçek Açtı* creates different images of men – reaching from patriarchal and demonising depictions of husbands to the pious and indulgent configuration of the father-in-law to the brotherly-modern attitude of the taxi driver Asaf and his wise friend Musa –, *When We Leave* creates a simplicistic functioning of the images of men through ethnicity. Umay falls in love with her German colleague Stipe with whom she works at a catering company. He constitutes a counter-image to the emotional fragile and tragical Turkish male characters in the film who internalised the patriarchal honour code. Stipe is child-friendly, courteous, humorous, romantic and is open to her wishes: He makes her son Cem laugh, helps Umay with her work and aspirations, he treats Umay's wound after her argument with her brother Mehmet and does not restrict her freedom, but tolerates and appreciates her display of wilfulness. Indeed, in moments of intimacy, when the Turkish men start to think abot Umay and the problems with her, they are shown as characters being at odds with themselves and revealed as victims of their restrictive social codex. We see Umays's father Kader smoking his cigarettes under the stress of the night Umay cut off her arteries. Her harsh and violent brother Mehmet is shown in a scene where he is crying on the sofa holding a picture probably of Umay the day before the attempt of the honour killing. However the men's social role as defenders of the familial honour seems not to be negotiable and their mental situation is that of the melancholy of the inevitable. Umay's persistence in not returning, the tragedies arising and in relevance of the very positive image of Stipe and the image of her Turkish husband being violent, the ethnicisation of good/bad images of men leads directly to the *"logic of representation"* which is known from the former *"Cinema of the Affected"*. From such a view, the film's semiotic energy as a kind of Barthesian mythological reality (Gramling, 2012) does not avoid the film's potential power of offering a representation of ethnicised and thus essentialised cultural differences for the viewer.

What becomes obvious with the comparison of both movies is the difference between the cultural milieus and the presented characters: emancipated young Umay vs. needy Mevsim, patriarchal, honour codex driven father Kader vs. pious and righteous father-in-law in *Mevsim Cicek Acti*. Such important cultural figurations as in *Mevsim Cicek Acti* are blocked out by the lack of consideration for Turkish films in the discourse about Turkish-German cinema. However these are necessary in order to understand the complexity of Turkish-German emigration as a visually constructed event. The grid or raster of the 'nation' seems not to be adequate for the nowadays transcultural films of Turkish-German cinema. In moments in which the basis for a Turkish-German visual epistemology is constructed only in a one-sided way, namely from a perspective of German films, the national perspective in the context of transnational questions can help make visible the blocked out fields of knowledges and constructions as it is suggested here for the case of Turkish Emigration Cinema in Turkish-German film discourse.

(Re-)writing Turkish-German cinema from the bottom up: A Plea

The topical academical view on Turkish-German cinema keeps one-sided as the Turkish films about emigration are not considered as a part of its history. Such perspective is Eurocentric. *"Home and the feeling for it"*, Edgar Reitz said analogously on the Turkish-German film festival in 2014 in Nuremberg, *"arise only there and then, where and when the stories of the people living there are known."* In the case of a "German" interest in Turkish stories which are told in Turkish film culture the result is sobering. Although there were four film festivals in Germany in 2014 (Essen, Nuremberg,

Frankfurt on the Main, Mannheim and Turkish Film Days in cities like Munih and Berlin) the academic interest in Turkish film culture as a whole could be characterised as "not existant" if one has a look at German literature about the general history of Turkish film.

One has to ask the question why the Turkish films and the perspective of the land of emigration are excluded from Turkish-German film discourse. Even if not considered as a fundamental part of what is tried to be defined as Turkish-German cinema, the comparison between *When We Leave* and *Mevsim Cicek Acti* on a level of the analysis of representations of men and women showed that a more or less unintended exclusion of films produced in Turkey produces an epistemological one-sided-ness. Only an interest in historical competences in transnational, but also national film cultures like the one of the home of the emigrants legitimises the use of discourses about transculturality and hybridity. What happens at the moment with the increasing academic discussions about Turkish-German cinema as "Transcultural Cinema" tends to be a kind of *"conceptual, theoretical and aesthetical (ab)use of postcolonial theory for the sake of academic complecance in respect of poststructuralist and postmodern celebration"* (cf. Steyerl, 2012: 47). The discourse about transculturality in the films seems to be the discussion about the appropriate representations of emigrants, but is rather a leveling and harmonious incorporation of the hybrid potentials of the Turkish-German emigrants in which the emigrants themselves are excluded from the discourse about them. Or to put it with Spivak's famous question: can the emigrant speak or are the intellectuals speaking with such films for them of which is thought that they represent and speak for them best (Spivak, 2007 [1985])?

Filmography

Akad, Ö. L. (1973). *Dügün [Wedding]*. Erman Film. Turkey. 84 min.
Akad, Ö. L. (1973). *Gelin [Bride]*. Erman Film. Turkey. 93 min.
Akad, Ö. L. (1974). *Diyet [Diet]*. Erman Film. Turkey, 90 min.
Akin, F. (2004). *Head On [Gegen die Wand]*. Germany. Wüste Filmproduktion. 116 min.
Aksoy, O. (1974). *Almanyalı Yarim [My German Love]*. Erler Film. Turkey, 82 min.
Aladağ, F. (2010). *When We Leave [Die Fremde]*. Independent Artists Filmproduktion. Germany, Turkey, 119 min.
Alakuş, B. (2001). *Anam [My Mother]*. Wüste Filmproduktion, ZDF. Germany. 86 min.
Algül, H. (2012). *Berlin Kaplanı [The Berlin Tiger]*. BKM Film, Acar Entertainment. Turkey, 102 min.

Arslan, T. (1997). *Brothers and Sisters [Geschwister]*. Germany. 84 min.

Arslan, T. (1999). *Dealer*. Germany. 80 min.

Arslan, T. (2001). *A Fine Day [Original: Der schöne Tag]*. FBB, Pickpocket Productions, Zero Film GmbH, ZDF. Germany. 74 min.

Arslan, Y. (1998). *Yara [Wound]*. Yılmaz Arslan Filmproduktion. Germany, Turkey. 99 min.

Ataman, K. (1999). *Lola und Bilidikid*. WDR, Boja Buck Filmproduktion, Zero Film GmbH, Germany. 90 min.

Baser, T. (1986). *40 Square Meters of Germany [40 m² Deutschland]*. Tevfik Baser Filmproduktion; Studio Hamburg Filmproduktion. Germany, Turkey. 80 min.

Baser, T. (1989). *Farewell to False Paradise [Abschied vom falschen Paradies]*. Ottokar Runze Produktion, ZDF. Germany. 92 min.

Baytan, N. (1978). *Yıkılış [Downfall]*. Sezer Film. Turkey. 72 min.

Bohm, H. (1988). *Yasemin*. Hamburger Kino Kompanie, ZDF. Germany. 83 min.

Çetin, S. (1993). *Berlin in Berlin*. Plato Film. Turkey, Germany. 117 min.

Dağtekin, B. (2013). *Fack Ju Göhte*. Germany. Constantin Film. 118 min.

Eğilmez, E. (1980). *Banker Bilo*. Arzu Film. Turkey. 95 min.

Elçi, I. (1990). *Düğün [Wedding]*. Wolfgang Krenz Filmproduktion. Germany. 90 min.

Elmas, O. (1974). *El Kapısı [Foreign Doors]*. Umut Film. Turkey. 73 min.

Fassbinder, R. W. (1969). *Katzelmacher*. antitheater-X-Film. Germany. 85 min.

Fassbinder, R. W. (1974). *Ali: Fear Eats Soul [Angst essen Seele auf]*. Tango-Film. Germany. 89 min.

Figenli, Y. (1980). *Deliler Almanya'da [The Crazies in Germany]*. Yavuz Film. Turkey. 80 min.

Gören, S. (1979). *Almanya Acı Vatan [Germany Bitter Home]*. Fatoş Film. Turkey. 90 min.

Gören, S. (1988). *Polizei [Police]*. Penta Films. Turkey. 90 min.

Günar, Sülbiye [aka Freytag, Verena S.] (2003). *Karamuk [Black Muk]*. WDR. Germany. 97 min.

Güney, G. (1991). *Bir Umut Uğruna [For a Hope]*. Em-Ra Film. Turkey. 76 min.

Güney, Y. (1971). *Baba [Father]*. Akün Film. Turkey, 96 min.

Gürsu, T. (1975). *Baldız [Sister-in-Law]*. Olgun Film. Turkey. 84 min.

Horst, H. (1987). *Aufbrüche [Awakenings]*. MedienOperative Berlin e. V. Germany. 90 min.

Kavur, Ö. *Amansız Yol [Unforgiven Way]*. Delta Film. Turkey. 87 min.

Kutlucan, H. (1998). *Ich Chef, du Turnschuh [I Chief, You Sneakers]*. ZDF. Germany. 95 min.

Okan, T. (1974). *Otobüs [Bus]*. Pan Film. Turkey, Switzerland. 75 min.

Okan, T. (1987). *Mercedes Mon Amour*. [Original: Sarı Mercedes/ Fikrimin İnce Gülü]. Promete Film, Odak Film. Turkey, Germany, Switzerland, France. 90 min.

Olgaç, B. (1984). *Yavrularım [My Children]*. Gülsah Film. Turkey. 83 min.

Pekmezoğlu, O. (1974). *Almanya'da Bir Türk Kızı [A Turkish Girl in Germany]*. Saner Film. Turkey. 93 min.

Refiğ, H. (1962). *Gurbet Kuşları [Birds of Exile]*. Artist Film. Turkey. 102 min.

Refiğ, H. (1972). *Acı Zafer [Bitter Glory]*. Turkey. 80 min.

Samdereli, Y. (2001). *Almanya – Welcome to Germany [Almanya - Willkommen in Deutschland]*. Roxy Film. Germany. 101 min.

Sanders-Brahms, H. (1976). *Shirin's Wedding [Shirins Hochzeit]*. WDR. Germany. 120 min.

Saner, H. (1966). *Turist Ömer Almanya'da [The Tourist Ömer in Germany]*. Turkey. 82 min.

Şoray, T. (1972). *Dönüş [Return]*. Akün Film. Turkey. 96 min.

Temelkuran, I. (2007). *Made in Europe*. Özen Film. Turkey. 85 min.

Tibet, K. (1981). *Davaro*. Basaran Film. Turkey. 80 min.

Tibet, K. (1985). *Gurbetçi Şaban [Foreign Saban]*. Uğur Film. Turkey. 88 min.

Turgul, Y. (1996). *Eşkiya - The Bandit*. Filma Cass. Turkey. 122 min.

Ucanoğlu, Y. (1984). *Gurbet [Foreign Country]*. Sine Ay Film. Turkey. 92 min.

Üngör, A. L. (2012). *Mevsim Çiçek Açtı [Blossom Season]*. Yalınayak Film. Turkey. 110 min.

Yapo, M. (2007). *Premonition*. Sony Pictures. USA. 96 min.

Yavuz, Y. (1998). *Aprilkinder [Children of April]*. Zero Film GmbH, ZDF. Germany, 85 min.

Chapter 12: Grounded theory and transnational audience reception

Deniz Özalpman

Introduction

The aim of this study is to shed new light on debates about Turkish migration studies using a grounded theory (GT) method. My case study for this research is *Magnificent Century*, an internationally viewed and acclaimed popular television series that refers to the sixteenth century Ottoman Sultan *Suleiman the Magnificent* associated with the pinnacle of Ottoman power in the world. The series dramatize the intrigues of his harem and court and most of the incidents and actions are based on real events and fictionalised subplots.

The series has received considerable attention after being targetted by Prime Minister Erdogan's critics as representing 'a distorted view of Ottoman history and blaspheming Turkish ancestors' and triggered considerable discussion not only in Turkey but outside as well in the global public sphere. In this sense the series became a 'reference point' (Koçak & Koçak, 2013:77) in public and political discussions in Turkey and abroad.

Magnificent Century has numerous symbols and elements historically related to Alevi culture and religion. These include, the depiction of Janissary corps and their rituals related to the Bektashi order, Şehzades' (Ottoman princes) oath-taking ceremony, the twelve Imams' scene and so forth. From this perspective, an analysis of an Alevi audience, positioned as genre-based interpretative communities, may ascertain sensibilities, desires and aspirations within their transnational positioning.

This study provides an important opportunity to advance our understanding of GT, specifically constructivist GT and to consider theoretical differences in its conceptualizations as the debate continues about the best strategies for the management of GT. The *traditional* version of GT is the Glaserian GT (Glaser, 1978: 1992: 1998) and the Straussian GT which in large part is developed by Strauss and Corbin as the *evolved* version (Strauss, 1987; Strauss & Corbin, 1990: 1998).

Constructivist grounded theory

A third version called constructivist GT was developed by Charmaz (2000: 2006: 2008: and 2009) and others (Bryant, 2003; Mills, Bonner, &Francis, 2006). Sharing the same conceptual framework, Thornberg (2012) calls it *informed* GT and Goldkuhl and Cronholm (2010) *multi-GT*. These scholars criticize the original idea of Glaserian GT as 'pure induction' and emphasize the inadequacies of 'delaying literature review till the end of the analysis' and the researcher's position as *tabula rasa* when entering the field of inquiry (Charmaz, 2000).

In constructivist GT, the motto of GT as 'all is data' (Glaser 1967) is replaced by the idea of 'all is construction'. Constructivist GT assumes that neither data nor theories are discovered, but are constructed by the researcher as a result of his or her interactions with the field and its participants (Charmaz, 2006: 2008: 2009; Mills et al., 2006; Thornberg & Charmaz, 2014). Data has been co-constructed by researcher and participants, and colored by the researcher's perspectives, values, privileges, positions, interactions, and geographical locations (Charmaz, 2008: 2009; Mills et al., 2006). The table below summarizes the main differences between Constructivist GT and the objectivist or traditional GT.

Table 12.1. Objectivist versus constructivist GT

Objectivist GT	Constructivist GT
Assumes an external reality	Assumes multiple realities
Assumes discovery of data	Assumes mutual construction of data
Assumes conceptualizations	Assumes researcher constructs categorizations
Views representation of data as unproblematic	Views representation of data as problematic, relativistic, situational and partial
Assumes the neutrality, passivity and authority of the researcher	Assumes the observer's values, priorities,positions and actions affect views
Views data analysis as an objective process	Acknowledges subjectivities in data analysis
Gives priority to researcher's views	Seeks participants views and voices as integral to the analysis
Aims to achieve context free generalizations	Views generalizations, as partial, conditional and situated in time, space, positions, action and interactions
Focuses on developing abstractions	Focuses on constructing interpretations
Aims for parsimonious explanation	Aims for interpretive understanding

Source: See Charmaz (2000: 2006).

Method

'Purposive sampling' (Lincoln & Guba, 1985) or 'theoretical sampling' (Glaser & Strauss, 1967) is the selection of participants according to the research question and the theoretical needs of the study. For this study, sample diversity was necessary to maximize differences of interpretation as the purpose was to ascertain consumption experiences and motivations within this genre-based community. Participants were selected from the *Alevi Culture Center* in Vienna *(Alevitisches Kulturzentrum in Wien),* which is the most populated among eight other Alevi culture centers in Austria. Participants were chosen based on their self-expression as regular viewers of the *Magnificent Century.*

The paper draws from focus group, paired/triad and in-depth interviews conducted in Vienna over a year period in 2013. The seven focus groups were divided between single-gendered adult female, male and mix-gendered groups. The focus groups were organized in two age groups: 18-30, 31-65.

All participants originate from Turkey, and all were settled in Austria, although among 52 participants, three came during the last decade and did not have citizenship rights. The older generation is high school graduated from Turkey, whereas the younger age group has graduated from high school and/or university in Austria.

Inside Alevi community, *dedes* (literally the `elder') manage the religious ceremonies (*Cem ayini*) that are followed as a spiritual guide. However, this *dede* position is as well shared by other older members of the community in respect to their age and knowledge. They make comments on issues related to politics, religion and popular themes. Initially, two focus groups were conducted with *dedes*, and then two more focus groups were conducted with women. The researcher found out after the fourth focus group that several common words and terms were repeated by female participants and that no new insights were presented. This finding was accepted as the signal of *saturation* and then the research was oriented toward the series' young audience with mix-gendered focus groups and in interaction with *dedes*.

For the internal validation of data, the findings were regularly and comparatively checked every time new interviews were added to the study. The questions asked fell within the following themes: Turkish `soap operas', Magnificent Century's relevance to their broader social life, experiences and motivations gained from this series. Participants were asked questions such as: 'How would you describe Magnificent Century?', 'What happened in the last episode and did you like it?' "What did you find as being relevant to Alevi/Bektashi traditions in the series?", 'What do you think about the comments of the critics on the series?'

In constructivist GT, there are two stages of data coding; open or initial coding applied by line-by-line analysis to the data and selective or focused coding which scrutinize the initial codes. Focusing on both the most frequent and the most telling codes provides tentative leads for exploration and checks during subsequent data collection. By including data in the memo, researchers build clear links to categories (Charmaz, 2008).

Following the GT protocol (Strauss 1987; Strauss & Corbin, 1990), seventy-eight pages of data were examined for identifiable units of meaning (clauses, sentences, or larger expressive units) and were coded into conceptual categories. The focused coding or selective coding identifies a few core categories and develops a central descriptive narrative of the phenomenon under study (Banks et al., 2000).

Results

After reading all the data at least twice, each meaningful unit was bracketed (often two or more sentences, a paragraph, occasionally and a clause) and labeled according to its apparent functional nature as a unit of communication. The open coding process generated 14 categories with a total of 539 coded units of analysis. Some instances from open categories and their frequency of occurrence are displayed below in Table 12.2, as an illustration.

Table 12.2. Open Coding Categories

Category number and description	Example	Codable units in category
1. Statement of motivations watching *Magnificent Century*	"I do not look at the way they are acting, I look at it as History, the way History has been represented but what I see there; this is not reality, lies were telling. There was a scene, they executed Alevis, and they did not show it properly. (1.Focus group)	39
2. Explicit statement of historical knowledge	"We studied till high school in Turkey so we know a lot from history, we read history and we are still reading, what has been lived in the past, is not reflected correctly in this series" (2. Focus group)	35
3. Statement of pleasure for the scenes related to *Alevi-Bektashi* order in *Magnificent Century*	"I was not expecting them to show that much *Bektashi* tradition in the series, as *gülbank* prayers (specific prayer chanted in unison), Sehzades (Ottoman princes) sermons on *Janissary* order" (From paired interview with young girls)	31

4. Indication of intergenerational differences	"Today young people mostly, who are born here or the ones who come here at very young ages; they do not know the truth. So they can really believe what they see in this series that is why I must revolt against it..." (1. Focus group)	28
5. Reference to Politics when discussing *Magnificent Century*	"People who are watching these series, someone from outside can think how rich they were Ottomans, but in reality, our generation, we did not have something to wear. In the series, they do not show Anatolia for example and how poor people were. I did not have a shoe to wear..." (3.focus group)	23
6. Warning and lessons to young generation	"A (*dede*): All Padişahs (Sultans) are murderers. Are they coming from Prophet's race? M: but we do not think like this in this period, they are all the same as kings A: but you misinform society, they are no saints, untouchable, you should not present them as saints! you should not deify them M: we are talking about seven hundred years before A: with this thinking you can also make saint Tayyip (Prime minister) M: but how can I judge history now?! Russian tsars or British kings they are all like this A: they were illerate, they do not know how to write and read, they were also just normal human beings" (Excerpt from 7.focus group)	35
7. Reference to personal experiences and politics	"After Premier' intervention, *Ramadan* came in the series, women show up more covered. While I was making my military service, during *Ramadan* I was having rest as I do not make it, I am Alevi and some soldiers insulted me, meanwhile as they take me as *Persian (Acem)* they were also afraid of me... However, my wife makes her *Ramadan*, my father too he was making it" (4.focus group)	24
8. Identity construction with reference to *Magnificent Century*	"As you know, we are Alevis-Kizilbash (Kızılbaş in Turkish), there is an oath-taking ceremony there, in the series, this part I appreciate, we share this feeling, we still live it exactly the same today, what they say in the sermon the Janissaries; do not tell a lie, do not steal... Nothing has changed for us, this is our philosophy" (1.focus group)	43
9. Transnational positioning	"Maybe here (Austria) we are foreigners, we are not in our country of origin but here I am respected, my religion is respected. Our children, our young	41

| | generation can ask them to write on their ID, their belief as Alevi. We will get buried respected to our Alevi traditions" (3.focus group) | |

Some units of discourse were vivid, almost defied naming; the difficulty in naming such units of analysis might seem to lie ambiguously between already established categories just as the example below from a female focus group discussion:

Ayşe: *My mother-in-law says sometimes; my daughter why you are watching this? They create conflict between daughter- and mother-in-law. I said, mother, we take these as a lesson, a good example; we don't look at it just to repeat what they did. I don't try to get the unfair but I take lesson, an example from that.*

This text could have been interpreted primarily as a 'Reference to family discussions' (Category 10), or 'Moral lessons related to the series' (Category 11), or 'Narrative pleasure' (Category 12). Following a principle of critical language analysis (Faircloth, 1989), the researcher examined the discoursal context in which the codable unit of analysis was embedded to aid the interpretation. As in the case of five similar codable units, this text was coded to 'Multiple categories' (Category 14), as the unit in question could clearly be interpreted as having multiple functions.

Selective coding

Focused or selective coding is the final operation in GT to identify the core category or categories. The responsibility through younger generations is the motivations of *dedes* and from their viewing experiences; they feel the necessity to produce an antidote against the poison which could derive from the amalgam of the real and fictional events. The narrative structure and the critical perspective of the series does not satisfy *dedes'* expectations and aspirations of the historical truths, however, in the least, for the community, the scenes related to the *Alevi-Bektashi* order partially refelects Alevi religion and culture correctly. The *Dedes'* background from Turkey helps them to develop a critical perspective against the series' narrative with reference to personal experiences and relate them to political discussions, while interpreting the series. The women and younger generation can better enjoy narrative and aesthetic pleasure of their viewing experiences as they are not responsible for others and do not have to make comments on the narration of the series in public.

136

Discussion

Constructivist GT gives the researcher an opportunity to conduct field research without preconceptions of the data with participants' words and terms, and to constantly check and compare the new findings with earlier theoretical and conceptual frameworks.

During the last decade, the shift on audience reception studies meant that migrants could be conceptualized from their 'multiple positions' (Mankekar, 1999), 'plural belongings' (Moores, 2005), 'multiple identities' (Rizvi, 2006), 'international frames of reference' (Robins &Aksoy, 2005) and 'cultural versus critical proximity' (Georgiou, 2012). Transnationals are defined as 'persons who live dual lives: speaking two languages, having homes in two countries, and making a living through continuous regular contact across national borders' (Portes et al., 1999, p.217).

This study has shown that after the official recognition of the religion as a sect and part of Islam, the Alevi community in Vienna feel more confident in their host country as citizens. However, as they are heavy viewers of the Turkish television channels, they are deeply attached to the problems with their country of origin, mostly regarding issues related to their Alevi identity and belonging. On the issue of *Magnificent Century*, the series made Alevi traditions of the past more visible to the global audiences, although the construction of truth did not entirely satisfy the community as 'being accurately represented'. Historical visibility with the whiff of the past is the basic motivation for their viewing experiences.

Chapter 13: Turkish Muslims in a German city: Entrepreneurial and residential self-determination[1]

Sarah Hackett

Introduction

Germany's Turkish communities have long been at the centre of vibrant political, academic and public deliberations. During the guest-worker years and the family reunification period that followed, and throughout their emergence as fixed attributes on German cities' landscapes, Turks secured a firm place in debates in a Germany that was a reluctant and hesitant country of immigration. In recent years, they have been the prime focus of discussions and reflections on integration, citizenship, multiculturalism, segregation, social cohesion and the place of Islam in Germany. On the whole, the history of Turkish migration to and subsequent settlement in Germany during the post-1960s era has conventionally been associated with economic exploitation and hardship, residential difficulties and segregation, educational underachievement, confusion, uncertainty, shortsighted political strategies and ad hoc social provisions (Herbert, 1986; Abadan-Unat, 2011). Turks have gradually come to be perceived as the ethnic minority group least likely to achieve integration into German society, and as recognizable and clear Ausländer.

This paper will provide an insight into the Turkish Muslim community in Bremen, a city that, apart from a few exceptions (Farwick, 2011; Hackett, 2013), has been neglected in the academic literature despite being home to a well-established and substantial Turkish population. Drawing upon a range of oral history interviews, it will expose the manner in which Bremen's Turkish Muslims have contended with and overcome the initial insecurity instilled by the overarching guest-worker framework, uncovering some of the more positive aspects of their entrepreneurial and residential patterns and behaviour. As well as investing in properties and businesses, they have progressively shaped and moulded individual neighbourhoods, and formed an engagement with the receiving society upon doing so. This paper's findings will be framed around two key points of discussion. Firstly, it will question the conventional thesis that Germany's Turkish migrants' business and housing careers have been shaped by discrimination and constraint (Kürsat-

---

[1] This chapter is reprinted with permission by *Migration Letters* journal: Hackett, S. (2015). Turkish Muslims in a German city: Entrepreneurial and residential self-determination. *Migration Letters*, 12(1), 1-12. Retrieved from http://www.tplondon.com/journal/index.php/ml/article/view/374.

Ahlers, 1996:123-6; Pütz, 2008). Secondly, it will query the long-term legacy of Germany's post-war guest-worker paradigm on Turkish Muslims at a local level.

Whilst the entrepreneurial and residential experiences and practices of Turks, and ethnic minorities more widely, in Germany have been awarded a significant level of attention in the academic literature, few works have drawn upon oral history. Instead, they have often used datasets, such as those provided by the German Socio-economic Panel (GSOEP) (Drever & Clark, 2002; Constant, Shachmurove & Zimmermann, 2007). Studies that have employed oral history interviews have tended to address other aspects of the Turkish migration process, such as political integration and ethnic identification (Doerschler, 2006; Ersanilli & Saharso, 2011). One notable exception is Patricia Ehrkamp's 2005 investigation into contemporary transnational ties and local attachments amongst Turks in Duisburg-Marxloh, which does discuss elements of both business- and neighbourhood-formation (Ehrkamp, 2005). This paper, however, will offer a grass-roots insight into Turkish Muslims' entrepreneurial and residential choices and behaviour, and findings will be contextualised within a historical framework.

Bremen: History, industry & identity

This paper draws upon the case study of Bremen, a Hanseatic city in North-western Germany. An industrial centre since the mid-seventeenth century, Bremen has been home to an active port and a wide variety of industries including steel, wool textile, craft and food production, tobacco and cigar manufacturing and ship construction (Leohold, 1986; Power et al., 2010). Although since the mid-1970s Bremen has become renowned for a continuous run of economic crises, including the closing of factories, shipbuilder bankruptcies and political controversies, as well as high levels of unemployment, poverty and social deprivation (Ireland, 2004:87), its initial post-war emergence as a renewed trade and industrial hub led to a vast increase in its immigrant population. Whilst slightly later than was the case in areas such as Hessen and Baden Württemberg in the industrial south, Bremen attracted a significant number of guest-workers. Some of the main recruiters in the city included AG Weser and Bremer Vulkan, two shipbuilding companies, Bremer Woll-Kämmerei, a wool textile company, the Klöckner steel- and metal-works, and the Bremen-Vegesacker Fischerei-Gesellschaft (Bremen Vegesack fishing company).

Perhaps as a result of this chronologically delayed recruitment and the fact that academic studies have tended to concentrate primarily on cities with neighbourhoods renowned for their Turkish communities, such as Berlin (Kreuzberg) and Frankfurt (Bahnhofsviertel) (Klopp, 2002; Mandel, 2008),

Bremen's Turkish ethnic minority population remains largely under-researched. Yet despite this academic neglect, the city is home to a well-established and sizeable Turkish community that for the most part has its roots in the guest-worker years. Since the 1970s, family members from Turkey have joined the original guest-workers, and the city's foreign-born population increased from constituting under 2 per cent of the total population in 1968 to 6 per cent in 1978 and almost 10 per cent in 1988 (Ireland, 2004: 86). With regards to the Turkish community specifically, it stood at 1,673 in 1966, 16,535 in 1976 and 36,406 in 2009.

As well as constituting a largely unexplored context in which to study entrepreneurial and residential patterns and behaviour amongst Turkish Muslims in Germany, there are other reasons for which the city of Bremen makes for a pertinent case study. Firstly, Bremen's local autonomy has long been prevalent in the devising and implementing of migration policies in that the city's government has been recognised for its early, persistent and forward-thinking attempts at promoting the integration of its Turkish population, and has traditionally taken great pride in the position of and provisions available for its migrants when compared to elsewhere in Ger-many (Interview with Mayor Hans Koschnick, undated; Ireland, 2004:90). Secondly, it has often been claimed that Bremen is home to a particular regional identity that has deep historical roots. This presumed identity is the consequence of the city's position as an international shipping and trading centre, and its political, economic and social distinctiveness (Buse, 1993).

Furthermore, clear links have been formed between Bremen's history and its more modern role as the home of ethnic minorities. This has recently been seen, for example, in the manner migrant businesses have been perceived as capable of building upon the city's role as an international port and foreign trade centre (Bremische Bürgerschaft Landtag 16. Wahlperiode. Drucksache 16/264). Overall, Bremen's government's approach has been one that has eagerly encouraged the integration of the city's Turkish com-munity, often escaping the widespread criticism that has been lavished upon policy in Germany at both a national and local level (Klusmeyer & Papademetriou, 2009). This particularism has undoubtedly sculpted the environment in which Turkish Muslims' entrepreneurial and residential experiences have played out.

The Research

This article draws upon 21 oral history interviews with Turkish Muslims that were carried out in Bremen in July and August 2010. Ten respondents were male, four of which were first-generation immigrants, and five and one of which were second- and third-generation respectively. Nine of the interviewees were female, with five being first-generation immigrants, three belonging to the second-generation and one to the third-generation. The remaining two interviews were conducted with married couples. One comprised a husband and wife who were both second-generation migrants. Regarding the other, the wife was a second-generation Turk who had grown up in Bremen whilst the husband had only lived in the city for a few years. The participants were contacted primarily through mosques, and Turkish and Muslim centres and organisations. After initial contact was es-tablished, snowball sampling was used in order to secure additional respondents. The majority of the interviews were conducted in the respond-ents' homes and places of employment, and were recorded when permission was given to do so. All respondents were informed that participation was voluntary and that they had the right to remain anonymous. The interviews consisted of open-ended questions that were loosely structured around the topics of employment, housing, integration, and general impressions of and experiences in Bremen. This format allowed for a range of possible responses, and enabled the interviewees to expand on themes and subjects they deemed important.

As is the case across Germany (Mandel, 2008:92), the Turkish com-munity in Bremen tends not to form part of mainstream middle-class socie-ty. The interviewees were primarily former guest-workers who arrived to Bremen during the 1960s and early 1970s, the majority of whom had rural origins, and the descendants thereof. As such, whilst some have middle-class aspirations and many have made vast progress with regards to their entrepreneurial and residential standings, they remain predominantly work-ing class. All of the respondents defined themselves as Muslims, yet it must be recognised that they do not constitute one homogenous group. Some were religiously active Muslims, whilst others had simply inherited their religion, but did not practice. Yet being Muslim often constituted an important part of their identities and they defined themselves as such on some level. Whilst the interviews most certainly do not represent the views of all Turkish Muslims in Bremen, they allow the exploration of specific themes and enable the uncovering of entrepreneurial and residential experiences and behaviour within a largely unexplored geographical context.

Key findings: Choice, success, and integration

An estimated 70 per cent of the European Union's self-employed Turks are in Germany and their entrepreneurialism has progressively been encour-aged by local-level government policies and measures (Constant, Shachmurove & Zimmermann, 2007). Recent years have also witnessed an increase in allegations of "parallel societies", a growing recognition that home ownership can lead to higher levels of integration, and the inclusion of the housing sector in the groundbreaking 2007 National Integration Plan (Schönwälder & Söhn, 2009; Constant et al., 2009). Yet despite this political and popular interest, the academic literature on migrant entrepreneurship and residential practices in Germany remains underdeveloped when compared to that addressing countries like the United States and Britain (Borjas, 1986; Bolt et al., 2010). Nevertheless, clear hypotheses have been established regarding the notions of choice, success and integration, or the lack thereof, in these areas. In both cases, the dominant argument has often been one of constraint, limited opportunities and a lack of acculturation.

Concerning entrepreneurship, whilst some studies have recognised that business-ownership amongst Turks is often an employment choice that stems from an inherent entrepreneurialism (Constant, Shachmurove & Zimmermann, 2007), many have argued that they are pushed into self-employment due to perceived discrimination in the German labour market (Constant & Zimmermann, 2006). Furthermore, although the Centre for Turkish Studies in Essen championed the argument that Turkish businesses convey a commitment to Germany, promote the emergence of a Turkish middle class, create jobs, and act as a bridge between Turks and Germans (Şen, 1991), there has long been a widespread belief that self-employment leads to segregation and ghettoization in that businesses serve a Turkish clientele and constitute ethnic enclaves (Abadan-Unat, 1997). Regarding residential practices, whilst some works have recognised the role played by personal aspirations in Turks' housing choices (Ehrkamp, 2005), academic research has overwhelmingly revelled in claims of enforced segregation, limited residential mobility and discrimination (Gans, 1987; Kürsat-Ahlers, 1996:123-125; Stowasser, 2002:58-59). Furthermore, little attention has been awarded to the growing practice of home ownership amongst Turks, perhaps because the rental market continues to dominate the German housing sector (for one exception, see Drever and Clark, 2002).

The oral history interviews drawn upon in this paper offer a more comprehensive and personalised account than can be attained from datasets, and go some way towards supporting the theory that Turkish migrants' entrepreneurship and residential practices have often been the consequences of consciously made choices, and have acted as evidence and conduits of success and integration. Whilst the interviewees cannot be perceived as one homogenous group, they overwhelmingly portrayed their self-employment and residential experiences in a positive light. For example, out of the 12 respondents who ran businesses at the time of the interviews or had previously done so, 10 portrayed entrepreneurship as their employment choice, and all maintained that their businesses enabled contact with and depended on the local German population in some way. Of the 23 interviewees, only two mentioned having lived in poor-quality housing, with a third having experienced overcrowded housing conditions. All of the respondents emphasised their ability to secure properties of their choosing in their preferred areas of the city, and seven of them, including one married couple, already owned properties, whilst three others expressed an ambition to soon do so. Overall, the interviewees emphasised their ability to develop and achieve their own entrepreneurial and housing aims and aspirations. They perceived their business and housing practices and behaviour as both indicators and conduits of success, integration and a long-term commitment to Bremen, and spoke about them with a sense of pride and satisfaction.

With regards to self-employment, not only was running a business a widespread practice, but it was also one that was deemed important on a personal level. A few of the interviewees portrayed self-employment as a consequence of discrimination and a lack of opportunities in the local la-bour market either in reference to themselves or others, and this is certainly the argument that has long dominated the academic literature on Turkish entrepreneurship in Germany (Pütz, 2008). Yet many others were keen to stress that their entrepreneurialism has been driven by a conscious desire to be economically independent. When asked why they had become self-employed, one interviewee stressed that it was because 'it's in my blood', whilst others cited a longing to be independent and receive good earnings as their primary motivations.

There are a number of ways in which the establishing and running of these businesses can be perceived as having been successful. Not only did respondents not report any problems in becoming self-employed, but also their businesses have long pertained to a variety of sectors and have included restaurants, shops, a discotheque, a sales office, a construction business, and media design and dressmaking services. Furthermore, whilst it has often been argued that Turkish businesses in Germany predominantly serve the Turkish community and are firmly rooted within the Turkish enclave economy (Hillmann, 2009:106), the interviewees were keen to emphasize the manner in which their businesses enabled and depended on contact with native Germans. One first-generation self-employed male, for example, had a German business partner. Others revealed that their businesses largely served a German clientele, with one respondent proudly divulging how the restaurant he used to run was regularly frequented by the city's football team, Werder Bremen's, manager. One second-generation male businessman explained that some Turkish entrepreneurs in Bremen purposely tailored their businesses in order to attract German customers. He claimed that some refused to hire Muslim women who wore headscarves because they 'want to give a better impression to their clientele'. He had done this himself by locating his business in an affluent part of the city, and by stocking and selling high-quality products.

Choice and success have also been present amongst Bremen's Turkish Muslims in the housing sector. Whilst some respondents acknowledged that their families had suffered poor quality housing and overcrowding during the early years of settlement, it is evident that Bremen's Turkish Muslims have since shaped their own residential experiences in a number of ways. The interviewees stressed the manner in which they had traditionally been either attracted to or deterred away from individual neighbourhoods as a result of what is recognized as their Turkish or Muslim identities. There were those who had lived in the west of the city for many years and could not imagine their lives unfolding anywhere else. Some had grown up in the West of Bremen, others had worked or had children go to school there, and this remained the case for many.

The western district of Gröpelingen especially, an area renowned for its multicultural streets, mosques, ethnic minority shops and restaurants, and migrant centres and organisations, has long been perceived as Bremen's Turkish hub. Having been home to the city's industrial harbour and numerous companies that employed Turkish workers during the Gastarbeiter years, namely the AG Weser shipbuilding company and the Klöckner steel- and metal-works, there were many interviewees who felt a strong sense of attachment to this city quarter in particular. For example, when asked why it was important to remain in Gröpelingen, one second-generation female respondent replied: 'This is home for me because I grew up here. I went to school here. I have my family here... I would not want to move to another area of the city...I'm active in a mosque so it's practical for me to get there and, because I grew up here, I know many local people. I know a lot of Germans...When I go to another area of the city, I feel like a stranger.'

Others had chosen to live in different areas away from the heart of Bremen's Turkish community. One couple listed the availability of better quality and more modern housing stock as one of their reasons for having done so. Yet many saw themselves as being a "different type" of Turkish Muslim to those who lived in Gröpelingen and thus had purposefully distanced themselves from this district, opting instead for areas like Osterholz in the east or for neighbourhoods in or near the city centre. For example, when comparing herself to Turkish Muslims in Gröpelingen, one second-generation female interviewee argued that 'my world is different'. For the most part, the neighbourhood was more important to the interviewees than individual properties, and was seen as both a representation and extension of their own identities.

As well as determinedly choosing their areas of residence, some respondents have succeeded in becoming owner-occupiers. When asked why they had decided to purchase property in Bremen, many mentioned that it had been an important step for them for a number of reasons. It had enabled them to live in close proximity to family, to achieve a sense of independence and many believed that it made long-term financial sense. Some identified home ownership as a sign of commitment to their local sur-roundings and Germany more widely. For example, one first-generation female stated: 'I want to live in Germany. That was the deciding factor for me.' At the time of the interviews, others still had ambitions of owning property, one of the reasons given for which was to become a landlord through the renting out of rooms. On the whole, respondents were overwhelmingly content with their residential standings. They had long been able to shape their own housing experiences and manipulate the housing market to serve their own interests, and were confident that they would continue to do so.

Conclusion

It is not the intention of this paper to claim that Bremen's Turkish Muslims' entrepreneurial and residential experiences have escaped constraint and discrimination. Indeed there have certainly been incidents of both, examples of which were discussed by some of the interviewees. Yet it is clear that these instances have long been overshadowed by a sense of choice, ambition and success to an extent that cannot simply be dismissed as what could perhaps otherwise be misinterpreted as a desire on behalf of the interviewees to overplay their parts in determining their own business and housing patterns and behaviour. It is evident that Turkish Muslims in Bremen have traditionally displayed a higher degree of self-determination and ambition in their entrepreneurial and housing performances than tends to be recognised for Turks in Germany as a whole. This might be the consequence of the city's particular historical characteristics, its local authority's proactivity with regards to migrant communities or its regional identity. Although the effects of these attributes prove impossible to measure, the interviewees certainly felt that their local surroundings provided them with opportunities that were not available to Turks in Germany more widely. They identified locality as an important factor, with many referring to themselves as "Bremer" and depicting the city as a distinguished location that had allowed them to thrive.

This local distinctiveness questions the extent to which Germany's post-war national immigration framework has had a lasting legacy at a city level. As was the case throughout West Germany, Bremen's post-war guest-worker history was one involving recruitment offices, medical examinations and temporary contacts, and was renowned for isolation, confusion, prejudice, racism and the everyday experiences of working for a company where one was considered nothing more than a temporary supply of manpower. Scholars have repeatedly emphasized the fact that, by their very nature, Gastarbeiter were expected to be temporary residents in a Germany that was "not a country of immigration", and whose labour importation scheme was shaped by short-term policies, unpreparedness and a neglect of future implications, which has had negative consequences on Turks' employment and housing performances (Castles, 1992:42; Fetzer & Soper, 2005:100-101). Indeed, Germany is frequently perceived as a nation that has only recently come to terms with its position as a "country of immigration" as a result of its reformed citizenship laws, its immigration law of 2005 and the unprecedented level of attention awarded to integration by Angela Merkel's government. Its Turkish Muslims remain at the centre of a frenzied debate regarding social cohesion and polarization, extremism and radicalization, and the alleged crisis of multiculturalism.

Yet this paper's historical approach and methodology expose how, irrespective of national-level political mandate and popular deliberation, entrepreneurial and residential experiences amongst Turkish Muslims in Bremen have long been both consequences and conduits of success, integration and a feeling of loyalty to their local German surroundings. In other words, the otherwise largely unexplored local context of Bremen offers a positive deviation from the traditional national immigration narrative in that it appears as though migrant choice and ambition soon surpassed the initial constraints of the guest-worker paradigm. This paper's scope and findings are timely in a number of ways. On an academic level, they support the recent, and increasingly prominent, call for scholarship to move beyond 'methodological nationalism', and do more to recognise the relationship that exists between migrants and the cities in which they live, as well as the role the local level can play in the migration process (Ireland, 2004; Glick Schiller & Çağlar, 2009; Çağlar & Glick Schiller, 2011). Furthermore, after decades of uncertainty and denial, Germany appears to have finally reached a political consensus on immigration and integration, with Muslim migrant communities in particular, as well as the employment and housing sectors, being awarded a significant level of attention. An enhanced understanding of individual migrant communities' entrepreneurial and residential patterns, behaviour and development certainly has the potential to inform these deliberations in a nation that continues to refine its 21st-century focus on integration.

Chapter 14: An Investigation on the Turkish Religious Foundation of the UK (Diyanet)

Yakup Çoştu and **Feyza Ceyhan Çoştu**

Introduction

People referred to as Turkish immigrants in Britain are comprised of Turks, Kurds emanating from the borders of the Turkish Republic and Turkish Cypriots. Turkish Cypriots migration to Britain started in the 1940s following the World War II and increased throughout the 1960s (Ladbury 1977; Robins & Aksoy 2001). Turkish migration from mainland Turkey to Britain started in the early 1970s (Mehmet Ali 2001; Issa 2005). Ethnic Kurds from Turkey began to immigrate in larger numbers during the late 1980s and early 1990s, often seeking refuge and asylum status (Robins & Aksoy 2001; Atay 2006). These increasing waves of migration have resulted in a significant social and cultural presence within British society (Çoştu, 2013a).

Turkish immigrants living in Britain have become permanent due to various factors such as waves of chain migration (family unification, marriage, etc.), economic migration, and the emergence of a second and third generation, thus increasing the number of people becoming British citizens. Immigrants such as these who becom permanent residents in a foreign country increasingly diminish the residual hopes of a return to homelands. Thus, they are induced to create their own identity. It was as a result of this process that Turkish immigrants have established a number of community organizations and solidarity networks within the framework of the legal rights granted to them by the hosting country, primarily to provide services in various areas. These organizations vary in terms of their functionalt purposes and subsequent activities (Küçükcan, 1999). One of the most significant outcomes of the services provided by these organisations can be considered to be the steps taken for identity formation. These voluntary organizations, concentrated in areas of settlement by Turkish migrants, have differed in accordance with their religious, ethnic, cultural, ideological and political discourses. These organizations include associations and foundations carrying out diverse activities such as education, culture, arts, sports and religious services (Küçükcan, 1999; Şahin, 2012). They have become more visible in the public sphere of the host country and more influential in their representation of wider Muslim interests. The tendency therefore, has been for Turkish immigrants to address some of their problems through these organizations, while preserving their identities and the continuity of their communities.

Some of these religious organizations also offer opportunities for establishing a common identity and a sense of belonging. They differ from other civil society and voluntary sector organisations in some respects such as their objectives, target groups, service types and service areas. These organisations are often founded around buildings or mosques promoting Islamic teachings. In his study of Turkish religious organizations in Britain, Çoştu (2013b) identifies four main Islamic tendencies among religious organizations established by Turkish immigrants: *i)* Sufi organizations[1], *ii)* Religious movement organizations[2], *iii)* Religio-political movement organizations[3] and *iv)* 'semi-official' religious organizations.[4] In addition, he argues that there are in Britain 10 Turkish religious organizations[5] linked to the various Islamic discourses to be found among Turkish Muslim immigrants in Britain (Çoştu, 2013b).

One of these religious organizations is "Turkish Religious Foundation of the United Kingdom (ITDV)". In this paper, we will be focusing on the founding and current status of ITDV. Then, we will try to examine the religious, social and cultural services of this religious organization carried out via imams or religious officials from Turkey and locally-trained staff using a macro-descriptive method. This research is based on a field research carried out in London from 09th July to 09th September 2012. Our field research

---

[1] Among them, there are the followers of the late Sheikh M. Nazım Kıbrıs, who is Naqshbandi Sufi religious figure in Northern Cyprus (see Atay, 1994), the followers of Mahmut Ustaosmanoglu, who is a Naqshbandi Sufi religious figure in Turkey (see for further information Küçükcan, 1999), and the followers of Muhammed Rasit Erol (Menzil), who is a Naqshbandi Sufi religious figure in Turkey (see Çakır, 2002).

[2] There are the followers of Süleyman Hilmi Tunahan (Süleymancı Group), who is a Naqshbandi Sufi religious figure in Turkey (see Küçükcan, 1999), the followers of Fetullah Gülen (Hizmet Movement), who is a religious figure in Turkey (see for further information Çakır, 2002) and Alevis (Alevi community), who are one of the Islamic religious discourses in Turkey (see Üçer, 2005).

[3] An example is National Vision (Milli Gorus) linked to the Islamic Community Milli Gorus in Germany-based and conservative religious-political discourse in Turkey (see for further information Küçükcan, 1999), Nationalists or Idealist Youth (Milliyetciler/Ülkücü Gençlik) linked to nationalist political discourse (Nationalist Movement Party) in Turkey (see Küçükcan, 1999).

[4] In this category there is Turkish Religious Foundation of the UK that is a semi-legal religious organization in relation to the Presidency of Religious Affairs of the Republic of Turkey in London.

[5] These Turkish religious organizations in Britain are: Sheikh Nazim Al-Haqqani Derghai (1972), London Islamic Turkish Association (1976), The UK Turkish Islamic Trust (1977), The United Kingdom Turkish Islamic Association (1979), UK Turkish-Islamic Cultural Centre Trust (1984), London Alevi Cultural Centre and Cemevi (1993), Islamic Community Milli Gorus UK (1994), The Menzil Trust (1999), Turkish Religious Foundation of the UK (2001), Anatolian Muslim Society (2004) (See Çoştu, 2013b).

includes interviews and observations conducted with the staff from this foundation and its and its service users.

Diyanet foundations in Europe

The *Presidency of Religious Affairs (DIB)* is an official institution providing   public service on religious affairs in Turkey. As an official and constitutional institution, DIB tries to meet societal needs and requirements through internal and external networks providing services. The external remit of DIB is organized in countries where Turkish citizens live, and are served by as the Counsellors of Religious Services connected to the Turkish Embassies (Çoştu, 2013a).

There are also semi-official religious foundations in relation to these Offices under the name of "Turkish Religious Foundations". In the early 1980s, DIB has started the practice of sending religious officials (i.e. imams) whose salaries are paid by Turkish government, abroad to serve at mosques and masjids.

Added to this, in the present period and in some Western European countries, such as Germany, Austria, Belgium, Denmark, France, Netherlands, England, Sweden, Switzerland, there are Turkish Religious Foundations and about 1500 mosque unions related to them (see Table 14.1).

Initially, Turkish people migrated to various European countries as 'guest workers' from the 1960s onwards. In the early years of immigration, both the sending country and the host countries did not focus on integration, since the shared expectation was that these immigrants would return to their home countries after a contractual period abroad. When it became clear that these guest workers were not temporary but rather permanent, host countries started to make arrangements regarding social security legislation, work documentation, legal status, and family reunification. The basic purpose of these policies was to facilitate the integration of the Turkish migrants to host country and establish the legal mechanisms to controlthe waves of immigration. At the same time, as an emigration country, Turkey has also took steps to help the integration of Turkish immigrants into host countries and to minimize the negative effects of immigration. It was in this context that the overseas branches of the DIB were set up (Aktay & Subaşı, 2006; Çoştu, 2013a).

From the early 1960s until the beginning of the 1980s, Turkey did not have any official policies in the field of religious services for emigrant citizens. During this period the activities of religious services were carried out by religious groups and communities of Turkish origin. On one hand, these activities have played an important role in finding solutions for immigrants' problems that surfaced during the integration process, kept their integrity, and ensured the continuity of their communities. On the other hand, divisions such as different ethnic, ideological and Islamic discourses among these groups and communities emerged with consequences on on Turkish Muslims immigrants' religious lives in the host country. These divisions diversified the religious services which were available for the migrants.

Table 14.1: Overseas Organizations of DIB (Continental Europe)

The Name of Foundation	Date of Establishment	Number of Mosque Unions	Number of Staff	Address
The Turkish-Islamic Union for Religious Affairs (DITIB)	1984	917	922	Subbelrather Str. 17, 50823, Köln, Germany. www.ditib.de
Austria Turkish Religious Foundation	1990	64	64	1100, Sonnleithnergasse 20 Wien, Austria. www.atib.at
Belgium Turkish Religious Foundation	1982	67	56	Chaussée de Haecht 67 – 1210, Bruxelles. Belgium www.diyanet.be
Denmark Turkish Religious Foundation	1985	30	28	Paul Bergsøesvej 14, 2600, Glostrup, Denmark. www.danimarkatdv.org
France the Turkish-Islamic Union for Religious Affairs	1986	214	191	58 RueLenine 93170, Bagnolet, France. www.fransaditib.com
Netherland Turkish Religious Foundation	1982	141	136	Javastraat 2, 2585 AM, Den Haag, Netherlands. www.diyanet.nl
Turkish Religious Foundation of the United Kingdom	2001	5	6	31 High Street, Hornsey, London, UK N8 7QB. www.diyanet.org
Sweden Turkish Religious Foundation	1984	19	15	Haradsvagen 15, 141 43, Stockholm, Sweden. www.isvecdiyanetvakfi.org
Switzerland Turkish Religious Foundation	1987	37	22	Schwamendingen strasse 102 Zürich 8050, Switzerland. www.diyanet.ch

(Source: DIB, 2012)

After nearly 20 years, with the external establishment of DIB in some Western European countries, it can be claimed that the Turkish state has taken immigrant citizens under its wings and has provided government-assisted religious services. . This can be considered as a step to eliminate the diversities observed in the Turkish communites concerned to provide a sense of uninty and solidarity (see for further information Costu, 2013a).

Turkish Religious Foundation of the United Kingdom

The Religious Services Office of the Embassy of the Republic of Turkey in London was founded in 1998. There are no other units such as religious services attaché office, vice- attaché and local secretariat within the Office (Çolak, 2005).

"Turkish Religious Foundation of the UK" (ITDV) affiliated to the Religious Services Office was established in North London in 2001 for religious and cultural activities. It promotes human resources, advocacy / advice / information, Islamic services for children and young people, for the elderly, and people with disabilities (Çolak, 2005).[6]

This foundation started its activities in a small residence at 149 Granville Road Wood Green in 2004. LaterITDV purchased a sizable estate that has administration offices, mosque, meeting rooms, classrooms and a cafeteria in 31 High Street Hornsey. The previous location was converted into a guest house for females.

The purpose of the establishment of ITDV is expressed that "the charity was established to enlighten immigrants of Turkish origin about their religion, and provide practical religious services in Turkish mosques and help them to achieve good and harmonious relations with the members of the British society" (see. www. charitycommission.gov.uk)

Charitable objectives of ITDV are "to advance charitable purposes for the public benefit, in particular those members of the public who are Turkish or of Turkish descent (the beneficiaries) by providing or assisting in the provision of services and facilities necessary to; (a) advance the Islamic religion as practised by the Turkish people (b) advance their education (c) assist those in conditions of poverty, need or distress, in order to improve the conditions of life of such persons" (see. www. charitycommission.gov.uk).

ITDV tries to execute its mission with the help of its official representatives in the London Turkish Embassy through the Office of Religious Affairs Counsellor, and with the support of well experienced and educated imams and other female staff. ITDV not only provides practical religious services in the mosques, but gives social and community services outside mosques as well (see Çolak, 2005). In this context, according to our

---

[6] According to the records of the charity commission of the UK, the registration of this foundation was held with charity number 1076377 on April 30, 2001 (see. www.charitycommission.gov.uk).

studies[7], it is possible to compile its activities under three main categories; religious, educational and socio-cultural.

Religious Services:

Mosque activities: ITDV has performed large scales of Islamic practices (such as perform pray/salat, preaching etc.) via mosques. Nowadays, there are five mosques belonging to the foundation, named as North London Diyanet Mosque, Luton Turkish Islamic Centre and Mosque, Bristol Somuncu Baba Mosque, Edinburgh Cultural Centre and Mosque, Newcastle Kotku Mosque. Also, the foundation's religious officials take charge in Aziziye Mosque in North London.

Hajj and Umrah Organization: ITDV has carried out these activities every year since 2005 in cooperation with DIB in Tukey.

Funeral Services: ITDV has a Funeral Services Fund which is to help community through a sharing system a type of solidarity fund. Members pay a subscription fee annually.

Services of al-adha: These services are provided by representatives in Turkey.

Religious Counselling and Guidance: ITDV has provided religious counselling and guidance via staff or religious officials. Some of these forms: radio talks (London Turkish Radio); publishing articles in Turkish newspapers (such as Olay, Haber, etc.); distributing printed publications and periodicals; doing socio-psychological support activities such as moral support visits in times of illness and death, participation in wedding ceremonies, circumcision and prayers in these ceremonies; prisons visits and religious wedding services.

Educational Services:

Educational Activities for Turkish Children: ITDV has some supportive activities for Turkish children in the educational field. It has carried out educational support for children through supplementary school programmes. This school programme has followed a curriculum including Turkish language, religious knowledge and Turkish national culture. It has also provided teaching Islam and the Quran in the foundation centre or its mosque unions.

---

[7] This information is based on findings of field research the authors conducted in London from July 9, 2012 to September 9, 2012 about the foundation. This field research includes interviews and observations done with administrators and staff members of the foundation and its participants. In addition, it has benefited from the foundation's official web site (www.diyanet.org) and information contained in relevant literature about the foundation.

Educational Activities for Turkish Adults: ITDV has organized seminars and meetings for adult immigrants on various topics such as teaching Islam and the Quran in the foundation centre or its mosque unions.

Socio-Cultural Services:

Activities of woman's branch: There is a woman's branch in the foundation centre. It has organized a variety of courses concerning knowledge and skills, such as ribbon embroidery classes, ceramics and jewellery course, housekeeping, cooking course, marbling course and English language course.

Family Information and Guidance Office: It has been carried out social/cultural/religious counselling and guidance for problems of Turkish immigrant families or family members by female employees.

Programs in the religious holidays and holy nights: ITDV has provided some religious festival programs for Muslim immigrants, such as holy birth week programs for the Prophet Muhammad, Islamic memorial service, etc.

Distribution printed publications: ITDV has distributed the Holy Quran, Catechism books, Hadith and other books, Diyanet Religious calendars, Ramadan timetables to Turkish immigrants free of charge or for a fee.

Student house for females: There is a 14-bed residence hall for girls for students or visitors from Turkey or other countries.

Turkish Muslim immigrants have been living in Britain for nearly half-a-century. During the early years of this migration, the religious life of Turkish community appears to be less organized and based on individual initiatives and endeavours. During these years, individuals performed Islamic practices limited to their daily prayers often in workplaces sometimes next to factory machinery. However, with increasing migration waves, an institutional restructuring in the religious field was required. While the first generation primarily built masjids in order to perform basic religious duties, the second and third generations have tended to construct institutional complexes integrated with their areas of residence and concentration (see Küçükcan, 1999; Çoştu, 2013a). Nowadays in Britain, there are quite a number of Turkish mosques and mosque-centred organizations. Çoştu (2013b) writing on Turkish Religious organizations in Britain, reports about 10 Turkish religious organizations and about 27 places of worship (Mosque, Cemevi, Sufi Centre) in the UK. If ranked by their founding dates, ITDV is ninth among ten such organizations. Despite its establishment in the early 2000s, ITDV[8], is the second largest Turkish religious organization in Britain. It could even be claimed that ITDV has a privileged position and special place

---

[8] ITDV have five mosques in Britain. Also, see for the number of mosques of other Turkish religious organizations Çoştu (2013b).

among those organizations with its policy of religious services (Çolak, 2005; Çoştu, 2013a).

Some divisions can be seen among the Turkish religious organizations which we have observed. These divisions reproduce the ethnic, ideological and Islamic discourses that Turkish immigrants have experienced in their homeland. Such factors have effects on the religious lives of and services provided for Turkish Muslims in Britain. According to our observations, ITDV has an important role due to the reason that it has an official religious policy adopted and declared by the Presidency of Religious Affairs (DIB). This is to promote tolerance and understanding and to reduce inter-communal confrontation. According to our observations, this policy has created a positive response from the Turkish migrant community in a relatively short amount of time. Nowadays, it can be seen that, Turkish migrants have a positive approach to ITDV. It is considered to be the most reliable foundation among Turkish religious organizations in Britain.

In addition, the ITDV is a member of the Federation of Turkish Associations in the UK (see www.turkishfederation.co.uk) and has taken part in various meetings and events under the leadership of the federation. It has also been involved in efforts to develop good relations with members of other religions and Muslim communities living in London within the framework of tolerance.

Conclusion

For immigrants living in foreign countries, religion plays an important role in identity formation and protection of national culture. As far as the authors could see, faith-based organizations and mosques play central roles as community hubs and venues. In these religious places, a large amount religious obligations are performed. In addition , religious organizations provide a wide range of services including supplementary schools, women's groups, advice centers, organizations specializing in job training, and informal groups which allow people to come together in order to discuss common problems and community events. It can be said that with their religious, social, cultural and educational functions, these religious organizations and their multi-functional mosques have played key roles to integrate Turkish community into Britain's social life.

ITDV is a civil organisation indirectly affiliated to the Presidency of Religious Affairs of Turkey. Before ITDV began to offer its religious and cultural services, different religious groups were competing with each other. Furthermore there was a lack of tolerance and compromise in their dealings with each other. When ITDV was established in 2001, it started to provide religious services in line with its established principles, such as 'suitability to the authentic religious sources, continuity, accountability and suitability to public interests'. Also, it carries out its activities via Imams/religious officials from Turkey, locally-educated staff and volunteers, similar to other Turkish religious organisations. It can be said that its comprehensive religious policy has had the effect of making the pre-existing religious organizations reconsider their policy identity, to transfer cultural values to the second and third generations, and to contribute the process of integration in the host country within its religious and initiate joint activities. ITDV aims to preserve Turkish religious and national policy. Turkish Muslim immigrants believe that the vital function of religious and cultural values is to preserve their national identities, and to ensure the continuity of their community. Therefore, it can be said that Turkish immigrants have perceived it as a shelter.

REFERENCES

Abadan-Unat, N. (1997). Ethnic business, ethnic communities, and ethno-politics among Turks in Europe. Ucarer, E. & Puchala, D. (eds.) *Migration into Western Soci-eties: Problems and Policies*. London: Pinter, pp. 229-251.

Abadan-Unat, N. (2011). *Turks in Europe: from guest worker to transnational citizen*. Berghahn Books.

Adams, R.H.Jr, Cuecuecha, A., & Page, J. (2008). The Impact of Remittances on Poverty and Inequality in Ghana (Working Paper No. 4732). *World Bank Policy Research.*

Adıgüzel, Y. (2010). Diyasporadaki Kimlik Algılamalarına Göç Tipinin Etkisi: Almanya ve İngiltere Türk Toplumlarının Karşılaştırması. *Sosyoloji Dergisi*, 3 (20), 97-119.

Ahmed, A. and Ekberg, J. (2009). "Fältexperiment för att studera etnisk diskriminering på den svenska arbets- och bostadsmarknaden", *Socialvetenskaplig Tidskrift*, 16, (2), 105 – 122.

Ahmed, N., & Phillipson, C. (2006). Transnational communities, migration and changing identities in later life: a new research agenda. In O. Daatland, & S. Biggs (Eds.), *Ageing and Diversity* (pp.157-174). Bristol, B: The Policy Press.

Akgönül, S. (2009). Turks of France: Religion, Identity and Europeannes. In *Turks in Europe: Culture, Identity, Integration*. Küçükcan, Talip, and Veyis Güngör, eds. Turkevi Research Centre. Pp.35-64.

Akgunduz, A. (2013). Bir Modernleşmeyi Hızlandırma Projesi Olarak Bati Avrupa'ya İşçi Göçü. In F. B. Zurcher (Ed.), *Modernizmin Yansimalari: 60'li Yillarda Turkiye* (pp. 191-211). Ankara, A.: Elif.

Akıncı, M.A., & Yağmur, K. (2003). Language use, choice, maintenance, and ethnolinguistic vitality of Turkish speakers in France: intergenerational differences. *International Journal of the Sociology of Language* 164,107-128.

Akıncı, M.A. (1996). *Les pratiques langagières chez les immigrés turcs en France. Ecarts d'Identité*, 74, 14-17.

Akıncı, M.A. (2003). Une situation de contact de langues: Le cas turc-français des immigrés turcs en France. In J. Billiez (Ed.), *Contacts de langues: Modèles, typologies, interventions* (pp.127-144). Paris: L'Harmattan.

Aksaz, E. (2006). Immigration familale turque et activités quotidiennes des femmes: Le souci de réputation dans une cite HLM de la banlieue parisienne. *Revue Européenne des migration internationals* 22(3):155-177.

Aktay, Y. & N. Subaşı (2006). *Referans Grupları, Avrupa'da Türkler, Dinsel Organizasyonları Soylem ve Tasavvurları*. Konya-Muğla: T.C. Diyanet İşleri Başkanlığı Dış İlişkiler Daire Başkanlığı Proje Raporu.

Alba, R., & Foner, N. (2015). *Strangers No More: Immigration and the Challenges of Integration in North America and Western Europe*. New Jersey, US: Princeton University Press.

Aleviler, Anayasal Hak İçin TBMM'de. (2013). Retrieved from https://www.youtube.com/watch?v=7QO7haOrSVg&feature=youtube_gdata_player

Alexander, J.C. (2013). "Struggling over the mode of incorporation: backlash against multiculturalism in Europe", *Ethnic and Racial Studies* 36 (4): 531–556.

Alkin, Ö. (2013). *Europe in Turkish Migration Cinema from 1960 to the Present. Journal of the LUCAS Graduate Conference 1(1), 56–66.* Received from *https://openaccess.leidenuniv.nl/bitstream/handle/1887/20536/JLGC-1-10%20Alkin.pdf?sequence=1 available on: 23.07.2014.*

Andreouli, E. (2013). "Identity and acculturation: the case of naturalized citizens in Britain", *Culture and Psychology* 19 (2): 165–183.

Anik, M. (2012). Türk Sinemasinda Yurtdisina Göc Olgusu [External Migration in Turkish Cinema]. *Yilmaz, E. (Ed.). Türk sinemasinda sosyal meseleler. Istanbul: Baska Yerler Yayinlari. pp. 31–58.*

Arslan, S. (2011). *Cinema in Turkey. A New Critical History.* New York: Oxford University Press.

Atay, T. (1994). *Naqshbandi Sufis in a Western Setting.* Unpublished Ph.D. dissertation, School of Oriental and African Studies, University of London, London

Atay, T. (2006). *Türkler, Kürtler, Kıbrıslılar İngiltere'de Türkçe Yaşamak.* Ankara: Dipnot Yayınları.

Attias-Donfut, C., & Waite, L. (2012). From generation to generation: changing family relations, citizenship and belonging. In C. Attias-Donfut, & L. Waite (Eds.), *Citizenship, Belonging and Intergenerational Relations in African Migration* (pp. 40-64). New York, NY: Palgrave Macmillian.

Augoustinos. M. (2009). "Racism(s). One or many?", *International Journal of Psychology* 44 (1): 43–45.

Aydın, M. Z. ve Mânço, A. (2002). Belçika'daki Türk yerleşiminin sosyal, ekonomik ve tarihî boyutları. (Social, Economic and Historical Aspects of Turkish Settlement in Belgium) *Türkler.* 20, 856-868.

Backus, A. (2005). Turkish as an Immigrant Language in Europe. In Tej, & W. Ritchie (Eds.), *The Handbook of Bilingualism* (pp. 689-724). Oxford: Blackwell Publishing.

Balibar, E. (1991). "Is there a 'neo-racism'? In: E. Balibar & I. Wallerstein (eds) *Race, Nation, Class. Ambiguous Identities.* London and New York: Verso, 17–28.

Baluja, F. K., Park, J., & Myers, D. (2003). Inclusion of immigrant status in smoking prevalence statistics. *American Journal of Public Health, 93,* 642–646. Received from http://www.pubmedcentral.nih.gov/ articlerender.fcgi?artid=1447804 available on: 24.03.2014

Baskin, F. (2014). *Ethnography Fieldnotes of Preliminary Fieldwork in Strasbourg and Wissembourg.* [Unpublished]

Bavelas, J. ve Gerwing, J. (2007). Conversational hand gestures and facial displays in face-to-face dialogue. *Social communication.* (Ed. K. Fiedler). New York: Psychology Press. pp. 283-308.

Bayram, N. et al (2009). "Turkish Immigrants in Sweden: Are They Integrated", *International Migration Review,* 43, 90-111.

Bebbington, A. (1999). Capitals and capabilities: A framework for analyzing peasant viability, rural livelihoods and poverty. *World Development 27*(12): 2021-2044.

Beck-Gernsheim, E. (2007). *Wir und die Anderen. Kopftuch, Zwangsheirat und andere Mißverständnisse [We and the others. Headscarf, forced marriages and other misunderstandings].* Frankfurt am Main: Suhrkamp.

Behlil, M. (2010). Close Encounters?: Contemporary Turkish Television and Cinema. *Wide Screen 2(2), 1-14.* Received from *http://widescreenjournal.org/index.php/journal/article/download/25/28 available on: 26.07.2014*

Bengtsson, T., Lundh, C., and Scott, K. (2005). "From Boom to Bust: The Economic Integration of Immigrants in Post-war Sweden" Chapter 2 in Zimmermann, K.F. (Ed) *European Migration. What Do We Know?* Oxford: Oxford University Press.

Berger, J. & Mohr, J. (1976). *Arbeitsemigranten. Erfahrungen, Bilder, Analysen. [Labour Emigrants. Experiences, Images, Analyses.].* Reinbek, Hamburg: Rowohlt.

Bilton, T., Jones, K. B., Lawson, P., Skinner, T., & Stanworth, M. (2003). *Sosyoloji.* Ankara: Siyasal.

Björklund, A. and Jäntti, M. (2013). "Country Case Study – Sweden", Chapter 6 in Jenkins, S., Brandeloni, A., Micklewright, J. and Noland, B. (Eds). *The Great Recession and the Distribution of Household Income*: Oxford: Oxford University Press.

Bohnsack, R. (1997). "Dokumentarische Methode". In: R. Hitzler & A. Honer (eds) *Sozialwissenschaftliche Hermeneutik*. Opladen: Leske and Budrich, 191–194.

Bohnsack, R. (2007). *Rekonstruktive Sozialforschung. Einführung in Qualitative Methoden.* Opladen and Farmington Hills: Budrich.

Bolt, G., Özüekren, S. & Phillips D. (2010). Linking integration and residential segrega-tion. *Journal of Ethnic and Migration Studies*, 36(2), 169-186.

Bora, T. (2006). *Taşralaşan ve taşrasını kaybeden Türkiye. Taşraya bakmak.* (Ruralized Turkey) (Der. T.Bora). İstanbul: İletişim Yayınları.

Borjas, G. (1986). The self-employment experience of immigrants. *The Journal of Human Resources*, 21(4), 485-506.

Bourdieu, P. (1987). *Die feinen Unterschiede. Kritik der gesellschaftlichen Urteilskraft.* Frankfurt/Main: Suhrkamp.

Bourdieu, P. (1991). *Language and Symbolic Power*. England: Polity Press, Cambridge.

Bozarslan, H. (1996). Femmes originaires de Turquie en France où en est l'intégration? Cahiers d'Etudes sur la Méditerranée Orientale et le monde Turco-Iranien. Received from http://cemoti.revues.org/560 available on 03.10.2014

Bremische Bürgerschaft Landtag 16. Wahlperiode. Drucksache 16/264. 'Kleine Anfrage der Fraktion Bündnis 90/Die Grünen vom 21. April 2004. Wirtschaftsförderung für Unternehmer und Existenzgründer mit Migrationshintergrund'.

Bryant, A., & Charmaz, K. (2007). *Handbook of grounded theory*. London: Sage.

Burns, A., & Mohapatra, S. (2008). *International Migration and Technological Process.* Washington, DC.: The World Bank

Burns, F., & Fenton, K. A. (2006). Access to HIV care among migrant Africans in Britain. What are the issues? *Psychology, Health & Medicine*, 11, 117–125.

Burns, R. (2007). The Politics of Cultural Representation: Turkish–German Encounters. *German Politics 16 (3), pp. 358–378.*

Burns, R. (2013). From two worlds to a third space: stereotypy and hybridity in Turkish-German cinema. *Karanfil, G. & Savk, S. (Eds.) Imaginaries Out of Place: Cinema, Transnationalism and Turkey. Newcastle: Cambridge Scholar Publishing. pp. 56–88.*

Buse, D. (1993). Urban and national identity: Bremen, 1860–1920. *Journal of Social History*, 26(3), 521-537.

Capdevila, R. & Callaghan, J.E.M. (2008). "'It's not racist, it's common sense': a critical analysis of political discourse around asylum and immigration in the UK", *Journal of Community and Applied Social Psychology* 18 (1): 1–16.

Castles, S. (1992). Migrants and minorities in post-Keynesian capitalism: the German case. Cross, M. (ed.) *Ethnic Minorities and Industrial Change in Europe and North America.* Cambridge: Cambridge University Press. pp. 36-54.

Cavanaugh, J. (2006). Little Women and Vital Champions: Gendered Language Shift in a Northern Italian Town. *Journal of Linguistic Anthropology* 16(2), 194-210.

Cemiloglu, İ. & Sen, Ü. (2012). Belçika'da yaşayan Türk çocuklarinin demografik özelliklerine göre türkçeye yönelik tutumları. [The attitudes of Turkish children who live in Belgium towards Turkish in terms of demographical features]. *Zeitschrift für die Welt der Türken. Vol. 4, No. 2, pp.7-26*

Charmaz, K. (2000). Grounded theory: objectivist and constructivist methods. In Denzin, N.K. and Lincoln, Y. S. (eds.) *Handbook of Qualitative Research*. Thousand Oaks, CA: Sage. pp. 509-536.

Charmaz, K. (2006). *Constructing grounded theory: a practical guide through qualitative analysis*. Thousand Oaks, CA: Sage.

Charmaz, K. (2008). Reconstructing grounded theory. In Alasuutari, P. et al. (eds.) *The Sage Handbook of Social Research Methods*, Sage. pp. 461-478.

Charmaz, K. (2009). Shifting the grounds: constructivist grounded theory methods for the twenty-first century. In Morse, J. Stern, P. Corbin, J. Bowers, B. Charmaz, K. & Clarke, A. (eds.) *Developing Grounded Theory: The Second Generation*, Walnut Creek, CA: Left Coast Press.

Christakis, N. A., & Fowler, J. H. (2008). The collective dynamics of smoking in a large social network. *New England Journal of Medicine, 358*, 2249–2258. Received from http://www.nejm.org/doi/pdf/10.1056/NEJMsa0706154 available on: 24.03.2014

Cinpoes, R. (2008). From national identity to European identity. *Journal of Identity and Migration Studies*. 2(1), 3-14.

Coll, C. & Falsafi, L. (2009). Learner identity. An educational and analytical tool. *Revista de Educación*, 353. pp. 211-233.

Constant, A. & Zimmermann, K. (2006). The making of entrepreneurs in Germany: are native men and immigrants alike? *Small Business Economics* 26(3), 279-300.

Constant, A., Roberts, R. & Zimmermann, K. (2009). Ethnic identity and immigrant homeownership. *Urban Studies*, 46(9), 1879–1898.

Constant, A., Shachmurove, Y., & Zimmermann, K. (2007). What makes an entrepreneur and does it pay? Native men, Turks, and other migrants in Germany. *International Migration*, 45(4), 71-100.

Çoştu. Y. (2013a). *İngiltere'deki Türk-Müslüman Gocmenler; Dini Organizasyonlar. (Turkish Muslim Immigrants in the UK; Religious Organizations).* Çorum: Lider Matbaası.

Çoştu. Y. (2013b). *"Turkish Muslim* Immigrants in Britain; Religious Life and Religious Organizations", *Sociology Study*, 3(7): 493-501.

Crul, M. et al. (2012). *The European Second Generation Compared: Does the Integration Context Matter?* Amsterdam: Amsterdam University Press

Çağlar, A. & Glick Schiller, N. (2011). Introduction: migrants and cities. Glick Schiller, N. & Çağlar, A. (eds.) *Locating Migration: Rescaling Cities and Migrants*. Ithaca NY: Cornell University Press, pp. 1-22.

Çakır, R. (2002). *Ayet ve Slogan; Türkiye'de Islami Oluşumlar.* İstanbul: Metis Yayınları.

Çelik, S. (2006). *Grenzen und Grenzgänger. Diskursive Positionierungen im Kontext türkischer Einwanderung.* Münster: Unrast.

Çinar, D. (1999). "Alter Rassismus im neuen Europa? Anmerkungen zur Novität des Neo-Rassismus". In: B. Kossek (ed.) *Gegen-Rassismen. Konstruktionen, Interaktionen, Interventionen*. Hamburg: Argument, 55–72.

Çolak, Y. (2005). *Din Hizmetleri Baglamında Ingiltere Dosyası. (Religious Services in England).* London. www.diyanet.org.uk/yazilar/ingilteredosyasi.pdf (available on: 15/02/2008).

Dagdelen, G., & Karakılıc, I. (2011). Disaggregating citizenship transnational partition of the "economic" from the "socio-cultural" in the case of a Turkish community in London. (pp. 1-22). Amsterdam: the International RC21 conference.

D'Angelo, A. et al. (2013). Welfare needs of Turkish and Kurdish communities in London. *Preliminary report*, London: Middlesex University, Day-Mer.

Davies, A., Basten, A., & Frattini, C. (2006). *Migration: a social determinant of the health of migrants.* Switzerland: IOM International Organistion for Migration.

De Acre R., & Mahias R. (2008). Determinants of Bilateral Immigration Flows between the European Union and Some Mediterranean Partner countries: Algeria, Egypt, Morocco, Tunisia, and Turkey. *FEMISE Project 2007/08, July, 2008.*

DIB. (2012). Dıs İlişkiler Genel Müdürlügü. (Directorate General for External Relations) Ankara (in Turkish).

DiFranza, J. R., Savageau, J. A., Fletcher, K., Ockene, J. K., Rigotti, N. A., McNeill, A. D., et al. (2002). Measuring the loss of autonomy over nicotine use in adolescents: The DANDY (Development and Assessment of Nicotine Dependence in Youths) Study. Archives of Pediatric and Adolescent Medicine, 156, 397–403. Received fromhttp://archpedi.jamanetwork. com/data/Journals/PEDS/4696/POA10271.pdf available on: 24.03.2014

Dinc, C. (2011). Avrupa kimligi: Çatışan perspektifler, güncel değerlendirmeler ve endişeler. [European identity: Conflicted perspectives, current evaluations and worries]. *Akademik Bakış*. 5(9), 31-58.

Doerschler, P. (2006). Push-pull factors and immigrant political integration in Germany. *Social Science Quarterly*, 87(5), 1100-1116.

Drever, A. & Clark, W. (2002). Gaining access to housing in Germany: the foreign-minority experience. *Urban Studies*, 39(13), 2439-2453.

Ehrkamp, P. (2005). Placing identities: transnational practices and local attachments of Turkish immigrants in Germany. *Journal of Ethnic and Migration Studies*, 31(2), 345-364.

Ehrkamp, P. (2007). Beyond the mosque: Turkish immigrants and the practice and poli-tics of Islam in Duisburg-Marxloh, Germany. Aitchison, C. Hopkins, P. and Kwan, M. (eds.) *Geographies of Muslim Identities: Diaspora, Gender and Belonging*. Aldershot: Ashgate. pp. 11-28.

Ersanilli, E. & Saharso, S. (2011). The settlement country and ethnic identification of children of Turkish immigrants in Germany, France, and the Netherlands: what role do national integration policies play? *International Migration Review*, 45(4), 907-937.

Esser, H. (2006). *Migration, language and integration*. AKI Research Review 4, Social Science Research Center Berlin

European Council on Refugees and Exiles (ECRE) (2002). *Position on the Integration of Refugees in Europe*, London. http://www.ecre.org/ component/downloads/ downloads/168.html, (Date Accessed: 12.09.2014)

European Union (EU) (2005). *A Common Agenda for Integration: Framework for the Integration of Third-Country Nationals in the European Union*, COM (2005) 389 final, Brussels, http://europa.eu/legislation_summaries/justice_ freedom_security/free_movement_of_persons_asylum_immigration/l14502_en.htm, (Date Accessed: 12.09.2014) p.3

Ezli, Ö. (2009). Von der interkulturellen Kompetenz zur kulturellen Kompetenz. Fatih Akins globalisiertes Kino [From intercultural competence to cultural competence. Fatih Akin's globalised cinema]. *Ezli, Ö., Kimmich, D. & Werberger, A. (Eds.). Wider den Kulturenzwang. Migration, Kulturalisierung und Weltliteratur [Against the constraint of culture. Migration, culturalisation and world literature]. Bielefeld: transcript (Kultur- und Medientheorie). pp. 207–230.*

Ezli, Ö. (2012). Peripherien zwischen Repräsentation und Individuation. Die Körper der Minderheiten in Fassbinders „Katzelmacher" und „Angst essen Seele auf" [Peripheries between representaton and individuation. The bodies of the minorities in Fassbinder's "Katzelmacher" and "Ali: Fear Eats Soul"]. *Colin, N., Schössler, F. & Thurn, N. (Eds.). Prekäre Obsession. Minoritäten im Werk von Rainer Werner Fassbinder [Precarious obsession. Minorities in the work of Rainer Werner Fassbinder]. Bielefeld: transcript (Film). pp. 93–123.*

Ezli, Ö. (Ed.). (2010). *Kultur als Ereignis. Fatih Akins Film "Auf der anderen Seite" als transkulturelle Narration*. Bielefeld: transcript.

163

Fagerström, K. & Schneider, N. (1989). Measuring nicotine dependence: A review of the Fagerström Tolerance questionnaire. *Journal of Behavioral Medicine*, 12(2), 159-181. Federal Office of Public Health. (2007). Strategie Migration und Gesundheit (Phase II: 2008 2013). Received from http://www.bag.admin.ch/themen/gesundheitspolitik/07685/07688/index.html?lang=d e available on: 24.03.2014

Faircloth, N. (1989). *Language and power*. London: Longman.

Faist, T. (2000). *The Volume and Dynamics of International Migration and Transnational Social Spaces*. Clarendon Press.

Faist, T., Fauser, M., & Reisenauer, E. (2013). *Transnational Migration*. John Wiley & Sons.

Farwick, A. (2011). The effect of ethnic segregation on the process of assimilation. Wingens, M. Windzio, M. de Valk, H. and Aybek, C. (eds.) *A Life-Course Perspective on Migration and Integration*. Dordrecht: Springer. pp. 239-258.

Favell, A. (2008). *Eurostars and Eurocities: Free Movement and Mobility in an Integrating Europe*. Oxford: Blackwell.

Ferraro, K. F., & Shippee, T. (2009). Aging and cumulative inequality: How does inequality get under the skin? *The Gerontologist*, 49 (3), 333–343. doi:10.1093/geront/gnp034

Fetzer, J., & and Soper, J. (2005). *Muslims and the state in Britain, France, and Germany*. Cambridge University Press.

Fiore, M. C., Bailey, W. C., Cohen, S. J., Faith Dorfman, S., Goldstein, M. G., Gritz, E. R., et al. (2000). Treating tobacco use and dependence. Clinical practice guideline. Rockville, MD: U.S. Department of Health and Human Services, Public Health Service. Received from http://www.treatobacco. net/de/uploads/documents/Treatment%20Guidelines/USA%20treatment%20guideline s%20in%20English%202000.pdf available on: 24.03.2014

Friedrichs, J. (1998). Ethnic Segregation in Cologne, Germany, 1984-94. *Urban Studies*, 35(10), 1745-1763.

Gal, S. (1978). Peasant Men Can't Get Wives: Language Change and Sex Roles in a Bilingual Community. *Language in Society* 7(1), 1-16.

Galloway, T., Gustafsson, B., Pedersen, P. and Österberg, T. (2009). "Immigrant Child Poverty in Scandinavia: A Panel Data Study." *IZA Discussion Paper* No. 4232. IZA, Bonn.

Gans, P. (1987). Intraurban migration of foreigners in Kiel since 1972. Glebe, G. and O'Loughlin, J. (eds.) *Foreign Minorities in Continental European Cities*. Wiesbaden: Steiner. pp. 116-138.

Georgiou, M. (2006). *Diaspora, identity and the media: diasporic transnationalism and mediated spatialities*. New Jersey: Hampton Press, Inc.

Georgiou, M. (2012). Watching soap opera in the diaspora: cultural proximity or critical proximity? *Ethnic and Racial Studies*, 35(5), 868-887.

Gingrich, A. (2003). "Grenzmythen des Orientalismus. Die islamische Welt in Öffentlichkeit und Volkskultur Mitteleuropas". In: E. Mayr-Oehring & E. Doppler (eds) *Orientalische Reise. Malerei und Exotik im Späten 19. Jahrhundert*. Vienna: Museen der Stadt Wien, 110–129.

Girstmair, S., Hametner, K., Wrbouschek, M. & Weigl, D. (2011). "Orientalismus am Beispiel der Türkei: Zur medialen Inszenierung europäischer Identität in der österreichischen Tageszeitung Kurier". In: R. v. Raden & S. Jäger (eds) *Im Griff der Medien. Krisenproduktion und Subjektivierungseffekte*. Münster: Unrast, 123–133.

Girstmair, S., Hametner, K., Wrbouschek, M. & Weigl, D. (2012). "Der gute und der böse Orientale. Zu Funktionalität und Wandelbarkeit des 'KurdInnenproblems' im EU-Beitrittsdiskurs der EU". In: K.-J. Bruder, et al. (eds) *Macht – Kontrolle – Evidenz.*

164

Psychologische Praxis und Theorie in den Gesellschaftlichen Veränderungen. Gießen: Psychsozial, 329–342.

Glaser, B.G. (1978). *Theoretical sensitivity: advances in the methodology of grounded theory*. Mill Valley, CA: Sociology Press.

Glaser, B.G. (1992). *Basics of grounded theory analysis*. Mill Valley, CA: Sociology Press.

Glaser, B.G. (1998). *Doing grounded theory, issues and discussions*. Mill Valley, CA: Sociology Press.

Glaser, B.G. (2001). *The grounded theory perspective: conceptualization contrasted with description*. Mill Valley, CA: Sociology Press.

Glick Schiller, N. & Çağlar, A. (2009). Towards a comparative theory of locality in migra-tion studies: migrant incorporation and city scale. *Journal of Ethnic and Migration Studies* 35(2), 177-202.

Glick Schiller, N. (2012). A comparative relative perspective on the relationships between migrants and cities. *Urban Geography*, 33(6), 879-903.

Gmel, G., Kuendig H., Notari, L., & Gmel, C. (2014). Suchtmonitoring Schweiz – Konsum von Alkohol, Tabak und illgalen Drogen in der Schweiz. Lausanne: Sucht Schweiz

Göktuna Yaylacı, F. (2012a). Belçika'daki Türklerin Dil Kullanımları (Language Usages of Turks in Belgium). *Uşak Üniversitesi Sosyal Bilimler Dergisi*, 5 (2), 63-88.

Göktuna Yaylacı, F. (2012b). Belçika'da yaşayan Türklerin yörecilik anlayışları ve toplumsal iletişim süreçleri: Belçika'daki Emirdağlılar ve Posoflulara ilişkin bir araştırma. Unpublished doctoral dissertation. Anadolu Üniversitesi İletişim Bilimleri Enstitüsü.

Göktürk, D. (2000a). Migration und Kino - Subnationale Mitleidskultur oder transnationale Rollenspiele? [Migration and Cinema – Subnational Culture of Pity or transnational Role Games?] *Chiellino, C. (Ed.). Interkulturelle Literatur in Deutschland. Ein Handbuch [Intercultural Literature in Germany. A Handbook]*. Stuttgart, Weimar: J. B. Metzler. pp. 329–347.

Göktürk, D. (2000b). Turkish delight - German fright. Unsettling oppositions in transnational cinema. Reframing "Minor" Cultures - from subnational to transnational. Received from http://eipcp.net/transversal/0101/goektuerk/en available on 25.09.2012.

Gramling, D. (2012). The Oblivion of Influence: Mythical Realism in Feo Aladag's Die Fremde (2010). *Hake, S. & Mennel, B. C. (Eds.). Turkish German cinema in the new millennium. Sites, sounds, and screens. New York: Berghahn Books*. pp. 32–43.

Granovetter, M. S. (1973). The strength of weak ties. *American Journal of Sociology*, *78*, 1360–1380.

Guarnizo, L. E., Portes, A., & Haller, W. (2003). Assimilation and Transnationalism: Determinants of Transnational Political Action among Contemporary Migrants. *American Journal of Sociology*, *108*(6), 1211–1248. doi:10.1086/375195

Guggisberg J, Volken T, Abdel T, Müller C et al. (2011). Gesundheitsmonitoring der Migrationsbevölkerung (GMM II) in der Schweiz: Schlussbericht, im Auftrag von Bundesamt für Gesundheit und Bundesamt für Migration . Received from http://www.bag.admin.ch/themen/gesundheitspolitik/ 07685/12533/12535/index.html?lang=de available on: 24.03.2014

Gundara, J., & Jones, C. (1992). *Long-term unemployment and the elderly in migrant communities in Europe*. Belgium: Council of Europe Press.

Gustafsson, B and Zhang, J. (2006). "Earnings of Immigrants to Sweden 1978-1999", *International Migration*, 44, 79 – 117.

Güngör, N. D., & Tansel, A. (2014). Brain drain from Turkey: Return intentions of skilled migrants. *International Migration*, 52(5), 208-226.

Ha, K.N. (2004). *Ethnizität und Migration Reloaded. Kulturelle Identität, Differenz und Hybridität im postkolonialen Diskurs*. Berlin: wvb.

165

Habermas, J. (1981). New Social Movements. *Telos*, *1981*(49), 33–37. doi:10.3817/0981049033

Hackett, S. (2013). *Foreigners, minorities and integration: the Muslim immigrant experience in Britain and Germany*. Manchester University Press.

Hake, S. & Mennel, B. C. (Eds.) (2012). *Turkish German cinema in the new millennium. Sites, sounds, and screens. New York: Berghahn Books.*

Hale-Williams, M. (Ed.). (2013). *The Multicultural Dilemma: Migration, ethnic politics, and state intermediation*. London: Routledge.

Halft, S. (2011). «40 qm Deutschland» - «Kanak Attack» - «Tatort». Filmischer Migrationsdiskurs im Wandel 1985-2008 [«40 Square Metres of Germany» - «Kanak Attack» - «Tatort». The changing of the filmic disccourse of migration 1985-2008]. *Nies, M. (Ed.). Deutsche Selbstbilder in den Medien: Film 1945 bis zur Gegenwart [German self-images in the media: film from 1945 to the present]. Marburg: Schüren Verlag GmbH (Schriften zur Kultur- und Mediensemiotik,* 4). *pp. 225–248.*

Hall, S. (1997): *Representation. Cultural representations and signifying practices. London, Thousand Oaks, Calif: Sage in association with the Open University (Culture, media, and identities).*

Hametner, K. (2012). "Rekonstruktive Methodologie als methodologisches Paradigma einer kritischen Migrationsforschung". In J. Dahlvik, H. Fassmann & W. Sievers (eds) *Migration und Integration. Wissenschaftliche Perspektiven aus Österreich*. Göttingen: V and R Unipress, 37–52.

Henwood, K.L., Pidgeon, N.F. (2003). Grounded theory in psychology. In Camic, P.M. Rhodes, J.E. Yardley, L. (eds.) *Qualitative Research in Psychology: Expanding Perspectives in Methodology and Design,* Washington, DC: American Psychological Association Press, pp.131-155.

Herbert, U. (1986). *Geschichte der Ausländerbeschäftigung in Deutschland 1880 bis 1980. Saisonarbeiter, Zwangsarbeiter, Gastarbeiter*. J.H.W. Dietz.

Herbert, U. (2003). *Geschichte der Ausländerpolitik in Deutschland: Saisonarbeiter, Zwangsarbeiter, Gastarbeiter, Flüchtlinge* [History of the policy on foreigners in Germany: Seasonal workers, forced labourers, guest workers, refugees]. Bonn: C. H. Beck.

Hess, S. 7 Moser, J. (2009). "Jenseits der Integration. Kulturwissenschaftliche Betrachtungen einer Debatte". In: S. Hess, J. Binder and J. Moser (eds) *No Integration?! Kulturwissenschaftliche Beiträge zur Integrationsdebatte in Europa*. Bielefeld: trancript, 11–25.

Higbee, W. & Song, H. L. (2010). Concepts of transnational cinema: towards a critical transnationalism in film studies. *Transnational Cinemas 1 (1). pp. 7–21. Received from http://www.ingentaconnect.com/content/intellect/trac/2010/00000001/00000001/art0 0002, available on: 26.09.2012.*

Hillmann, F. (2009). How socially innovative is migrant entrepreneurship? A case study of Berlin. MacCallum, D. Moulaert, F. Hillier, J. and Haddock, J. (eds.) *Social Innovation and Territorial Development*. Farnham: Ashgate. pp. 101-114.

Holert, T. (2005). Kulturwissenschaft/Visual Culture [Culture Studies/Visual Culture]. *Sachs-Hombach, K. (Ed.). Bildwissenschaft. Disziplinen, Themen, Methoden [Visual Studies. Disciplines, issues, methods]. Frankfurt am Main: Suhrkamp. pp. 226–235.*

Holtz, P. & Wagner, W. (2009). "Essentialism and the attribution of monstrosity in racist discourse: right-wing internet postings about Africans and Jews", *Journal of Community and Applied Social Psychology* 19 (6): 411–425.

Howarth, C. (2004). "Re-presentation and resistance in the context of school exclusion: reasons to be critical", *Journal of Community and Applied Social Psychology* 14 (5): 356–377.

166

Howarth, C. (2006). "Race as stigma: positioning the stigmatized as agents, not objects" *Journal of Community and Applied Social Psychology* 16 (6): 442–451.

Howarth, C. (2009). "'I hope we won't have to understand racism one day': researching or reproducing 'Race' in social psychological research?" *British Journal of Social Psychology* 48 (3): 407–426.

İçduygu, A., Sirkeci, I. & Aydıngün, I. (1998). *Türkiye'de İçgöç*. İstanbul: Tarih Vakfı Yurt Yayınları.

Interview with Mayor Hans Koschnick (undated). Staatsarchiv Bremen, 4,63/2 N-284, *Gastarbeiter 1971-1973*.

Ireland, P. (2004). *Becoming Europe: immigration, integration, and the welfare state*. University of Pittsburgh Press.

Issa, T. (2005). *Talking Turkey: The Language, Culture and Identity of Turkish Speaking Children in Britain*. Staffordshire: Trentham Books.

Jandt, F. E. (2010). *An introduction to intercultural communication: identities in a global community*. California: Sage Publications.

Joppke, C. (2007). Transformation of Immigrant Integration in Western Europe: Civic Integration and Anti-discrimination Policies in the Netherlands, France and Germany. *World Politics* 59(2):243-273.

Kanmaz, M. (2003). *Does a Turkish diaspora still exist? Turkish immigrants in Belgium: Between Europe and Turkey*. International Summer Seminar 'Christianity, Islam and Judaism: How to Conquer the Barriers to Intercultural Dialogue? Antwerpen: Universitair Centrum Sint-Ignatius.

Kastoryano, R. (2002). *Negotiating identities: States and immigrants in France and Germany*. Princeton University Press.

Kaya A. ve Kentel, F. (2005). *Euro –Türkler: Türkiye ile Avrupa Birliği arasında köprü mü, engel mi?* (Euro-Turks: Obstacle or Bridge between Europe and Turkey) İstanbul: Bilgi Üniversitesi Yayınları.

Kaya, A. (2000). *Berlin'deki Küçük İstanbul: Diyasporada Kimliğin Oluşumu*. İstanbul: Büke Yayıncılık.

Kaya, A. (2004). Avrupa Birliği, Avrupalılık ve Avrupa-Türkleri: Tireli ve Çoğul Kimlikler. [EU, Europeans, euro-Turks: multi-identities] *Cogito Avrupa'yı Düşünmek Özel Sayısı*. 39.

Kaya, A. (2012). "Backlash of multiculturalist and republicanist policies of integration in the age of securitazion", *Philosophy and Social Criticism* 38 (4–5): 399–411.

Kaya, İ. (2008). Avrupalı Türkler: misafir işçilikten Avrupa vatandaşlığına. [European Turks: from guest workers to European citizenship] *Eastern Geographical Review*. 13(19), 149-166.

Kayaoglu, E. (2012). Figurationen der Migration im türkischen Film [Figurations of Migration in Turkish Film]. *Ozil, S., Dayioglu-Yücel, Y. & Hofmann, M. (Eds.). 51 Jahre türkische Gastarbeitermigration in Deutschland [51 Years Turkish Gastarbeiter-Migration]. Göttingen, Niedersachs: V&R unipress (Türkisch-deutsche Studien*, 2012). *pp. 81–104*.

Khemlani D., et al. (2003). Language Maintenance or Language Shift among the Punjabi Sikh Community in Malaysia? *International Journal of the Sociology of Language* 161, 1-24.

Kibria, N. (2011). *Muslims in motion: Islam and national identity in the Bangladeshi diaspora*. Rutgers University Press.

Kim, Y. Y. (1977). *Inter-ethnic and intra-ethnic communication: a study of Korean immigrants in Chicago*. Phoenix: Annual Meeting of Western Speech Communication Association.

King, R., Thomson, M., Mai, N., & Keles, Y. (2008a). *'Turks' in London: Shades of invisibility and the shifting relevance of policy in the migration process.* London: University of Sussex.

King, R., Thomson, M., Mai, N., & Keles, Y. (2008b). 'Turks' in the UK: Problems of definition and the partial relevance of policy. *Journal of Immigrant & Refugee Studies, 6* (3), 423-434. doi:10.1080/15362940802371895

Klopp, B. (2002). *German multiculturalism: immigrant integration and the transformation of citizenship.* Praeger Publishers.

Klusmeyer, D., & Papademetriou, D. (2009). Immigration policy in the Federal Republic of Germany: negotiating membership and remaking the nation. Berghahn Books.

Koçak, D.Ö., Koçak, O.K. (2013). Glorifying the past on screen: conquest 1453. In Morey, K.A. (ed.) *Bringing History to Life through Film: The Art of Cinematic Storytelling (Film and History).* UK: Rowman & Littlefield Publishers. pp. 71-89.

Koopmans, R. (1999). Germany and its immigrants: An ambivalent relationship. *Journal of Ethnic and Migration Studies.* 25(4), 627-647.

Kucukcan, T. (1999). *Politics of Ethnicity, Identity and Religion Turkish Muslims in Britain.* Aldershot: Ashgate.

Kürsat-Ahlers, E. (1996). The Turkish minority in German society. Horrocks, D. and Kolinsky, E. (eds.) *Turkish Culture in German Society Today.* Oxford: Berghahn Books. pp. 113-135.

Ladbury, S. (1977). "The Turkish Cypriots: Ethnic Relations in London and Cyprus". Watson, J. L. (ed.), *Between Two Cultures: Migrants and Minorities in Britain.* Oxford: Blackwell, pp. 301-331.

Lancaster, T., & Stead, L. F. (2005). Individual behavioural counselling for smoking cessation. *Cochrane Database of Systematic Reviews, 2.* Art. No.: CD001292. doi:10.1002/14651858.CD001292.pub2

Laniado-Laborín, R. (2010). Smoking cessation intervention: An evidence-based approach. *Postgraduated Medicine, 122,* 74–82.

Leeds-Hurwitz, W. (1992). Forum introduction: Social approaches to interpersonal communication. *Communication Theory,* 2, 131-139

Leeson, G.W. (1989). *Atbliveældrei et andethjemland* (Growing old in a second homeland), Senior Forlaget, Copenhagen.

Leohold, V. (1986). *Die Kämmeristen. Arbeitsleben auf der Bremer Woll-Kämmerei.* VSA-Verlag.

Lindquist, M. and Sjögren Lindquist, G. (2012). "The Dynamics of Child Poverty in Sweden", *Journal of Population Economics,* 25, 1423-1450.

Liversage, A. (2009). Life below a `Language threshold'? Stories of Turkish marriage migrant women in Denmark. *European Journal of Women's Studies, 16* (3), 229-247. doi:10.1177/1350506809105307

Livingston, G., Leavey, G., Kitchen, G., Manela, M., Sembhi, S., & Katona C. (2002). Accessibility of health and social services to immigrant elders: the Islington Study. *Britih Journal of Psychiatry,* 369-373.

Lundborg, P. (2013). "Refugee's Employment Integration in Sweden: Cultural Distance and Labor Market Participation", *Review of International Economics,* 21, 219-232.

Makal, O. (1994). *Sinemada Yedinci Adam. Türk Sinemasinda Ic ve Dis Göc Olayi [The Seventh Man in Cinema. Internal and External Migration in Turkish Cinema].* Second ed. Izmir: Ege Verlag.

Manço, A. (2002). Göçmen Türklerin Belçika eğitim sisteminde yeri. [Turkish migrants in the Belgian educational system] *C.Ü. Sosyal Bilimler Dergisi.* 26(1), 61-68.

Mandel, R. (2008). *Cosmopolitan anxieties: Turkish challenges to citizenship and belonging in Germany*. Duke University Press.

Mankekar, P. (1999). *Screening culture, viewing politics: television, womanhood and nation in modern India*. New Delhi: Oxford University Press.

Martin, I. (2009). Labor Markets Performance and Migration Flows in Arab Mediterranean Countries. A Regional Perspective. Robert Schuman Centre, European University Institute. Florence, Italy.

Massicard, E. (2007). *Türkiye'den Avrupa'ya Alevi Hareketinin Siyasallaşması*. Iletisim Yayinlari.

Mau, S. (2010). *Social Transnationalism: Lifeworlds Beyond the Nation-State*. London and New York: Routledge.

McCallin, A.M. (2003). Grappling with the literature in a grounded theory study. *Contemporary Nurse*, 15(1-2), 61-69.

McDonald, M. (1994). Women and Linguistic Innovation in Brittany. I P. Burton, K. K. Dyson & Sh. Ardener (Eds.), *Bilingual Women Anthropological Approaches to Second-Language Use* (pp. 95-110). Oxford: Berg.

MEB (2006). Yurt dışı eğitim personeli rehberi. [Guide for educational personel in abroad] Received from http://strazburg.meb.gov.tr/habers/RehberKitap.pdf on 20.02.2014.

MEB (2014). Yurt dışında görevlendirilecek öğretmenlerin mesleki yeterlilik sınavı ve temsil yeteneği mülakatı başvuru kılavuzu. [Guide for professional competence exam for the teachers to be appointed abroad] Received from http://www.meb.gov.tr/meb_duyuruindex.php? KATEGORI=&BIRIM=80&ID=80 on 20.12.2014.

Mecheril, P. (1997). "Rassismuserfahrungen von Anderen Deutschen". In: P. Mecheril and T. Teo (eds) *Psychologie und Rassismus*. Reinbeck bei Hamburg: Rowohlt, 175–201.

Meer, N. & Modood, T. (2013) 'Interacting interculturalism with multiculturalism: observations on theory and practice', in M. Barrett (ed.) *Interculturalism and multiculturalism: similarities and differences,* Council of Europe.

Mehmet Ali, A. (2001). *Turkish Speaking Communities and Education -No Delight*. London: Fatal Publication.

MFA (2014). *Yurtdişinda yaşayan Türkler*. Minister of Foreign Affairs. [Turks living abroad] Received from http://www.mfa.gov.tr/yurtdisinda-yasayan-turkler_.tr.mfa avaliable on 15.01.2014.

Migration Policy Institute, www.migrationpolicy.org.

Mills, J., Bonner, A., & Francis, K. (2006). The development of constructivist grounded theory. *International Journal of Qualitative Methods*, 5(1), 1-10.

Modood, T. (2013). *Multiculturalism*, 2nd eds. Bristol: Polity Press

Moores, S. (2005). *Media/theory, thinking about media and communications*. New York, NY: Routledge.

Morawska, P. E. (2011). *A Sociology of Immigration: (Re)making Multifaceted America* (Reprint edition.). Basingstoke: Palgrave Macmillan.

Mosselson, J. (2011). Conflict, education and identity; Resettled youth in the United States. *Conflict and Education*. 1(1)

Mukherjee, D. (2003). Role of Women in Language Maintenance and Language Shift: Focus on the Bengali Community in Malaysia. *International Journal of the Sociology of Language* 161,103-120.

Nassar, H. (2009). Migration and Financial Flows: Egypt in the MENA Region. European University Institute/ CARIM (Euro-Mediterranean Consortium for Applied Research on International Migration): San Domenico de Fiesole.

National Board of Health and Social Welfare (Socialstyrelsen) (1999). *Social och ekonomisk förankring bland invandrare från Chile, Iran, Polen och Turkiet*, Seires: Invandrares Levnadsvilkor 2., Stockholm.

Neuliep, J.W. (2006). Values, cultural identity and communication: a perspective from philosophy of language. *Halvor Nordby Journal of Intercultural Communication*, 17.

Neumayer, E. (2006). Unequal access to foreign spaces: How states use visa restrictions to regulate mobility in a globalized world. *Transactions of the Institute of British Geographers, 31* (1), 72-84. doi:10.1111/j.1475-5661.2006.00194.x

Nierkens, V., de Vries, H., & Stronks, K. (2006). Smoking in immigrants: Do socioeconomic gradients follow the pattern expected from the tobacco epidemic? *Tobacco Control*, *15*, 385–391.

Nierkens, V., Stronks, K., van Oel, C. J., & de Vries, H. (2005). Beliefs of Turkish and Moroccan immigrants in the Netherlands about smoking cessation: Implications for prevention. *Health Education Research*, *20*, 622–634.

Nohl, A.-M. (2006). *Interview und dokumentarische Methode. Anleitungen für die Forschungspraxis*. Wiesbaden: Verlag für Sozialwissenschaften.

Oca, V. M., García, T. R., Sáenz, R., & Guillén, J. (2011). The Linkage of Life Course, Migration, Health, and Aging: Health in Adults and Elderly Mexican Migrants. *Journal of Aging and Health*, 20 (10), 1–25.

OECD (2014). "Education Database: Foreign / international students enrolled", OECD Education Statistics (database). DOI: http://dx.doi.org/10.1787/data-00205-en (Accessed on 27 April 2015).

Okan, M. (2004). *Türkiye'de Alevilik: Antropolojik bir Yaklaşım*. İmge Kitabevi.

Okulda Avrupa Değerleri Projesi (2014). Okulda Avrupa Değerleri Projesi Avrupa Birliği Öğretmen Bilgi Araştırması. [European values in school project EU teacher information research] Received from http://www.sabah.com.tr/Egitim/2014/02/26/demokrasiyi-gelistirir avaliable on 16.02.2014.

Öztürk, S. A. ve Sevim, N. (2009). Almanya'daki Türk göçmenlerin medya kullanımı: etnik özdeşleşme, dil tercihi ve kalma süresi etkisi. (Media Using of Turkish People in Germany). *Avrupa'da medya, kültür ve kimlik*. (Ed. S. Arslan; V. Aytar, D. Karaosmanoğlu; S. Kırca-Schroeder). (Media, Culture and Identity in Europe) İstanbul: Bahçeşehir Üniversitesi Yayınları.

Papadopoulos, S. L. (2007). Ethiopian refugees in the UK - Migration, adaptation and settlement experiences and their relevance to health. *Ethnicity & Health, 9* (1), 55-73.

Phillips, C. (2012). *Into the Quagmire: Turkey's Frustrated Syria Policy*. Chatam House.

Pişkin, G. (2010). Türkiye'de Göç ve Türk Sinemasına Yansımaları: 1960-2009 [Migration in Turkey and Reflections in Turkish Cinema: 1960-2009]. *E-Journal of New World Sciences Academy: Humanities 5(1), 45–65.*

Portes, A. (2003). Conclusion: Theoretical Convergencies and Empirical Evidence in the Study of Immigrant Transnationalism. *International Migration Review*, *37*(3), 874–892. doi:10.1111/j.1747-7379.2003.tb00161.x

Portes, A., Guarnizo, L.E., & Landolt, P. (1999). The study of transnationalism: pitfalls and promise of an emergent research field. *Ethnic and Racial Studies*, 22(2): 217-237.

Power, A., Plöger, J., & Winkler, A. (2010). *Phoenix cities: the fall and rise of great industrial cities*. Policy Press.

Pötzschke, S., Duru, D., Cesur, N. S., & Braun, M. (2014). *Cross-Border Activities and Transnational Identification of Turkish Migrants in Europe*. EUCROSS Working Paper, 7. Retrieved from http://www.eucross.eu/cms/index.php? option=com_docman&task=doc_download&gid=79&Itemid=157. (2014/1/31).

Pries, L. (2008). *Die Transnationalisierung der sozialen Welt: Sozialräume jenseits von Nationalgesellschaften* [*The transnationalization of the social world: Social spaces beyond national societies*]. Frankfurt am Main: Suhrkamp.

Przyborski, A. & Slunecko, T. (2009). "Against reification! Praxeological methodology and its benfits". In: J. Valsiner, P. Molenaar, M. Lyra & N. Chaudhary (eds) *Dynamic Process Methodology in the Social and Developmental Sciences*. New York: Springer, 141–170.

Przyborski, A. & Wohlrab-Sahr, M. (2008). *Qualitative Sozialforschung. Ein Arbeitsbuch*. München: Oldenbourg Verlag.

Przyborski, A. (2004). *Gesprächsanalyse und dokumentarische Methode. Qualitative Auswertung von Gesprächen, Gruppendiskussionen und anderen Diskursen*. Wiesbaden: Verlag für Sozialwissenschaften.

Pütz, R. (2008). Transculturality as practice: Turkish entrepreneurs in Germany. Al-Hamarneh, A. and Thielmann, J. (eds.) *Islam and Muslims in Germany*. Leiden: Brill. pp. 511-535.

Ratha, D. (2005). 'Workers' remittances: An important and stable source of external development finance'. In S. M. Maimbo & D. Ratha (Eds.), *Remittances: Development Impact and Future Prospects*. World Bank: Washington.

Ratha, D., & Xu, Z. (2008). Migration and Remittances Factbook 2008. World Bank: Washington.

Räthzel, N. (2006). "From individual heroism to political resistance: young people challenging everyday racism on the labour market", *Journal of Education and Work* 19 (3): 219–235.

Recchi, E., & Favell, A. (2009). *Pioneers of European Integration: Citizenship and Mobility in the EU*. Cheltenham: Elgar.

Reese, A., Spallek, J., & Razum, O. (2005). Changes in smoking prevalence among first- and second-generation Turkish migrants in Germany—An analysis of the 2005 Microcensus. *International Journal for Equity in Health*, *8*, 26.

Reuter, J. & Villa, P.-I. (2010). "Provincializing Soziologie. Postkoloniale Theorie als Herausforderung". In J. Reuter & P.-I. Villa (eds) *Postkoloniale Soziologie. Empirische Befunde, theoretische Anschlüsse, politische Interventionen*. Bielefeld: transcript, 11–46.

Rizvi. F. (2006). Epistemic virtues and cosmopolitan learning. *The Australian Educational Researcher*, 35(1): 17-35.

Robins, K. and A. Aksoy (2001). "From Spaces of Identity to Mental Spaces: Lessons from Turkish-Cypriot Cultural Experience in Britain". *Journal of Ethnic and Migration Studies*. 27(4), pp. 685-711.

Robins, K., Aksoy, A. (2005). Whoever looks always finds: transnational viewing and knowledge-experience. In Chalaby, J.K. (ed.) *Transnational television worldwide: towards a new media order*. London, New York: IB.Tauris. pp. 14-43.

Rooth D. and Ekberg J. (2003). "Unemployment and Earnings for Second Generation Immigrants in Sweden: Ethnic Background and Parent Composition", *Journal of Population Economics*, 16: 4, pp. 787-814.

Rutherford, J. (1990). The Third Space. Interview with Homi Bhabha. *Rutherford, J. (Ed.). Identity. Community, culture, difference. London: Lawrence & Wishart. pp. 207–221.*

Ryan, L. (2011). Migrants' social networks and weak ties: accessing resources and construction relationships post-migration. *The Sociological Review*, 59: 707-724.

Sahin-Hodoglugil, O. N., & Polit, K. (2005). Health, Wealth or Family Ties -Why Turkish Work Migrants Return from Germany? *Journal of Ethnic and Migration Studies, 31* (4), 719-739. DOI: 10.1080/1369183050109894

Saïd, E. (1978). *Orientalism*. New York: Vintage.

Said, E. (1998). Krise des Orientalismus [Crisis of Orientalism]. *Conrad, C. & Kessel, M. (Eds.). Kultur & Geschichte. Neue Einblicke in eine alte Beziehung [Culture & History. New views into an old relationship].* Stuttgart: Reclam Verlag (*Universal-Bibliothek*, 9638). *pp. 72–96.*

Schaffer, J. (2008). *Ambivalenzen der Sichtbarkeit. Über die visuellen Strukturen der Anerkennung [Ambivalences of visibility. About the visual structures of recognition].* Bielefeld: transcript (Studien zur visuellen Kultur, 7).

Scheibelhofer, P. (2007). "A question of honour? Masculinities and positionalities of boys with Turkish background in Vienna". In: C. Riegel and T. Geisen (eds) *Jugend, Zugehörigkeit und Migration. Subjektpositionierung im Kontext von Jugendkultur, Ethnizitäts- und Geschlechterkonstruktionen.* Wiesbaden: VS, 273–288.

Schiller, N. G., Basch, L., & Blanc, C. S. (1995). From Immigrant to Transmigrant: Theorizing Transnational Migration. *Anthropological Quarterly, 68*(1), 48. doi:10.2307/3317464

Schnoz, D., Schaub, M., Schwappach, Ph.D. & Salis Gross, C. (2011). Developing a Smoking Cessation Program for Turkish-Speaking Migrants in Switzerland: Novel Findings and Promising Effects. *Nicotine & Tobacco Research, 13(2),* 127-134.

Schönwälder, K. & Söhn, J. (2009). Immigrant settlement structures in Germany: general patterns and urban levels of concentration of major groups. *Urban Studies,* 46(7), 1439-1460.

Schramm, C. (2005). Migration from Egypt, Morocco, and Tunisia: Synthesis of Three Case Studies. World Bank: Washington.

Schütz, A. (1962). *Collected Papers (Vol. 1): The Problem of Social Reality.* The Hague: Martinus Nijhoff.

Schütze, F. (1983). "Biographieforschung und narratives Interview", *Neue Praxis* 13 (3): 283–293.

Seedsman, T. (2014). Yaşlı Göçmenler: Değişim, Dönüşüm, Kayıp ve Keder Uzerine Yaklaşımlar. In N. Korkmaz, & S. Yazıcı (Eds.), *Küresellesme ve Yaşlılık–Eleştirel Gerontolojiye Giriş* (pp. 280-310). Ankara, A: Utopya.

Shimanada, A. (2010). The Transfer of the Remittance Fee from the Migrant to the household. *Journal of Economic Integration,* 25 (3): 613-625.

Shooman, Y. (2011). "Keine Frage des Glaubens. Zur Rassifizierung von 'Kultur' und 'Religion' im antimuslimischen Rassismus". In: S. Friedrich (ed.) *Rassismus in der Leistungsgesellschaft. Analyse und kritische Perspektiven zu den rassistischen Normalisierungsprozessen der "Sarrazindebatte".* Münster: edition assemblage, 59–76.

Shutika, D. (2011). *Beyond the borderlands: migration and belonging in the United States and Mexico.* University of California Press.

Sinclair-Webb, E. (2003). Sectarian violence, the Alevi minority and the left: Kahramanmaras 1978. In J. Jongerden & P. J. White (Eds.), *Turkey's Alevi Enigma: A Comprehensive Overview.* BRILL.

Sirkeci, I. & Açık, N. (2015). İngiltere'de göçmenlerin ekonomik uyumu ve işgücü piyasasında azınlıklar. In: Şeker, B., Sirkeci, I. & Yüceşahin, M. eds. *Göç ve Uyum.* London: Transnational Press London, 143-164.

Sirkeci, I. & Cohen, J.H. (2016). Cultures of migration and conflict in contemporary human mobility in Turkey. *European Review,* Vol. 23, No.3 (forthcoming).

Sirkeci, I. & Zeyneloglu, S. (2014). Abwanderung aus Deutschland in die Türkei: Eine Trendwende im Migrationsgeschehen? In: Alscher, S. & Krienbriek, A. (eds.) *Abwanderung von Türkeistämmigen: Werverlässt Deutschland und warum?* Germany: BAMF, pp. 30-85.

Sirkeci, I. (2003). *Migration, ethnicity and conflict: the environment of insecurity and Turkish Kurdish international migration* (Doctoral dissertation, University of Sheffield, UK).

Sirkeci, I. (2009). Transnational mobility and conflict. *Migration Letters*, 6(1), 3-14.

Sirkeci, I. et al. (2016). *Little Turkey in Great Britain*. London: Transnational Press London.

Sirkeci, I., & Esipova, N. (2013). Turkish migration in Europe and desire to migrate to and from Turkey. *Border Crossing: Transnational Working Papers*, No 1301, 1-13. http://tplondon.com/journal/index.php/bc/article/viewFile/89/88.

Smeeding, t. et al. (2009). "Income Poverty and Income Support for Minority and Immigrant Children in Rich Countries", *Institute for Research on Poverty, Discussion Paper* no 1371-09.

Smets, K.; Meers, P.; Winkel, R.V.; Van Bauwel, S. (2009). Çok kültürlü Avrupa kentinde diasporik Türk sinema kültürü: Belçika'daki Türk filmi gösterimlerinin yapısal bir analizi. (Diasporic Sinema Culture in Multicultural European City). *Avrupa'da medya, kültür ve kimlik.* (Ed. S. Arslan; V. Aytar, D. Karaosmanoğlu; S. Kırca-Schroeder). (Media, Culture and Identity in Europe) İstanbul: Bahçeşehir Üniversitesi Yayınları.

Smith, R.W. (2000). The influence of teacher background on the inclusion of multicultural Education: A case study of two contrasts. *The Urban Review*. 32(2).

Soysal, L. (2003). Labor to culture: Writing Turkish migration to Europe. *The South Atlantic Quarterly, 102* (2/3), 491-508.

Soysal, Y. N. (2000). Citizenship and identity: living in diasporas in post-war Europe? *Ethnic and Racial Studies, 23*(1), 1–15. doi:10.1080/014198700329105

Sökefeld, M. (2008). *Struggling for Recognition: The Alevi Movement in Germany and in Transnational Space*. Berghahn Books.

Statistics Belgium (2012). *Key figures. Statistical Overview of Belgium.* http://statbel.fgov.be/en/statistics/figures/ (10.12.2013).

Stead, L. F., & Lancaster, T. (2005). Group behaviour therapy programmes for smoking cessation. *Cochrane Database of Systematic Reviews, 2.* Art. No.: CD001007doi:10.1002/14651858.CD001007.pub2

Stead, L. F., Perera, R., Bullen, C., Mant, D., & Lancaster, T. (2008). Nicotine replacement therapy for smoking cessation. *Cochrane Database of Systematic Reviews, 1.* Art. No.: CD000146. doi:10.1002/14651858.CD000146.pub3

Stevens, W., Thorogood, M., & Kayikki, S. (2002). Cost-effectiveness of a community antismoking campaign targeted at a high risk group in London. *Health Promotion International*, 17, 43–50. Received from http://heapro.oxfordjournals.org/cgi/reprint/ 17/1/43 (Accessed 24.03.2014).

Steyerl, H. (2003). Postkolonialismus und Biopolitik. Probleme der Übertragung postkolonialer Ansätze in den deutschen Kontext [Postcolonialism and Biopolitics. Problems of the transfer of postcolonial approaches to the German context. *Steyerl, H., Gutiérrez Rodríguez, E. & Kien, N. H. (Eds.). Spricht die Subalterne deutsch? Migration und postkoloniale Kritik [Can the subaltern speak German? Migration and Postcolonial Critics]. Münster: Unrast Verlag. pp. 38–55.*

Stowasser, B. (2002). The Turks in Germany: from sojourners to citizens. Haddad, Y. (ed.) *Muslims in the West: From Sojourners to Citizens*. Oxford: Oxford University Press. pp. 52-71.

Strauss, A. (1987). *Qualitative analysis for social scientists.* Cambridge, UK: Cambridge University Press.

Strauss, A., Corbin, J. (1998). *Basics of qualitative research: techniques and procedures for developing grounded theory* (2nd ed.). Thousand Oaks, CA: Sage.

Şahin, B. (2010). Almanya'daki Türk Göçmenlerin Sosyal Entegrasyonunun Kuşaklar Arası Karşılaştırması: Kültürleşme. *Bilig.* 55, 103- 134.

173

Şahin, B. (2010). *Almanya'daki Türkler: Misafir İşçilikten Ulusötesi Bağların Oluşumuna Geçiş Süreci,* Ankara: Phoenix Yayınevi.

Şahin, İ. (2012). "From Tradition to Religion: Organisational Transformation of the London Turkish Migrant Community", *Zeitschrift für die Welt der Türken* (Journal of World of Turks) Vol. 4, No. 2, ss. 53-78.

Şen, F. (1991). Turkish self-employment in the Federal Republic of Germany with special regard to Northrhine-Westphalia. *International Migration,* 29(1), 124-129.

Şenay, B. (2002). Avrupa Birliği'nin 'dini kimliği've Avrupa'da dinler: Hristiyanlık, Yahudilik, Hinduizm, Budizm ve İslam. [Religious identity of EU and religions in Europe] *Uludağ Üniversitesi İlahiyat Fakültesi Dergisi.* 11(1), 121-166.

T.C. Anayasa Mahkemesi. (2013). Retrieved 27 October 2014, from http://www.anayasa.gov.tr/en/Introduction/

Taguieff, P.-A. (2000). *Die Macht des Vorurteils. Der Rassismus und sein Double.* Hamburg: Hamburger Edition.

Taylor, E.J., Rozelle, S., & de Brauw, A. (2003). Migration and incomes in source communities: A new economics of migration perspective from China. *Economic Development and Cultural Change, 52*(1), 75-101.

Taylor, C. (1997). The Politics of Recognition. In: A. Heble, D. P. Pennee, & J. R. Struthers (Eds.), *New Contexts of Canadian Criticism.* Broadview Press, pp.25-73.

Terkessidis, M. (1998). *Psychologie des Rassismus.* Opladen/Wiesbaden: Westdeutscher Verlag.

Terkessidis, M. (2004). *Die Banalität des Rassismus. Migranten zweiter Generation entwickeln eine neue Perspektive.* Bielefeld: transcript.

Thornberg, R. (2012). Informed grounded theory. *Scandinavian Journal of Educational Research*, 56(3), June, 243–259.

Thornberg, R., Charmaz, K. (2014). Grounded theory and theoretical coding. In Flick, U. (ed.) *The SAGE Handbook of Qualitative Analysis.* London: Sage. pp. 153-169.

Toksöz, G. (2006). *Uluslararası Emek Göçü.* Istanbul: Bilgi Üniversitesi Yayınları.

Topal, K., Eser, E., Sanberk, I., Bayliss, E., & Saatci, E. (2012). Challenges in access to health services and its impact on quality of life: a randomised population-based survey within Turkish speaking immigrants in London. *Health Qual Life Outcomes*, 10(11).

Torres, S. (2006). Culture, Migration, Inequality, and "Peripher" in a Globalized World: Challenges for Ethno- and Anthropogerontology. In J. Baars, D. Dannefer, & C. P.Walker (Eds.), *Aging, Globalization and Inequality* (pp. 231-244). New York, NY: Baywood.

Tribalat, M. (2013). *Assimilation, la fin du modèle français.* Les éditions du Toucan.

TTK (2009). *Yurt dışındaki Türk çocukları için türkçe ve Türk kültürü dersi öğretim programı.* [Turkish and Turkish Culture Lesson Teaching Program for Turkish Children in Abroad]Ankara: Milli Eğitim Bakanlığı Talim Terbiye Kurulu Başkanlığı.

Turkish Embassy in Brussels (2014). *Türkiye-Belçika Siyasi İlişkileri.* Turkish Embassy in Brussels. http://www.bruksel.be.mfa.gov.tr/ShowInfo Notes.aspx?ID=121215

United Nations High Commissioner for Refugees (UNHCR) (2013). *A New Beginning: Refugee Integration in Europe, www.refworld.org/pdfid/522980604.pdf,* Date Accessed: 12.09.2014).

Urry, J. (2007). *Mobilities.* Cambridge, Malden: Polity Press.

Urso, G. & Schuster, A. (Eds.) (2013). *Migration, Employment and Labour Market Integration Policies in the European Union (2011),* International Organization for Migration, Brussels, *ec.europa.eu/social/BlobServlet? docId=9989&langId=en,* (Date Accessed: 12.09.2014).

Üçer, C. (2005). *Geleneksel Alevilik.* Ankara: Ankara Okulu Yayınları.

Van Bruinessen, M. (1996). Kurds, Turks and the Alevi Revival in Turkey. *Middle East Report,* (200), 7. doi:10.2307/3013260

Van Dalen, H.P., Groenewold, G., & Fokkema, T. (2005). The effect of remittances on emigration intentions in Egypt, Morocco, and Turkey. *Population Studies, 59*(3), 375-392.

Vertovec, S. (2001). Transnationalism and identity. *Journal of Ethnic and Migration Studies,* 27(4), 573-582.

Vertovec, S. (2004). Migrant Transnationalism and Modes of Transformation1. *International Migration Review,* 38(3), 970–1001. doi:10.1111/j.1747-7379.2004.tb00226.x

Vertovec, S. (2009). *Transnationalism.* Routledge.

Wahlbeck, Ö. (1999). *Kurdish Diasporas: A Comparative Study of Kurdish Refugee Communities.* St. Martin's Press.

Warnes, A., Friedrich, K., Kellaher, L., & Torres, S. (2004). The diversity and welfare of older migrants in Europe.*Ageing & Society* (24), 307-326.

Watters, C. (2011). Towards a new paradigm in migrant health research: integrating entittlement, access and appropriateness. *International Journal of Migration, Health and Social Care* (7), 148-159.

Weber, M. (2007). "Ethnisierung und Männlichkeitsinszenierungen. Symbolische Kämpfe von Jungen mit türkischem Migrationshintergrund". In: C. Riegel & T. Geisen (eds) *Jugend, Zugehörigkeit und Migration. Subjektpositionierung im Kontext von Jugendkultur, Ethnizitäts- und Geschlechterkonstruktionen.* Wiesbaden: VS, 307–321.

Wenger, E. (1998). *Communities of practice: learning, meaning, and identity.* Cambridge University Press.

Westin, C. (2003). "Young People of Migrant Origin in Sweden", *International Migration,* 37, 987-1010.

White, K.K. & Zion, S. & Kozleski, E., (2005). *Cultural identity and teaching.* National Institute for Urban School Improvement.

Wiking, E., Johansson, S. – E., and Sundqvist, J. (2004). "Ethnicity, Acculturation, and self reported Health. A Population Based Study among Immigrants from Poland, Turkey, and Iran in Sweden", *Journal of Epidemiol Community Health,* 58, 574-582.

World Bank. (2011). Migration and Remittances Factbook. Washington. Available at: http://www.google.co.il/books?hl=enandlr=andid=xlaAt _bEF0cCandoi =fndandpg= PR5anddq=Migration+and+Remittances+Factbook+andots=xAJYJJUiTJandsig=qpH WpUiFdhFVeihI66J-H0cKycandredir_esc=y#v= onepageandq=Migration%20and%20Remittances%20Factbookandf=false.

Yağmur, K. (2010). Batı Avrupa'da Uygulanan Dil Politikaları Kapsamında Türkçe Öğretiminin Değerlendirilmesi. *Bilig.* 55, 221- 242.

Yaren, Ö. (n. d.). "Die Fremde": European Space and Women Victims in Migrant Films. Received from https://www.academia.edu/2179613/Die_Fremde_European_ Space_and_Women_Victims_in_Migrant_Films available on: 12.9.2013.

YTB (T.C Basbakanlik Yurtdisi Turkler ve Akraba Topluluklar Baskanligi) (2011). *Avrupa'da Yasayan Turkler Saha Arastimasi.* http://www.ytb.gov.tr/documents/ytb/files/ yayinlar/kitaplar/Avrupada _Yasayan_Turkler_ Anketi. pdf) (Accessed:31.01.2015).

Zentrum für Türkeistudien. (2001). Türkische Unternehmer in Bremen und Bremerhaven. Eine Analyse ihrer Struktur, ihrer wirtschaftlichen Situation sowie ihrer Integration in das deutsche Wirtschaftsgefüge - Ergebnisse einer standardisierten telefonischen Befragung im Auftrag der Ausländerbeauftragten des Bundeslandes Bremen.

Zeyneloğlu, S. & Sirkeci, İ. (2014). Türkiye'de Almanlar ve Almancılar. *Göç Dergisi,* 1(1), 77-118. http://tplondon.com/dergi/ index.php/gd/article/view/5 (accessed: 15/01/2015).

Zirh, B. C. (2008). Euro-Alevis: From Gastarbeiter to Transnational Community. In Remus Gabriel Anghel (Ed.), *The making of world society: perspectives from transnational research*. Transcript Verlag.

Zohry, A. (2007). Egyptian irregular migration to Europe. *Migration Letters,* Vol.4, pp. 53-63.

Zuercher, K. (2009). The Linguistic Construction of Gender in Azerbaijan: Sociodemographic Factors Influencing Russian Language Choice. *International Journal of the Sociology of Language* 198, 47-64.

www.ingramcontent.com/pod-product-compliance
Lightning Source LLC
Chambersburg PA
CBHW021559210326
41599CB00010B/508